The Peopleware Papers

ISBN 0-13-060123-3

9 780130 601230

90000

The Peopleware Papers

Larry L. Constantine

Professor of Computing Sciences
University of Technology, Sydney

Director of Research and Development
Constantine & Lockwood, Ltd.

YOURDON PRESS
Upper Saddle River, New Jersey 07458

Library of Congress Cataloging-in Publication Data

CIP Data available

Editorial/production supervision: *Mary Sudul*
Cover design: *DesignSource*
Cover design concept: *Larry Constantine*
Cover design direction: *Jerry Votta*
Manufacturing manager: *Alexis Heydt*
Acquisitions editor: *Paul Petralia*
Marketing manager: *Debby van Dijk*
Editorial assistant: *Justin Somma*

 Published by Prentice Hall P T R
Prentice-Hall, Inc.
Upper Saddle River, New Jersey 07458

Prentice Hall books are widely used by corporations and government agencies for training, marketing, and resale.

The publisher offers discounts on this book in bulk quantities. For more information contact: Corporate Sales Department, Phone: 800-382-3419; Fax: 201-236-7141; E-mail: corpsales@prenhall.com; or write: Prentice Hall PTR, Corp. Sales Dept., One Lake Street, Upper Saddle River, NJ 07458.

Printed in the United States of America

10 9 8 7 6 5 4 3 2 1

ISBN 0-13-060123-3

Prentice-Hall International (UK) Limited, *London*
Prentice-Hall of Australia Pty. Limited, *Sydney*
Prentice-Hall Canada Inc., *Toronto*
Prentice-Hall Hispanoamericana, S.A., *Mexico*
Prentice-Hall of India Private Limited, *New Delhi*
Prentice-Hall of Japan, Inc., *Tokyo*
Prentice Hall (Singapore) P.T.E., Ltd.
Editora Prentice-Hall do Brasil, Ltda., *Rio de Janeiro*

Dedication

To the memories of Dennis Davie and Ken MacKenzie—
and to all those others who opened doors.

Contents

Acknowledgments

No book is the work of a single person, and this one, with its focus on collaboration and the collective enterprise, has been an appropriately collaborative effort from the start. The book owes its existence to the columns I wrote, which exist because of the persistence and vision of my editors, Larry O'Brien and Marie Lenzie. Larry seduced me into the world of regular deadlines by offering me the prime real estate of *Computer Language Magazine* to write about whatever interested me. Marie plugged me into *Object Magazine* as a people-oriented misfit among a stable of process and technology mavens. Both Larry and Marie have been not only good editors but also good friends over the years. Larry was abetted by a succession of talented and long-suffering people at Miller Freeman Publications—including Gretchen Bay, Nicole Freeman, Michele Gahee, and Nicole Claro—who coped with my convoluted constructions and suffered my sometimes insufferable e-mail lectures.

To Paul Petralia, my editor at Prentice Hall, go my thanks for the enthusiasm with which he helped breathe new life into an old project. For adding the final polish of professionalism to the manuscript, I am grateful for the hard work of Mary Sudul, production editor for this edition, and Harriet Tellem, who contributed so much to the first edition.

To the list of all those editors who have helped along the way, I would add my best critic and advisor, Lucy Lockwood. My partner in both life and business, Lucy is usually the first to read anything I create and the first to recognize when my writing soars and when it sinks. Thanks Lucy. Thanks all.

Introduction

The Other Side of Software

This book is about the other side of computer software, the side facing outward. This face of computing touches and is touched by people—technology people, like you and me, and ordinary people, like you and me. The essays here compiled explore the many diverse aspects of peopleware—that interface between software and its developers and between software and its users.

My editors, both at the magazines in which this material originally appeared and at Prentice Hall, have allowed me to range widely in my explorations. The enormous breadth of the topic of peopleware has enabled me to write about almost anything I desired: from organizational culture and project organization, coding chaos and coding discipline, programming tools and programming techniques, to users, usability, and user interfaces. This far-reaching landscape spans the peculiar in-between world where the boundaries between technical and social issues blur, where psychology meets cybernetics, and where theory and practice intermix. The picture reflects my enduring personal and professional interests in both people and in computer software.

This book is a revised, expanded, and updated successor to *Constantine on Peopleware* (Prentice Hall, 1995). It is too radical a revision to be called a second edition, yet too closely related not to be connected with its forerunner. For the readers of *Constantine on Peopleware* and new readers alike, a wealth of new material is included to round out the subject matter. To the chapters from the original volume, this compilation adds 25 new essays being published here for the first time in book form. These incorporate all 52 of my original "Peopleware" columns from *Computer Language* magazine and *Software Development* magazine, including a "lost column" from the very end of that series (see the Appendix). In addition, I have assembled seven closely related essays from *Object Magazine* that might otherwise be difficult for readers to obtain. These are particularly important in providing an overview of usage-centered design. This approach, first introduced in my columns, has been refined and expanded into the award-winning book, *Software for Use: A Practical Guide to the Models and Methods of Usage-Centered Design* (Addison-Wesley 1999), written with Lucy Lockwood.

One of the great advantages to writing about people is that people change far less rapidly than technology. In rereading and editing the material for this compilation, I was often struck by how little has changed during the many years over which I have been writing about the people side of technology. Projects are still running way over budget, products are still delivered unconscionably late, resources are still hopelessly inadequate for the job, and managers are still wrestling with how best to inspire and channel the creative potential of their counter-dependent developers. Developers, for their part, still chafe at the constraints of design diagrams, modeling tools, and disciplined methods for developing software. Users, in turn, still struggle with making sense of software that speaks well with computers but poorly with ordinary human beings.

Nevertheless, while people have changed little, the technology has altered so radically as to make some of the examples and references in the earliest columns seem almost quaint. An essay on the move from monochrome to full-color monitors, for instance, may seem like a return to prehistory for newcomers to software development, even though the use and misuse of color, the central subject, is as current as the Web. So, with full respect for the original intent and flavor, I have updated the essays where needed for currency and correctness.

This expanded collection has been organized into nine topic areas, with the reprinted columns arranged within each section to form a more-or-less logical unfolding of ideas. New sections—on usability in relation to software objects and on organizational culture—have been added. The reader will quickly learn that each of the essays, while interwoven with others, stands on its own. I suspect this was part of the appeal of my original column and of the first compilation—each chapter could be read independently of the others and in the time of a short cab ride or a break between meetings.

New chapters have also been interspersed in meaningful blocks to make them easier for readers of the first volume to locate them. The new chapters are: 22-25, 31-32, 40-41, 43-49, and 53-61, as well as the Appendix.

In assembling this material from its scattered resting places, I hope I have created a resource of lasting value, a book that will continue to provoke and inspire and enlighten the wonderful people who work in the software industry. It is for them—the designers, developers, and managers who invent and implement software—that I wrote in the first place and that I continue to write today.

Original Introduction

Hardware, Software, Peopleware

Good software does not come from CASE tools, visual programming, rapid prototyping, or object technology. Good software comes from people. So does bad software. In 1992, I started writing a regular column with this simple premise: since software is created by people and used by people, a better understanding of people — how they work, how they do their work, and how they work together — is a basis for better software development and better software. The subject of the column was not hardware, not software, but peopleware.

In a field peppered with neologisms, peopleware is one of those few that really needed to be invented. Peter G. Newmann, perhaps best known for his regular reports on the human risks and real hazards of computers and computer programs, appears to have been the first to use the term in print, in a 1976 paper called "Peopleware in Systems" in an obscure book that took its title from the paper. The word seems to have been independently coined by Meilir Page-Jones, who used it in the 1980 edition of his *Practical Guide to Structured Systems Design,* the book that finally made my work on structured design understandable to the average programmer. But peopleware most likely became lodged in the permanent lexicon of our field with the 1987 publication of a great little book by that title from Tom DeMarco and Tim Lister. In calling my column "Peopleware," I was cribbing from the best.

Peopleware is really the third frontier of the computer revolution. First came the hardware crisis. At one time we thought our problems were really due to hardware. If only we had faster and more powerful computers, we thought, with more memory and better peripherals, then we could build better systems; we could solve our problems. Well, we got better computers. Year after year the hardware grew swifter, the memories larger, and the peripherals more versatile and ergonomic. And our problems persisted. We still delivered hard-to-use systems; we still ran late and over budget with our projects. So we concluded that the real problem was software, and the front lines in the revolution shifted to what many came to call "the software crisis." If only we had better tools, higher level languages, richer component libraries, and programs to help us build programs, then we could solve our problems and deliver good systems on time and within budget. The third-generation languages grew more sophisticated and begat 4GLs. Compilers grew faster and more clever. Libraries of reusable components expanded, editors became context-sensitive, and computer-aided software engineering tools sprang up from every point of the compass. On the heels of the structural revolution that gave us structured design and analysis, object orientation began to mature and gained in popularity. Still, schedules kept slipping and budgets kept busting, and everywhere the bugs remained stubbornly bugs.

At last, like Pogo and his fabled friends from Okeefenokee, we were forced to recognize where the problem lay. "We have met the enemy and they is us," said the unwittingly wise little possum. Indeed. Peopleware is the real issue. We are the problem and we are the solution. How convenient.

Peopleware spans a pretty broad panorama. Anything that has to do with the role of people in the software and applications development process is within the purview of peopleware. The column, like this book, touches on an assortment of issues scattered around that landscape: quality and productivity, teamwork, group dynamics, personality and programming, project management and organizational issues, interface design and human-machine interaction, cognition, psychology, and thought processes.

All of these things interest and excite me. They always have. I took my degree in management in part because it allowed me to mix computers and systems theory with psychology. My thesis was on the psychology of computer programming. I introduced psychologist George Miller and his magical number (7 ± 2, of course) to thousands of students and dozens of colleagues over the years. The structure of structure charts was carefully devised to aid visual concept formation and problem solving. Coupling and cohesion, those venerable metrics at the heart of structured design, are really about computer programs as viewed by people. What makes programs complex or simple is precisely whatever is complex or simple to the minds of the programmers who write, maintain, and modify them.

In a sense, I can't stay away from the people issues any more than I can stay away from computers. I thought I had escaped when I bid farewell to the computer field in July of 1976, declaring my independence even as America celebrated the bicentennial of its independence. Trained as a family therapist, I ended up spending more than a decade in private and agency practice working with couples and families and troubled adolescents. But the forces of the universe conspired to steer me back toward the technological frontier.

Peopleware is a crossroads on that frontier, a junction where highways from my different worlds intersect. Management, organization development, personality, modeling, tools, methods, process, human-computer interaction, whatever. At one time or another I've written and worked and taught in all of these areas. The column has given me the excuse to wander again over the landscape, like a Charles Kuralt, stopping to explore interesting ideas, taking up challenges where they arose, cruising the interstates and county roads of software and applications development.

This book logs the journey so far, starting out in *Computer Language Magazine* and continuing in the retitled *Software Development*. The column was still just called "Peopleware." Here are the Peopleware columns and a few closely related side trips published in other places. The essays and articles have been edited for continuity, and some material that was deleted when they were cut to length for magazine publication, has been restored. This, then, is the "director's cut," arranged into quasi-logical sections that contribute to a certain illusion of organization. But this is no encyclopedia or textbook, not even a road map of the vast territory of peopleware, just the journal of one pilgrim.

The pilgrimage continues.

I

Group Development

Introduction

Michelangelo, that paradigm of the lone genius, did not work alone. The Sistine Chapel was not the lonely labor of an isolated artist, but a group effort overseen and coordinated by Michelangelo. His genius, it turns out, was not for art alone, but the art of managing a team. He called his artists and artisans by their first names or nicknames. He encouraged initiative, cooperation, and pride in workmanship. He would have been at home in a meeting on software quality management.

Software development is group development. Whether it's a matter of art or engineering, most software comes out of a collective enterprise in which a group of developers work together or at odds on a common system. How the group carries out its discussions, its decisions, and its digressions will have a lot to do with how good the work turns out. It is easier to build good software if you have a group that works well together, one that copes with conflict without collapse, one that uses its resources efficiently and effectively.

Group development also refers to the development *of* groups, to the processes and practices that can transform a mere assemblage into a high performance team. Many programmers view group development and team building with a certain skepticism. They don't cotton to cheerleading or chants or group games that seem only to support a superficial team spirit. Such touchy-feely stuff is not for them. They were selected for their programming skills not their social skills, for coding more than for cooperation.

Because understanding the language of groups and group processes may be every bit as important as understanding a programming language, this book starts with an exploration of how groups work and how they can work better to develop better software.

1

Decisions, Decisions

There is more than one way. There is always more than one way. This simple credo has been a practical beacon throughout my professional life, leading me to consider alternatives in how software might be organized and how people might be organized. But recognizing alternatives also carries a burden, the burden of making decisions. Developing better software means making choices among alternatives and, better still, finding that creative synthesis that integrates the best of several approaches and thereby exceeds them all. Well-organized teams that base decision making and problem solving on consensus have the best shot at making quality decisions and building such a creative synthesis, but they need to know how to avoid certain traps common to groups. The secrets of consensus-based teamwork are worth exploring.

I have always considered the ability to make decisions to be one of the most essential of basic life skills. There is no way to learn how except by doing it, which means that successful families and companies make sure there is plenty of opportunity to practice the real thing. By mid-career, the typical professional programmer has solved countless problems and along the way has probably made many thousands of decisions. Naturally, we expect professionals to become good at it. But most of these decisions will have been made individually, by the programmer on her or his own, and problem solving and decision making in groups are different animals altogether.

Risks of Mediocrity

In the dark ages, when I was first learning about management and group dynamics at M.I.T.'s Sloan School, much study and concern were focused on supposed defects of group problem solving and decision making, particularly the effects of the so-called risky shift and the counter-tendency of groups to pull toward a mediocre mean. In those conservative days, even democratically minded managers worried more about the risky-shift than about creeping mediocrity. The upheavals of the 1970s lay ahead, and groupthink was the zeitgeist.

According to the research, collective decisions often seemed to be skewed toward more risky alternatives than would be selected by members deciding independently. If this model applied to programming, we would expect groups to produce software that used more exotic data structures or more unconventional algorithms or more obscure language features. However, other research on group dynamics seemed to show that groups had a leveling effect on problem solving and decision making that reduced results to a kind of lowest common denominator of individual contributions and abilities. Either way, the lone decision maker seemed to have an edge.

It turns out that both effects depend largely on the way a group is organized and led. In Russia, where I have worked with consultants and managers involved in new enterprises, the mediocre mean appears to have dominated the old Soviet-based system. To many of the managers trained under the old regimes, teamwork meant being dragged down to levels of common incompetency. In Soviet management, teams were often a way to avoid responsibility; sometimes they actively conspired to limit performance. To take a stand or advance a novel or controversial idea in such a team, indeed to stand out in any way, was not only to risk the resentment of peers but perhaps to be held accountable and then expected to repeat the performance on future efforts. With the ultimate job security of the typical Soviet sinecure and no rewards for practical performance, why bother?

The social and organizational climate in which a group works is what really shapes the ability to perform up to potential. For best results, the corporate culture and group leadership must actively encourage and support innovation and collaboration. In a sense, the Soviet teams did perform well, meeting the *real* expectations of bosses and enterprise policy makers, which were based more on covering the backside than achieving results. Soviet managers told me they all learned "never be the last link in a chain."

Leading Lightly

In consensus design and decision making, the role of the group leader is crucial, not only in establishing the overall climate for collaboration but also in the detailed way in which leadership is exercised. Consensus design and decision making is at its best when the solution derives from the talents of all team members and reflects the experience, creativity, and critical thinking of all, not just an average of their contributions, but a genuine synthesis that combines their best. When group leaders, however talented and brilliant, push their own agenda, the quality of teamwork goes down.

The effect of group leadership can be as insidious as it is subtle. Even just expressing an opinion at the wrong time can bias a group and lead to a poorer outcome. Research has shown that merely having leaders delay tossing in their own ideas until after all or most group members have presented theirs will improve the group solutions. That means that a leader who merely speaks too soon is probably degrading the quality of teamwork. Confident leaders, sure that they are right or know best, may cause the most difficulty.

Most project leaders and mid-level managers in software development are really techies at heart. Nearly every one of them was promoted up from programming, systems analysis, and software engineering. They got where they are by being good at software development. For many, it is hard to let go of the keyboard, letting someone else actually do the work and make the technical choices.

We now know that one of the most important factors in achieving first-rate problem solving through consensus is having neutral leadership. The position of discussion leader is so powerful that whoever leads or facilitates meetings and discussions must be assiduously neutral about the outcome in order that the best of what the group has to offer can emerge.

Such a leader is everyone's friend and nobody's advocate. Such a leader draws out the contributions of all without favoring any. Such a leader helps the group to build its own technical consensus without biasing the outcome or pushing a private agenda.

Ironically, what this means is that project managers and official team leaders are probably the worst choice for leading any discussions or meetings directed at technical problem solving and decision making. They have too much at stake. In a sense, they probably also know too much. The stronger they are as leaders, the more likely they are to actually dampen the free-spirited exploration of alternatives and the building of technical consensus that lead to the best results.

Some managers take a completely hands-off approach and try to stay out of the technical problem solving altogether; however, this is not ideal for their teams, who are deprived of the manager's experience and expertise, or for the managers, who miss out on much of the fun. The best of them will turn over meetings and discussions to a neutral facilitator, then practice staying in the background, learning how to contribute without dominating. Some may never learn how to do this, but many with whom I have worked actually enjoy being able to be "one of the bunch" again, taking part in technical discussions on equal footing with the rest of the team.

There is life after promotion.

From *Computer Language Magazine,* Volume 9, #3, March 1992.

2

Consensus and Compromise

Getting the most from a software development team depends on the ability to build technical consensus among the professionals on the project. But why should it matter whether you and your office mate agree on the layout of an entry form or the best way to report error messages? Technical consensus is not about getting along together or feeling close to your fellow programmers. (Not that there is anything wrong with getting along or feeling good about each other.) Technical consensus is about taking full advantage of all the skills and experiences of every team member. It's about building better software.

Software professionals may understand good software, or at least claim to know it when they see it, but technical consensus is a lot less well understood among developers. Probably most software developers have had some bad experiences with what they thought was design by consensus. They'll tell you tales of brilliant ideas being lost in discussions, about compromising their artistic integrity, about six-month projects that took years, and about groups that settled for less than the best. Listen carefully and you'll realize that what they are talking about is not consensus at all, but compromise. What's the difference?

Unpromising Compromise

Compromise is neither one thing nor another but something halfway in between, which often means in the middle of nowhere. Consider this variation on a classic example. Your team is designing a graphical user interface. One group strongly advocates placing the control buttons across the bottom of the screen, another is pushing for a panel down the left side. Between these horizontal and vertical extremes, a perfectly objective compromise can be struck: just place the buttons along a diagonal across the middle of the screen!

A compromise, like this one, is frequently worse than any of the original alternatives, but a consensus solution can be better than all of them. Technical compromises often fail to account for the merits in each of the alternatives, and their advantages are lost by taking some kind of average position. True consensus is not based on compromise, in which everyone and every position loses a little, but on synthesis, in which everyone wins big. The payoff, of course, is better software.

A synthesis is something original that incorporates essential features of each contributing idea or proposal. In the interface design example given above, it's easy to see a creative synthesis in which the placement of the button panel is an option selectable by the user. Not only does a consensus based on synthesis incorporate the best of the alternatives, but new features or capabilities typically emerge from the combination. Out of the synthesis of horizontal and vertical button panels might emerge end-user customization. The product thus incorporates the best of both worlds, not the worst.

Building real consensus is not easy, as politicians and labor negotiators know all too well. Building a technical consensus is a little different from building political consensus, but it has some of the same elements. Both take a commitment to working things out; both require a certain faith in the process.

True Believers

Team members need to believe that it is possible to reach a technical synthesis incorporating the best elements and aspects of everyone's contributions. Believing this, they will stubbornly look for something better, rather than settle on compromise or cling needlessly to personal favorites. By persisting, they build their understanding of the problem and the nature of the strengths and weaknesses of each approach. From this, they enhance the odds of finding that creative something that exceeds them all.

Consensus design also works best when each of us believes that building a better piece of software is more important than getting our own favorite ideas into the result in some predetermined form. This investment in the quality of the outcome makes it easier to see the merits of whatever ideas emerge from the group process.

It helps, of course, if teamwork is applauded over individual pyrotechnics. Companies that reward individual performance instead of group success, or those that promote the lone wolf programmer over the team player, typically end up with a staff of uncompromising loners who probably will not and cannot play team sports. Such companies will rightly conclude that the best software is produced by their frontier-type geniuses. What they don't realize is that they've set it up to come out that way. Other outcomes are possible, of course.

One essential rule in building technical consensus is: No horse trading! Trading votes or support or influence is one of the classic tactics for political success, but it can destroy technical effectiveness. For example, we might work a trade in the interface design. I'll agree to your stupid idea of having the button panel across the bottom, if you agree to my clever design for icons without labels. The result is an interface that is less than the best in not one, but two features. Horse trading is just compromise in another disguise, but compromise made worse because decisions in one area contaminate those in another. Good technical consensus must see each issue as a separate problem, to be resolved on the merits, not as part of a point scoring system in which concessions in one area can be traded for obstinacy in another.

Just the Facts

One likes to think that technical decisions are made on the basis of technical issues—facts, measurable quantities, practical considerations. The truth is that feelings, opinions, intuition, and just plain biases are part of any decision-making or problem-solving process involving people. This is the reality of what it is to be human, and although some people try to deny, control, or suppress these nonrational aspects, it never works completely.

An essential skill of any team that hopes to build technical consensus is to learn to separate fact from opinion. If the group, collectively, is to make the best decisions and solve problems creatively, they need access to the best information and to know what kind of information they have. Opinions aren't bad; team members should be able to express them freely. Opinions can even be useful, especially when weighted by hard-won experience, but they must not be confused with facts or data or analyses. Facts, too, have their limitations. In the areas of aesthetics or marketing appeal, facts may be in short supply. Unfortunately, once some group members have made up their minds, they do not want to be bothered by facts.

Calling something a fact doesn't make it so, and groups have to learn to cut through the bull and agree not to abuse the language. My first wife learned in our early years to be suspicious of any statement I made that started with something like, "The facts in the matter clearly indicate ..." This was a warning that what followed was probably a bald-faced personal opinion unsupported by either data or evidence. Failing with this opening gambit, I was sometimes known to fall back on another tactic, which we came to know as the "Ninety-five-percent-of-all-scientists" move. Some of you may recognize it. "You know, the vast majority of professional software engineers, certainly more than ninety-five percent, favor this approach." Of course, to have any hope of continued effectiveness with this clever ruse, you have to vary the percentages. "Nearly seventy-eight percent of WordPerfect users know that the one best way is ..." "If we took a survey, better than two-thirds of C programmers would agree ..." Sometimes it seems that if you squint just right you can almost see those legions of scientists or software engineers or end users lining up behind the speaker to lend support to his or her position.

But that's just my opinion.

From *Computer Language Magazine,* Volume 9, #4, April 1992.

3

Negotiating Consensus

You can't reach consensus unless you recognize it when you have it in your grasp. This means that software development groups trying to reach collective decisions are wise to agree, in advance, on the criteria by which technical matters will be decided. What is important? What matters? What is "good" and what is "bad" within the confines of this particular project?

Many times, when a group gets bogged down trying to reach a conclusion on an analysis or design problem and says, "We can't decide which way to go," I ask them, "How will you know which approach is better?" Engineering is about trade-offs—trading off a little more of this for somewhat less of that. Resolving trade-offs requires knowing something about the value, within a given project, of whatever is gained or lost in the trade-off.

In almost all engineering, projects are driven by competing criteria. It is not possible to meet all of them equally well in every detail at every juncture. Most projects pursue a mixture of technical and economic objectives. They want on-time delivery, run-time efficiency, ease of use, marketability, extensibility, and maintainability, along with a host of other goodies next to godliness. How are these to be weighed?

Straight Priorities

It helps to have your priorities straight. The metrics mavens will probably push you to reduce the decision criteria to a mathematical formula with weights and exponents for each factor, but this is generally neither necessary nor particularly useful. A simple rank ordering of the criteria is sufficient. During analysis and design, when most trade-offs are and should be resolved, we seldom, if ever, have enough data to quantify our assessments with any precision or confidence anyway. Plugging a bunch of seat-of-the-pants "guesstimates" into a bogus formula can give the dangerously deceptive appearance of disciplined objectivity. It can even become an escape hatch by which development teams avoid accountability. "Well, we just did what the formula said we should; it's not our fault that each screen update takes 17 seconds."

Accountability is promoted when development teams participate in establishing their principal goals and, on the basis of these, rank the criteria by which issues are to be decided. Once agreed upon, the criteria and their ordering are no longer open to debate. Most of the time they won't even enter into technical discussions. It is not necessary to analyze every little trade-off in terms of seven or eight criteria. The agreed-on list of criteria is taken off the shelf only when needed to help resolve a decision that is unclear or is taking too long.

Debate and Dialogue

Lack of clarity or agreement on criteria is not the only thing that can hinder negotiation to technical consensus. Free-wheeling discussions are not only the heart of consensus teamwork, but they're fun. Vigorous discussion, however, can cross the line into rancorous debate. Neither the courtroom nor the political podium offers a good model for consensus-based teamwork. Whether or not the adversarial approach works in the justice system, it is essential that design and development groups not end up as debating societies.

In one training class in object orientation, a member of a student design team complained to me that his group was getting nowhere. They were repeatedly getting bogged down in seemingly endless wrangles. Even what little progress they were able to make was seriously substandard compared to other teams in the same class.

As I watched them work—or try to work—I realized that the discussions were being dominated by one man who was an arguer par excellence, but his ideas were not up to his debating skills. Some other members of the team had a sense of the shortcomings in his thinking but, outgunned by his argumentation, kept falling back on opinions and feelings: "I don't think so." "It just doesn't feel right."

The original complainant had the motivation to see it work better, so I asked him to be group facilitator. His job had two parts: to make sure that no one person or side dominated the discussion, and to help the less active or less aggressive members articulate the real content and logic of their ideas.

If you are trying to build the best systems, you don't want to reduce technical solutions to whichever side can argue better, any more than you would want to base them on who has the most power or can shout the loudest. To avoid this, the power of logic and argumentation should belong to the group collectively, not to individuals or factions in a decision. The goal is to level the playing field so the merit of ideas and analyses in themselves carries the weight, not the cleverness of the argument or the loudness and long-windedness of the advocate.

If people can't seem to find a common ground arguing their own positions, one useful technique is to have advocates reverse roles and argue each other's positions. Or strong debaters can be assigned to argue the case of technically interesting but weakly defended notions. "Look, Mavis, you're good at this, so see if you can convince us about the real advantages of Greg's idea." Yet another twist is to say, "Let's apply this same line of reasoning to the other proposal."

Technical consensus is better thought of in terms of dialogue and negotiation than in terms of debate and argumentation. Some of the things that have been learned about negotiation in other areas can be very useful. Two excellent books from The Harvard Negotiation Project are highly recommended: *Getting to Yes* and *Getting Together* (Fisher and Ury 1981; Fisher and Brown 1988).

A perennial problem in negotiations is that the negotiating parties often come to the table already committed to a position, a proposal in which much thought and consideration may already have been invested. Instead of being genuinely open, each arrives with a predetermined solution. Negotiating from a position is thus a problem in itself. It tends to promote compromise at best, rather than consensus, and it is all too easy for things to degenerate into a shootout of one approach versus another.

Some of the simplest devices can make a big difference. The Harvard Negotiation Project learned that negotiations progressed better when disagreeing parties sat side-by-side, facing "their common problem," rather than facing each other over a table. I have found that placing factions in a technical dispute together facing a whiteboard or display screen can facilitate more productive discussions and speedier resolution.

Putting It Together

Sometimes starting from a set of prior proposals or already worked out solutions cannot be avoided. Two parts of the same company may have done prior work that we would not want to discount or waste, for example. Some companies even promote design competition in a kind of internal free market of ideas. When the time comes to build one system, usually the authors or competitors make their own pitch, introducing and describing their approaches. It can facilitate consensus building to have one person, someone who is less invested than the proponents, present all the alternatives before inviting the proposers into the discussion. Setting the right tone for what follows can help progress toward a consensus design. Participants can be encouraged to look for the strengths and advantages in other proposals before moving on to any critique. Realism about the starting positions can be encouraged: "Since it is more important for us to know about technical weaknesses in our systems than to pretend to have everything perfect, would each of you tell us about the weaknesses of your own approach?"

Where distinct subgroups or teams have been involved in preparing proposed solutions, after the initial discussions each subteam can be invited to go back and improve their own proposal by incorporating what they think are some of the best features of opposing approaches. This means that the next meeting starts with the opposing positions already moved closer together.

In general, technical consensus is built from alternatives by finding ways that combine or even transcend the best features of each. Instead of starting with positions, with specific technical proposals, it is often more efficient and effective to start with issues. The team's first job is to explore and settle on what are the essential technical issues represented in the various possibilities, the underlying reasons and technical rationale that are reflected in stated positions or proposed solutions.

The stage for creative synthesis is set even before the first meeting. Instead of having team members think about approaches to, say, the file structure, they might be asked to come with a catalog of the issues involved in designing an efficient file structure. They might list and prioritize specific decision criteria. They may even have to be discouraged from coming up with design ideas or proposed solutions. With many of the more maverick software developers, the problem is not so much spurring them on as reining them in before they stampede.

4

The Lowly and Exalted Scribe

Remember Bob Cratchit toiling away on the books at the august firm of Scrooge and Marley, fingerless gloves on his hands to keep them from freezing between entries? I am a real nut about *A Christmas Carol* and was recently given a video of the marvelous black-and-white version starring Alistair Sim. Watching it started me to thinking about old Bob and all the other "clarks" who kept the records for so many enterprises over the centuries. These scribes were really the computers of their day. Without them, businesses would have been thrown into bankruptcy and whole industries cast into chaotic disarray. Their real power and importance went far beyond either their meager wages or their lowly status. If anything, what good old Bob and his compatriots did had more to do with the continued success of Scrooge and Marley than whatever Ebenezer contributed.

Things are hardly different today. Those who keep the records are held in low regard. Yet, in their pens and markers and keyboards can reside the power to spell success or failure for software development.

Software development groups, if they keep any records at all, are likely to limit their files and notes to results and conclusions, the work product or deliverables generated by their efforts. Programmers, especially, are loathe to write down anything other than the code itself unless they are threatened with a fine or imprisonment. Getting them to draw diagrams can be akin to getting an elephant to do pencil sketches. After all, isn't good code self-documenting?

Vital Statistics

This view tends to lose sight of vital information. In general, when only the work product is preserved, we know what we got in the end but not how we got it. How the software was generated, the decisions along the way, are essential parts of the process. Do we want to trust to memory? Do we care only about our mistakes or do we also want to learn from them?

A particular problem with groups that keep only the end product of software development is that they do not preserve a record of what they didn't do. Often it can be as important to know what approaches were rejected and for what reasons as to know which were selected. This is vital information to have when it comes to future versions or systems or to preserve for when the current system goes down the tubes.

You have probably had occasion to examine some of your own code some years or months after you wrote it. Have you ever had the experience of spotting something that you just knew must be wrong and you wondered how the software ever squeaked by without crashing because of it? If you gave in to the temptation to "correct" such a latent bug, as I have on occasion, then you may have found that "fixing" it brought the system to its knees. The problem, of course, is that the code only *looked* wrong, but the code did not explain why it was actually right. It does not help to have a comment in the code like the one I once saw that read, "Do not change this decision; it looks wrong but is really right." If the programmer knew why it was right and why the alternative was wrong, then why wasn't that logic recorded in the comment? We need to know what alternatives were considered and rejected and why if we are going to be able to maintain a system for years or build its successor five years later after all the original development staff are long gone.

Business consultants today talk about organizational learning as a key to enterprise success over the long run. Organizations, like individuals, can learn from their experiences, accumulating knowledge and improving performance. To the extent that organizational learning resides solely in the brains of individual employees, the organization is vulnerable. Employees get sick, take vacations, and change jobs. They forget.

In truth, the learnings of an organization are embodied in its records, its policies, and its practices or processes, not solely in its people. The more we document and record what happens as we go along, the more likely such learning is to survive the group or team that produced it.

Scribbles

Enter the lowly scribe. Fanfares and cheers!

The function of the scribe or recorder on a software development team is to be responsible for the team's collective memory, the repository of its work product as well as of the processes that generated the results. The scribe keeps the books. In the Structured Open teamwork model devised independently by Rob Thomsett and myself (Constantine 1989, 1991a; Thomsett 1990), the role is referred to as Information Manager. This newspeak title is intended to raise the status of the role, somewhat akin to the ad for a garbage truck driver calling the job a "sanitation transport engineer."

It is easy to see the scribe in a meeting as a mere functionary, hardly more than a human dictaphone, but this position actually draws on many skills. You can't keep effective notes on things you don't understand, so software scribes have to be fully trained developers. And they must know how to record and manage information for a real development project. The quality of the records determines the quality of the group's permanent collective memory of what happened and how. A scribe who captures a full account of what the group did, complete but without excessive detail, well organized and understandable, is a team member worth his or her weight in C++ code.

A good group memory must carry a lot of information. Some of this is volatile or temporary storage, some is permanent. Some of it is active and worked with dynamically in meetings and the day-to-day tasks of the team, while some is more passively filed. The information management functions can be divided for convenience into session memory and project memory. Session memory consists of the records generated and manipulated during group sessions, whenever the team is meeting and solving problems as a group. Project memory covers the permanent records and documentation produced and used by the group. It includes the work product, which means not only code but also all the design and analysis models and documents generated along the way to the code. Project memory also covers inputs to the project, such as requirements and specifications, and other background documents. Managing the project memory really requires a librarian, and often the role is known by that title.

Modular Memory

An essential part of the session memory is the process record, a log of the discussions and decisions made by the group (Doyle and Strauss 1982). The idea of keeping process records is probably new to most software development groups, but it has been a part of meeting management for decades. In creating a process record, new scribes tend to fall into one of two traps. Either they try to write down everything as if they were taking dictation, or they wait until the group reaches some conclusion and just summarize. For technical teamwork, a "he-said/she-said" kind of record is neither necessary nor ideal. A good process record keeps track of key events along the way to an outcome, especially the alternatives considered, decisions made, and arguments presented. These are essential contributors to group learning and may be invaluable when it comes time for a project "post mortem" or design review.

For software development, a continuous and unstructured process record is not ideal. Some categories of information are so commonly generated by development teams working in collaborative sessions that they warrant separate recording for special attention. It is useful to keep a "do-list" for noting those things that come up in discussions but are not acted on right away. This alone can justify the frustration of keeping session records because it can save projects from those embarrassing oversights that tend to show up in systems integration or after product shipment. "Oops, I thought we took care of that dangling pointer problem!"

A good session memory also records deferred decisions, which are best kept separate from the heap on the "do-list." A formal storage place for deferred decisions can also speed up decision making. Instead of wasting time with endless discussion driven by inadequate understanding or missing information, the group can put the issue on the deferred decisions list. Often, by the time the group returns to the issue, enough has been learned to make a swift decision. A third special record that proves useful on development teams is a "parts bin," where bits and pieces of bright technical ideas or partial solutions can be set aside temporarily without disrupting the main thread of discussion. The "reject bin" is just the opposite, a place to note all those unused ideas and paths not taken, along with that vital rationale for rejection.

All four of these special records—the do-list, the deferred decisions, the parts bin, and the reject bin—serve to record things that might otherwise be lost or forgotten. They also help the group to make efficient use of time. By recording digressions and distractions in one of these specialized bins, the group can stay on track with the main problem without losing useful information. It can also keep a group from getting stuck on discussions that are going nowhere. Instead of more wheel-spinning, an issue can be moved to one of the "bins" for later attention. The bins themselves also serve as quality assurance mechanisms. By the end of a project, everything in the bins must have been crossed off or otherwise accounted for.

So who is the lucky person who gets to be a scribe? Some approaches, such as *Joint Application Design* (Wood and Silver 1989), bring in outside facilitators and scribes, trained specialists who are good at it and can free up project members to concentrate on creating software solutions. Some groups permanently assign the job to one person on the team, often a junior member or trainee. For most software development teams, a compromise between these approaches can be more effective. The function of information management can belong to the team as a whole, with the actual responsibility rotated among members of the project team. No one is exempted from playing the scribe, but no one is stuck with the job for too long. The job of Session Recorder is one that may actually change from moment to moment with the flow of the meeting, or it may stay in one set of capable hands for an entire working session. However, for the sake of sanity and good teamwork, it probably should switch at least with each new meeting. In longer meetings, it probably should rotate at least every hour or so. The truth is that being a good scribe takes extraordinary concentration, and very few people on the planet actually enjoy the role.

Taking care of the archives, the off-line or project memory, can be rotated less frequently. Passing the torch on a daily basis would only ensure chaos or nonperformance. During a one-year project, the overall job, what might be termed the Project Information Manager or Project Scribe, might change hands only once or twice at the most.

So, take a scribe to lunch. Next week it could be you.

From *Computer Language Magazine,* Volume 9, #6, June 1992.

5

Official Space

Your office mate chews gum, plays "Where-in-the-World-is-Carmen-San-Diego?" on his desktop machine, and interrupts with burps, groans, and stupid questions whenever you are trying to logic your way through some obscure bug. You've been with the company several years and feel it's high time you had a private office. You go to your boss saying you need more room and more freedom from distracting noise and interruptions. You say it's cost effective, that if you had more space and fewer distractions you'd be more productive. You mention studies to prove it. You need at least a hundred square feet of dedicated work space and thirty square feet of desk-and-table-top. A window would be good, too. In Denmark they legislate that you inform your boss. In Denmark she would have to give you a window.

In the folk wisdom of software development, more space, more quiet, and fewer interruptions yields higher programming productivity with fewer defects. A hundred square feet of office and thirty square feet of work surface has become the plea of programmers around the world. This notion was made a permanent part of industry folklore by Tom DeMarco and Tim Lister in their 1987 classic, *Peopleware*. Drawing on several sources, but primarily their own annual "coding war games," they concluded that programmers with privacy, more elbow room, and more space to spread out their diagrams and listings were more productive.

Shaping Process

At work, at home, in a restaurant, or in a classroom, physical space shapes what happens and can happen among people. At a long banquet table you may be able to converse with a couple of people on either side and a few across from you, but it's not likely that you'll be able to carry on a meaningful exchange with anyone clear down on the other end. King Arthur made his table round as a statement about equality. It also made it easier for all the knights to talk with each other.

How buildings or offices are designed and furnished can have a powerful effect on communication and collaboration. I once lived in an apartment building for two full years but met few of the neighbors. The entryway of the building was a tiny little airlock, barely big enough for one person and a bag of groceries; the halls were narrow, dark, and sterile. There was simply no place for people to bump into each other, no place for serendipitous interaction.

Offices do not usually suffer from tiny entrances and gloomy hallways, but modern high-tech offices have their equivalent architectural inhumanities. The flexible-partition, open-office design dominates modern office layout. Despite its appealing name, the system is usually neither flexible nor open.

One computer company has buildings with miles of corridors crisscrossing acres of cubicles, all marked out by those sand-colored acoustic partitions that make you crane your neck to see over but that merely dampen conversations to the distracting murmur of an opera house just before curtain time. There's not only no privacy, but there's not much that's open, either. People in offices separated by more than twenty feet in this beige warren can go for years without ever crossing paths. Visitors have to be escorted—not for security reasons but to keep them from becoming lost. Mail stops have designations like KK14-HDQ:117N\BB.R3, an arcane code referenced to floors, pillars, and rows. The flexibility of flexible office layout is largely illusory. Moving a partition would require uprooting and rerouting ethernet and telco cables, to say nothing of revamping mail-stop designations. The walls may be flexible, but the mailroom personnel are decidedly not.

From the standpoint of using office space to leverage developer productivity, these inflexible "flexible" systems are usually laid out to be about as bad as anyone could devise. They do not make it easy to work alone, and they do not make it easy to work together. They do not make it easy to get away or to meet casually.

The whole story on office layout and developer productivity is more complex than just more space and more isolation. First, there is that old bugaboo of all social science research, the cause-and-correlation conundrum. The high performers in the coding war games may have had bigger offices and fewer distractions *because* they were high performers, not vice versa. Or their performance may have contributed to their companies' ability to afford quieter and more spacious facilities.

Even more important, the findings reported in the DeMarco and Lister book were based on coding and testing, not on the complete process of software development. Their annual competitions required that each competitor work alone—no teamwork. So space and quiet seem to support isolated coders, but what about collaborative teams?

Collaborative Communication

For efficient collaboration, project teams do need space: space of their own as a team, space laid out to their needs as a team. The best evidence points to the need for a mix of open and closed spaces for smooth collaboration. Offices should support groups of two or three people working together intensively for shorter or extended periods and have at least one locale for meetings of the entire project staff. If there is no place where the entire team can meet comfortably, building the team into a cohesive working unit will be much harder.

One software manager ardently supported project teamwork but was disappointed with the quality of collaboration among his software developers. The floor where they worked was a fun-house maze of narrow corridors with tiny little glass-walled offices—isolated but not private. Few offices were big enough for two, and those that were large enough often held office mates who were assigned to different projects. I observed one team scheduled for a meeting in the largest conference room on the floor. Eleven developers crammed into a room that held a conference table and six chairs with about seven inches clearance all around. Between the end of the table and a small whiteboard was barely room for the team leader to pace and turn. Needless to say, the meeting was brief.

One crucial office need of collaborative teams is a common meeting space dedicated to the team "for the duration." They need a place to serve as headquarters, a "situation room" where the whole team can convene for meetings and discussions and a protected territory where members can retreat from outside distractions and interference. Intermittent use of a conference room shared with various others is a poor substitute.

A dedicated project "situation room" of sufficient size is especially important for teams using "system storyboarding" (Zahniser 1990, 1993) and other group analysis and design approaches. The walls and whiteboards of the team HQ become the repository for the group's work, its visible, external "group memory," preserving essential parts of the work product and the process through which it evolves. The walls of the team HQ might be covered with everything from the team flag and mission statement to essential design documents. The room and its decorations become part of the team culture, contributing to a sense of shared identity that helps members work together smoothly and efficiently.

When team members are split between buildings, spread across different sites, or scattered around the globe, collaboration—even communication — becomes more difficult and more expensive. Other things being equal, spreading a project among multiple sites—even just different buildings or different floors—can add as much as 50–100% to the cost. Because spatially distributed project teams will almost invariably be less efficient than comparable groups at a single site, dispersed teams need compensating mechanisms. Good e-mail and teleconferencing facilities can help, but nothing can substitute for coming together to meet face-to-face and press the flesh at least once.

Back in the dark ages of software engineering when I was at M.I.T., studies of engineering and R&D groups had established that productivity improved with better communication and that communication improved when groups worked in the right environment. The best arrangements had central open spaces that facilitated or even forced engineers to bump into each other. Buildings with fixed walls and management with closed minds can be deterrents, but creative compromises are possible. Risa Hyman describes one group that made inventive use of the conventional string of offices arrayed along a central corridor (Hyman 1993). The hallway itself was outfitted with whiteboards along the walls and was used as the primary meeting space!

Having the right physical layout can help teamwork, but it's up to managers and team members to determine whether walls become barriers or bridges to more effective teamwork.

From *Software Development*, Volume 1, #12, December 1993.

6

Irksome Interruptions

Interruptions can be irksome. On the other hand, a bug that doesn't come to your attention may stay in the code, and an idea that you never hear about won't help you solve a problem. How well and how efficiently people communicate within an office or on a project team can make a real difference in performance. Sharing an office makes it easy to share information. Sometimes that's a plus, sometimes not. The kind of intense and focused thinking that is necessary for good code construction or for ferreting out elusive bugs benefits from sustained and undivided attention. When the words of an article or the lines of code just seem to flow from the fingertips, the last thing you want is someone throwing in a casual comment about something Robert X. Cringely wrote. At other times, the fresh perspective of someone else's off-hand remark may get you thinking along new lines. Sometimes, talking through a design with an attentive listener can help you see what is missing or where hidden problems might lurk.

Good office teamwork requires easy access without irritation. People who work together or share the same working space have many legitimate reasons to interrupt each other: asking for help, tossing out ideas, checking on status, and, in general, coordinating the work at hand. On the other hand, uninterrupted time to think and create is essential. An ill-timed interruption can erase a great idea, kick an elusive thought just out of reach, or make you lose track completely within a complicated line of reasoning.

This problem isn't new and isn't special to software development groups, but developers may have advantages in coming up with better ways to manage group communication. Of course, computer people love to solve social and organizational problems by using computers, so the first thing that probably comes to mind is a fast network with fancy e-mail facilities. But sometimes a very simple system can go a long way. Maybe all that is needed is some better vocabulary.

Word Warriors

Technical fields often have a rich interaction with ordinary vocabulary. The computer field has usurped many everyday words for narrow technical purposes. We have taken over "object" and "entity," leaving nothing to refer to those ordinary things in the physical world around us. We've appropriated "method" and "message," arrogated "protocol" and "file." It works the other way, too, of course. Technical terms enter the mainstream to the point that computer jargon now peppers conversations on the street.

Tech weenies in the computer field have a special passion for interpolating their jargon into ordinary conversation, extending and expanding the meaning of the terminology to cover social purposes. They struggle to "parse" a garbled voice-mail message or maniacally "multiplex" two conversations. Habitual patterns of behavior are "hard coded" in "ROM." Programmers will "port" a tape deck from one car to another rather than buy a new one. They will do a "core dump" to write a first rough draft of a report on yesterday's design meeting. This can get pretty tedious or sound awfully silly, but technobabble occasionally enriches ordinary language in useful or interesting ways.

I remember my first experience with an attempt to import programming terminology into conversation management. Our group was experimenting with commercial applications of Lisp and became so enamored with the language that we talked in lists and dotted pairs. Our conversations became punctuated by oddball exclamations. We'd "cons" two ideas together and "car" and "cdr" our way through conversation so multithreaded that eventually someone would complain of stack overflow and call for garbage collection. For those of you who never learned to thpeak with a lithp, "car" means "the first thing off the list" or "the left branch" while "cdr" (pronounced "could-er") means "the rest of the list" or "the right branch." The funny names have stayed with Lisp, even though they refer to hardware registers in the long defunct IBM 709/ 7090/7094 computers, namely "contents of address register" and "contents of decrement register."

Our short-lived affectation probably sounded pretty dorky and wasn't terribly useful, except in helping us to learn the jargon and anchor the concepts of Lisp firmly in our minds. I haven't "cadadr-ed" an idea in decades. If you hang around our offices nowadays, though, you're apt to hear some equally weird but maybe more useful idiomatic interjections.

Office Protocol

The usual ways of interrupting in polite society are just too long and clumsy for efficient collaboration. "Excuse me. Are you busy? I hope you don't mind. I just have a quick question. It will only take a second." A second? It has already taken six and a half! By this point, the interruption is a *fait accompli*. By the time your brain has parsed and processed all that noise and reached a decision on what to do about it, you've forgotten which line of code you were looking at and which method of which subclass you were intending to invoke.

Working groups need a vocabulary of interruptions that is short, sweet, and simple. What works for hardware seems to work for people, so in our offices we IRQ, we ACK, and we NAK.

"IRQ" is short for "interrupt request"; it's pronounced, appropriately, "irk." As in "I'd like to irk you?" All you need say is just the one word, "IRQ?" A rising intonation makes it more polite, an explosive final consonant makes it more imperative. The word is sharp enough to penetrate through the hiss of cooling fans and the whine of laser printers, yet it's short enough to barely deflect your mental processes. The possible responses are "ACK" or "NAK" (pronounced "ack" and "en-ack" or "nack"), meaning, "Okay, go ahead!" or "Not now!" respectively. You barely have to be conscious of your surroundings to burp out either an ACK or a NAK. Both ACK and NAK have an appropriate phonetic flavor that seems to fit with the situation of being interrupted.

The interrupt protocol is simplicity itself. An interrupter says "IRQ!" and waits for a response. The interrupted person may continue for a short time before completing the handshaking, perhaps marking a spot in the text, completing a title box, or making a quick note about what they were doing. As soon as they are ready to service the interrupt, they respond by saying "ACK." A response of "NAK" means, "No, don't interrupt me now." We regard it as a polite version of "Go away. Don't bug me!" All this may seem too silly for words, but it is remarkable how such a simple system can contribute to smoother resource sharing in a working group. Although we haven't found the need for it in day-to-day work, an obvious extension would be to provide for an occasional "NMI" (pronounced "nimmy"), that is, a "nonmaskable interrupt." Good etiquette would save "NMI" for true emergencies or top-priority issues that justify grabbing the full foreground processing capacity of your poor colleague's wetware CPU. The recommended protocol would be to pause briefly before beginning to talk, although no ACK or NAK is required.

People who IRQ you more often than necessary are dubbed, appropriately, IRQsome. These you deal with by doing your Bill-the-Cat impersonation, loudly crying, "ACK, NAK. NAK! ACK!" while tearing at your hair. If you can come up with a fur ball at the right moment, it's all the more effective.

End of interrupt.

From *Software Development*, Volume 2, #6, June 1994.

II

Cowboys and Cowgirls

Introduction

One of the great things about doing a column in a computer magazine is that readers respond by electronic mail, creating a lively immediacy in the relationship between reader and writer. Over the years, *Peopleware* has generated a steady exchange with an intelligent and interested readership who frequently and repeatedly get excited or incensed enough to inquire or comment. I have come to look at reading the regular e-mail (and irregular snailmail) as a part of writing the column.

I was totally unprepared, however, for the deluge triggered by my first column on "coding cowboys." In fact, that column and its successor broke records for reader response. Suddenly, I was in the wild west of an earlier epoch. For the intensity of reaction, I might as well have been talking with hunters about gun control or cattle ranchers about charging for grazing rights on public lands. Some of the "flaming" that swept over the electronic prairie was too intense for verbatim reproduction in a family-oriented publication like *Software Development*. Clearly, the issue touched some archetypal anarchy among software developers. My vocabulary grew as I caught some of the more trendy insults of the electronic age and was surprised to learn that "commie pinko" was still in the lexicon of contempt of some programmers. *Plus c'est change, plus c'est même chose.*

The topic turned out to be a rich enough lode to be mined in multiple columns and a full-length article. Along the way I made some friends and I probably made some enemies. And I will most probably never get an invitation to lunch in Redmond with "The Bill."

7

Cowboy Coders

The millennium arrived and you didn't even know it! Software reliability became, at long last, a reality. And how was this breakthrough in software engineering achieved? I quote from a 16-page marketing blurb from Nanomush, Inc., mailed to millions of benighted users and developers: "One of the most powerful additions to Blerbbleflox 3.1 is 'parameter validation.' Parameter validation means that when information is passed from an application to the Blerbbleflox operating system, Blerbbleflox checks the information to make sure it is valid." What a novel idea! Why didn't you think of that, eh? (Of course, everyone knew I was talking about Microsoft and Windows 3.1. LLC).

This bit of attempted self-congratulation revealed that Nanomush, one of the world's largest developers of languages and operating environments, had finally begun to practice the rudiments of sound software engineering, techniques so basic that those worthy of the name programmer have known and practiced them since shortly after they learned to code. Could this cast some light on the shortcomings of earlier releases of similar software? But we should rejoice rather than carp, lauding the efforts of all fledgling software engineers, encouraging them to continue to mature, perhaps even to try to learn about coupling and cohesion or information hiding.

One wonders how the computer world arrived at this sorry state of affairs in systems software until one looks more closely at the character of the developers responsible for some of the products on which we depend so much. My colleagues who deal with organizational dynamics would call them "cowboys." Cowboys, the last of the rugged and untamable individualists, are found in various fields, but nowadays many of them are punching assembly language cattle on the silicon frontier. Please note that the sobriquet ends in "boys" not "men."

In the spring of 1992, at Miller Freeman's Software Development Conference, I found myself part of a panel on the putative topic of "structured" versus "unstructured" management of software development. I was paired with one of the development managers from Nanomush. His position, wholly on the side of the cowboys, was that what kept programmers from reaching their full potentials were managers who tried to impose standards, expectations, or restrictions. Just get out of the way and let them programmers do their thing. Structured methods, disciplined development, paper-and-pencil model building, and software metrics are all unjustified impositions on the free artistic expression of our brilliant programming cowboys. No wonder there is such unpredictable performance and variability in quality within the products being shipped by such companies.

Why does it take four releases and 12,000 (no kidding) beta test sites to discover that something less cryptic than "unrecoverable application error; okay?" is needed? But cowboys don't like to be reined in by specific quality criteria or by being expected to think out in advance what is really needed. No, let's just jump into that old development corral and cut some code, wranglers! The GUI may be pretty and the coding clever—after all, we are artistic geniuses—but to hell with real usability or reliability; those might require planning or, heaven forbid, discipline.

And we need not single out any one software company in this regard; the market abounds with countless examples. It is rare, however, when promotional literature or panel presentations give us such candid glimpses into the maturity of developers and their development methods.

Maverick Maturity

Maturity is a central issue for the field of software development. Methodologists are wondering how long it will take for software engineering to mature as a discipline, managers are concerned about the level of "process maturity" in the approaches to development used within their organizations, and project leaders wonder about the maturity of the individuals whom they are called on to lead.

One large corporation surveyed their software development groups to determine how much and at what level of sophistication groups were making use of established systematic or disciplined software engineering approaches. The most advanced in their use of software engineering methodologies were the MIS and business information departments. Engineering support groups were intermediate in their use. Rock bottom last were—you guessed it—the people who wrote the operating systems, compilers, and utility software. Surveys of CASE tool penetration show similar patterns. Where engineering discipline and process maturity count most, software development is a wild-west side show dominated by coding cowboys.

Our culture lionizes the lone genius who does everything from start to finish on the development of some brilliant theory or machine or piece of software, but the truth is, nobody really makes it on their own. Even the eremitic teenaged hacker, cranking out code in the isolation of his bedroom on the machine he assembled himself, is dependent on the army of engineers who designed and built the chips, the legions of programmers who went before to create the tools. For those who are monitoring my LSI (Latent Sexism Index), it is not accidental that I use the masculine pronoun here. Most young hackers are male, and the particular mentality associated with cracking on-line computer systems or hacking clever new worms to bring networks to their knees is almost exclusively a male psychopathology. Boys also commit the majority of vandalism, and let's face it, writing viruses or trashing corporate files or invading government computers is just vandalism, nothing more. Unfortunately, it is only a matter of time before such computer vandalism results in loss of life; we've already come close on several occasions.

Coeducation

So, how did we get, in just a few paragraphs, from software engineering and methodological maturity to these gender issues? Because, at the heart of it, the immaturity of the cowboy mentality that shuns discipline and collaboration alike is largely a male thing.

At one meeting of a planning group within a software company, the assembled "team" went through 40 minutes of the men playing competitive games, debating definitions, jockeying for position, showing off their knowledge and erudition, and generally trying to score points off each other. Slowly, one by one, the men drifted away, excusing themselves with one rationale or another, usually something ostensibly "more important" having to do with "real work." When only women were left, one of them said, "Now, we can get something done." They wrapped up the real job of the meeting quickly and efficiently, while enjoying themselves in the process.

Of course it's a stereotype, but let's face it, guys, women understand collaboration a lot better than we do. For whatever reasons, little boys compete and little girls collaborate. Females, as a rule, are much better at building relationships, supporting and motivating each other. (So, one wonders why more of them aren't managers and project leaders in our field. Think about it, you middle and upper managers: all other things being equal, a female may have a decided edge over a male as a team leader—even with those Neanderthal programmers who claim they can't work for a woman.)

In my years as a marriage and family therapist I came, reluctantly, to the conclusion that most modern men basically do not know all that much about parenting, or, for that matter, relationships in general. This is not a matter of male bashing, just one of those statistical facts of life. I've been lucky to know uncommon males who really understood about *relating*, and I've also known my share of interpersonally inept females. Neither sex has a monopoly on either sensitivity or relationship bungling. But the odds favor women, at least in most cultures, when it comes to finesse with the people issues.

Now I expect to hear it loud and long from all those coding cowboys out there who insist that rugged individualism and the free market of programming independence are the only hope for American business (or humankind, if they're less provincial in their outlook). These are precisely the ones who insist that working collaboratively cramps their style, that building consensus drags them down to the lowest common denominator, that having to design before they code slows them down. Strange that so many of them produce such ordinary software or even fundamentally flawed systems.

True, there are some scattered few, women and men alike, with the genius, the vision, the talent, and the creativity to go it alone and do credible and laudable work. For most of us, though, releasing our real potential lies in learning how to build off each other's ideas in a creative synthesis that goes beyond what each of us might be capable of doing alone. *Our* work is likely to be better than either *my* work or *your* work.

So, grow up, cowboys. Learn how to stand on each other's shoulders instead of each other's toes. And, please, all the women out there, lend us a hand. We have so much to learn.

From *Computer Language Magazine*, Volume 9, #8, August 1992.

8

Cowboy Homecoming

When I first rode out onto the software range to write about the problem of "cowboy coders," I had no idea what a hornet's nest I was poking. Cowboy coders are those industry denizens who denigrate discipline of any kind, spurning methods and models and management alike. They would rather quit than cooperate. The thought of designing before cutting code is enough to make them feel downright claustrophobic. My suggestion that these mostly male code punchers might learn from their more collaborative female counterparts triggered a dust storm of protests. The protesters, nearly all male themselves, accused me of everything from sexism to communism, so it should not be surprising that I held off returning to the subject for a spell. But circumstances seem to impel me once more to think about the untamed wilds of the programming frontier.

For starters, my younger daughter graduated from college. Commencement was filled with its Kodak moments. I remember particularly that swell of paternal pride as she received her degree in psychology, then the relief-filled realization that the last of a long series of distressingly large checks had been posted to the college. And I remember the commencement speech.

Chimp Tales

Commencement speeches are rarely memorable. They're usually either pious, platitudinous, or political; some particularly deadly ones may be all three. But Wheaton's new president had prevailed on a former Cornell colleague to help launch her first Wheaton graduating class. Carl Sagan filled his remarks with wit and intelligence and kept them brief. Inspired by the graduating class, only the second to go through four years of coeducation at Wheaton, Sagan started by looking at gender and behavior. He focused on women and men and the world they make for themselves by first turning the spotlight onto chimpanzees. Chimps, of course, are our genetic brothers and sisters; 99.6% of the active genes are identical in chimps and humans. The behavior of chimps and humans is not all genetics, of course, but neither is it all simply learned. Just as looking at our own parents can tell us something about ourselves, we can learn something about *homo sapiens sapiens* by looking in the mirror of our primate relatives.

When stressed by crowded conditions, male chimps grow increasingly aggressive and competitive, gathering rocks to throw and keeping other males at a distance. Sagan described a male chimp, arms loaded with rocks, confronted by a quiet female blocking his way. Slowly, gently, she pries open the fingers of his clenched fists and deposits the rocks on the ground, then walks away. For some males, this is enough, and they turn to other chimpish interests, but a few just don't get it. Slower to learn, they have to be gently disarmed a number of times before they get the message. It reminded me of some of the men I know.

Sagan returned from chimpanzees to the subject of people and the widely demonstrated differences in how little boys and little girls play, the tendency for women to promote cooperation where men are prone to compete. He wondered whether the world might be more collaborative if women had truly equal access to positions of power and influence. Not a few senators and token female CEOs, but an honest fifty-fifty split of the leadership pie.

And I wondered where Carl Sagan was last year when I needed him, when I was being pelted by troops of software chimps, males all, for saying many of the same things. I guess they must have felt crowded by talk of cooperative coding.

If all cowboy coders were lone rangers, they would not present so many problems. Many of them are darned good. In isolation, on self-contained applications, cowboys can turn in whirlwind performances. Even one or two on a larger team can spice up a development project. Managed with judicious attention to the software interfaces and personal connections, cowboys can add diversity in ideas and perspectives without undermining the integrity of the system.

Unfortunately, cowboys have been known to gather not only at rodeos and roundups but also at large software houses, where they create complex system software—with the emphasis on complex. It seems just possible that some of the slipped schedules and bug-ridden software that plague our industry might be related to the wild-hair programming practices of undisciplined cowboy coders and the maverick managers who encourage them. Cowboy coders can be creative, no doubt. That's not always a good thing. In the system software on which everything else depends we want peerless performance and, at the bottom of it all, rock-solid reliability. Performance can sometimes be bought through cowboy tactics, but reliable software generally comes from the discipline that cowboys disdain. Code that's both fast and flawless requires the very best software engineering practices carried out with consistent rigor.

Lots of cowboys also means lots of code—whether it's needed or not. It means great quantities of unstructured code, conceived on the fly and created independently, all of it different, all of it with the unique stamp of some cowboy's personal style.

Trail Bosses

Imagine, if you will, trying to produce a major new operating system, not with a closely coordinated team of disciplined professionals, but with a couple hundred coding cowboys. It's tough enough to lead a small posse of cowboys. Imagine trying to manage a whole ranch full of them. It might take a lot just to get their attention.

Perhaps, then, we should sympathize with the head of the Windows NT project who harangued his herd continually and even reportedly punched a hole in an office wall. Maybe as an ex-programmer with a reputation for clever code he understood the maverick mentality.

Alas, understanding may not be enough. As described by the *Wall Street Journal* (26 May 1993), the entire project seemed doomed to produce a gargantuan, overly complicated, and defect-ridden result. With some 200 programmers furiously cutting code to specs generated on the fly, the project promoted a cacophonous free-for-all.

Like the cattlemen and sheep herders of yore, coders and testers were turned into competing camps, pitted against each other in pitched battles. Such a division of labor can be effective in reducing software defects. But in the project pecking order, coders—mostly male and mostly cock-sure—came first. When coders complained that testers were trying too hard, the testers were overruled, presumably in the interest of meeting deadlines or performance goals.

With schedules slipping and problems proliferating, the NT staff went into "ship mode"—and stayed there for nearly two solid years. Since error rates rise when humans are fatigued and stressed, long hours under pressure will only multiply the number of defects injected into code. Some weeks they were finding and "fixing" on the order of a thousand bugs. But, even the best regression testing protocols detect only a fraction of injected bugs. The undiscovered residue of all those long weekdays and weekends awaits future users.

There are alternatives. Discipline works. As reported by Al Pietresanta at the 1989 Software Development Conference in Boston, by using "clean room" coding techniques and continuous process improvement, coding defects even in very large systems can be cut to less than one in ten thousand lines of code.

Maturity pays off. Large projects carried out by mature organizations using mature processes have been found to cut development costs by factors of 20–30 compared with more free-form hack-and-slash approaches.

There may be many bastions of coding cowboyism, but in the case of Rancho Redmond, it's now a matter of record. Mitchell Duncan, chief builder on the NT project, is quoted by the *Journal* as saying, "We have all these cowboy developers, just slinging code like crazy."

And sling they did—4.3 million lines worth. Just be careful where you step.

From *Software Development*, Volume 1, #10, October 1993.

9

Unity in Diversity

What does it take to be a leader? What kind of leadership leads to effective teamwork and successful problem solving? Back in the late 1970s, British management consultant R. Meredith Belbin (1976) was asked by the Administrative Staff College in England to find answers to just these questions through formal observations and experiments.

Using the best scientific knowledge and thinking of the day, he assembled experienced middle to senior managers into teams to take part in competitive activities that could be objectively rated. Beginning with an "A-Team" that brought together the best and the brightest, the truly outstanding performers, he assigned participants to various teams until there remained only an assortment of leftovers who did not seem to fit with any of the carefully defined high-performance teams. These last he threw together to form one last team, a motley crew of undistinguished misfits.

At the end of extensive tests and exercises, the teams were ranked on their objective performance. To the surprise of all, the all-star team ended up dead last in the rankings, while the motley crew topped the charts.

Required Roles

Careful study of the results revealed that the key ingredient was diversity. Teams whose members showed greater diversity in leadership style performed better, while teams whose members all showed basically similar ways of leading and participating within the group performed less well. Going back to his observations and data on the team members, Belbin identified eight distinct "leadership roles" or team functions that team members seemed to play in the most diversified, most successful teams.

Belbin's leadership roles represent functions needed by a team for peak performance, and they also represent styles in which those leadership functions can be carried out. Four of these resemble conventional notions of how real leaders behave. A *driver* is a team member who typically defines things, steering and shaping the team thinking and the discussion toward a particular end or outcome, imposing specific patterns of work or approaches. We all know drivers in this sense, and often they are people seen as dominant in teams. But there are other important forms of team leadership. An *originator* is a leader in ideas, an innovator and inventor who advances new ideas or approaches. A *coordinator* is a leader in terms of process, a facilitator who helps move the problem solving forward by drawing on the entire team as human resources. A *monitor* is an evaluator who applies critical review and analysis to the group work, in effect; a leader in quality assurance.

The other four roles that Belbin regarded as forms of legitimate leadership are more often thought of as supporting roles. In fact, one of them is sometimes called just that. A *supporter* provides emotional leadership, fostering team spirit and nurturing team members as individuals. An *implementer* leads in transforming concepts and plans into practical systems and solutions, carrying out group plans as agreed. A *finisher* sees that work of the group is completed and maintains the group's focus and sense of urgency. An *investigator* manages the interfaces with other groups and resources, exploring and conducting research.

For the highest performance, team leadership is a multifaceted function. Typically, the varied forms of essential leadership are distributed among team members rather than being concentrated into one "superleader" who can do it all. Indeed, this "shared leadership" model has been found as the hallmark of more successful groups of many kinds.

Two distinct senses of diversity are essential to effective teamwork. High-performance teams need varied technical skills and backgrounds. This seems to be the easy part for most people. From diverse experiences and abilities the team is able to cover more of the technical landscape than one person ever could. Of course, there are always those superstars who are driven to try to do it all and be expert at everything, but scant few are very successful. The price of too many interests is often a sacrifice in depth or rigor, and the dilettante risks being singled out for criticism. (There are some who have opined, for instance, that the eclectic and versatile author of this book is really just "intellectually promiscuous.")

In addition to diverse skills and knowledge, Belbin's work—and numerous other studies that followed—suggests that variety in *style* is at least as important as variety in content. By style I mean not only personality, but also interpersonal proclivities. If everyone is trying to lead the way through the door, the entire team jams up at the jamb. If everyone is of the sort who looks for something to play off of before committing support, the entire crew may end up waiting at the bottom of the stairs while the plane takes off without them.

Liking Alikes

These findings pose some challenges for software developers. One difficulty is that most everybody seems to prefer to work with people who are essentially like themselves, while better team performance seems to result from putting together people who are essentially different. Having a variety of skills and a variety of working styles in which to carry out those skills gives team flexibility.

I think of this matter of team diversity as not unlike ethnic diversity in the larger world, especially the contribution of ethnicity to the richness of culture and cuisine. It would be a much impoverished world without chiles rellenos, tom kah gai, szekely goulash, pesto sauce, lamb vindaloo, coq au vin, strange-flavored beef, pasta primavera, paella, and feijoada. If we are to learn how to function well in diversified teams, we need to learn to value the diversity in skills, background, and style as much as we value diversity in diet.

Of course, I also knew a prince of a man who worked as a systems analyst with the post office and ate the same thing for lunch every day for 17 years. There are those people who just prefer to stick with the same foods all the time, and I am not sure where they fit in. A good teamwork model has room for them, but I am not sure how much they would like working on a truly diversified team—or eating at my house.

It is not always easy to tell when variety shades over into incompatibility. People often think of *The Odd Couple* as the classic case of fundamental incompatibility, yet Felix Unger and Oscar Madison really functioned quite well together considering that they perpetually drove each other crazy. In teamwork, perhaps, individual frustration may not be as important as collective performance.

Against this background must be written the growing body of disturbing evidence that programmers and computer professionals are strongly skewed in the direction of certain personality types. Australian consultant Rob Thomsett found that more than three out of five of those people in the computer field share the same basic personality profile. They are practical, logical, matter-of-fact, and realistic. They concentrate and maintain focus on useful subjects and practical issues. They are not particularly "people-oriented." Less than 20% of the general population fit this profile. This group of typical computer people also tends to perform within only certain of the team leadership roles. They are likely to be implementers, finishers, monitors, or drivers; few if any go for the coordinator or supporter styles, which are crucial for smooth and effective interpersonal functioning of a team, or for the originator role, which is essential for creative problem solving.

Thomsett blames the selection process of training and higher-level education, but there may be other factors operating here. I have management consulting colleagues in Russia who argue that computer programming represents a subculture of such power that it may have greater influence and claims to allegiance than even national culture. Their position is that programmers in Moscow are more like programmers in Minneapolis than either are like their nonprogramming compatriots from the cities in which they live and work. Whatever the causes, this trend toward uniformity may be a real handicap to our profession, especially as we work in teams.

Joshua Jacobson, conductor of Boston's Zamir Chorale and also one of my favorite philosophers, put it this way at one of our rehearsals. If everyone sings the same note, you do not get harmony. For harmony you need people singing different notes that fit together. In this he echoes another of my favorites, Heraclitus, The Obscure. He was called The Obscure not because he is any more difficult to understand than the next Greek philosopher, but because so little is known of him except indirectly and by attribution. This may account for why he is credited with so many wise and wonderful insights that seem to support such varied positions. Supposedly he said, "Εχ των διαφεροντων χαλλιστη αρμονια." Loosely translated from the Greek, this says, "From differing songs arises the highest harmony."

Amen, Heraclitus! Selah, Jacobson!

From *Computer Language Magazine*, Volume 9, #9, September 1992.

10

Coding Cowboys
and Software Sages

Quality has become a watchword of the hour in software development. Some of the concern with quality is genuine, and some is merely panicky chief executives lunging after the bandwagon rolling by; some "quality programs" will make a difference, and some will only make for good public relations. As issues of software quality come to the fore, matters of maturity will loom larger, because an effective commitment to quality requires maturity from organizations and individuals.

Managers of software development face many new challenges as software systems become larger and more complex. Organizations are moving toward greater "process maturity" using more disciplined and sophisticated models of software development. The question in the minds of many managers is whether development professionals will live up to their name and mature with the methods. Programmers, analysts, and designers are often a breed unto themselves, and managing an entire herd of such mavericks can tax the resources of even the best managers. The problems of dealing with diehard independents who would rather quit than collaborate are major issues facing software development groups today.

Even with the surplus of loners in the field, most software is produced by groups of people working together. Some of it is produced by groups of people working separately. Some is even produced by groups of people working against each other. Very little software is developed by individuals working alone.

This obvious, simple, and seemingly inconsequential fact would not be worth stating were it not for the way in which the field of software development is dominated by myths of giants, by a mythology that glorifies the brilliant genius who single-handedly conceives and codes clever new systems in sweaty and sleepless weekends of nonstop programming. We are blessed and cursed by the promethean images of these nerdy pioneers bringing us new languages, new tools, and new paradigms for computer applications. And we are blessed and cursed by a larger cadre of lesser godlings, programmers of more limited talent but nevertheless indomitable spirit, determined individualists who insist on doing things their way, alone, without interference, without help, without the hindrances of supervision, methodology, or discussion.

Management and organizational consultants often refer to such people as "cowboys." Cowboys, the last of the rugged and untamed, are found in various fields, but nowadays many of them are punching assembly language cattle on the silicon frontier. They have also been called "human cougars," for their solitary and sometimes wary ways. They are the mavericks who either go it their own way or not at all.

In case there are any doubts, it is important to make clear that I am a maverick myself, or so I have been told. In fact, I have been officially branded a maverick by methodologist-become-historian Paul Ward in his history of structured analysis (Ward 1992). He has personally assured me that it is to be taken as a compliment. I certainly have been a nonconformist most of my professional life. Modern software engineering may have embraced many of the basic principles of structured design, with CASE tools and integrated development environments enshrining data flow diagrams and structure charts as the technical iconography of development orthodoxy, but such was not always the case. Difficult though it may be to believe, these were once the unorthodox, even radical ravings of a maverick.

I believe in mavericks; many of my best friends are mavericks. And I believe in the maverick imagination, in individual creativity as the well-spring of nearly all genuine innovation. I also recognize it as the well-spring of much monumental lunacy. For every Einstein there are a gaggle of Velikovskys. Sometimes the innovation and idiocy even spout from the same font, as from a Tesla or a Wilhelm Reich. One way or another, mavericks have enriched our lives, if not always by invention then by entertainment.

Being a cowboy is not the same as being independent or an individualist. The definition does not hinge on whether or not someone uses a particular software methodology or even any methodology at all. Being a cowboy is a frame of mind and a style of life. Cowboy coders are simply those oppositional developers who can't abide being fenced in by standards, constraints, or discipline, who resist all efforts at being reined in by supervision or collaboration with others, who put idiosyncratic originality above usability or reliability.

Of course, not every programmer who prefers to work alone is a coding cowboy. Some people are loners by temperament. Some are perhaps better described as hermits, others just prefer their own company, and many simply find the company of others distracting or even overwhelming. Some of my best work has been done with no one in the room but me and my trusty computer.

Managing Mavericks

Why is it important to manage mavericks? Why not merely turn them loose, let them join their cowboy companions as contract programmers and independent consultants? For one thing, there are so many of them. For another, a lot of them are good, and potentially could be a heck of a lot better if their creative contrariness could be tempered by a little more cooperation. Mavericks and coding cowboys have a real contribution to make to software development. Good management creates a context for capturing and utilizing this contribution for the benefit of both the organization and the cowboys.

Some managers advocate a laissez faire approach to coding cowboys. Expecting discipline or imposing standards just keeps programmers from reaching their full potential as brilliant programming cowboys.

I think managers have better options—at least I hope so. The free-rein approach probably accounts for a lot of the poor performance and unreliability of the products being shipped by many such major software companies. It shows also in the user interfaces of major software products that suffer from creeping featurism and are covered with a hodge-podge of unreconciled hooks and handles contributed by each and every member of the old programming posse.

As the size and complexity of software products grows, it is more important for project managers to learn how to use the isolated developer wisely. Even where the dominant project model is collaborative teamwork, the best managers will find ways to accommodate the needs of loners. It may not be possible to allow them to work in complete isolation, but it also may not be necessary to make them attend every meeting or code walkthrough.

Loners can do good work and they can do poor work. It is up to the manager to find ways to utilize them so that they do good work. Part of the trick is in how the work is broken down and assigned. Those who work best in isolation need to be given tasks that are more or less separable, portions of the system that can be defined as black boxes with simple interfaces and well-defined external specifications. They need to work on components that are only weakly coupled with other parts of the system, that do not require close coordination or frequent communication with others.

Another part of the trick is careful monitoring and review. Limiting the interdependencies between independents and the rest of the development team does not mean ignoring them. In fact, when part of a system is developed separately, it is even more important to monitor the interfaces and interconnections that remain. Managers often understand this when working with outside contractors or telecommuters who work at home, but tend to forget it when dealing with the independent who sits in the office down the hall.

When work is done openly in groups, increased visibility tends to reduce defects and increase quality (See Chapters 26 and 33). Work completed in some degree of isolation from a development group therefore warrants greater scrutiny in terms of conformance to external specifications and closer inspection in terms of implementation quality. It is not enough that the code works as far as acceptance testing can verify; quality assurance must also study the code itself for conformity to standards of clarity and reliability.

Mavericks and Methods

Working alone does not imply working without discipline or without good methodology, any more than working in a group guarantees results. Working in a group only guarantees there are more people involved. From the manager's perspective, however, using systematic development methodology assumes greater importance when there are developers working in isolation. Regression testing and implementation walkthroughs can only do so much in assuring quality. True quality cannot be achieved after the fact; it has to be designed and built in from the beginning. Systematic and formal methods for software development are proven ways of building in quality. The work of even the most independent coding cowboy will probably be improved and can certainly be trusted more if a systematic methodology is used.

In order to get the coding cowboys to use systematic development methods, management may have to compromise on *which* method is used. It is better that independent operators use their own idiosyncratic methods than no methods at all.

Design models not only can speed development and improve quality but can also aid traceability by providing a partial record of a developer's thought processes, an audit trail of the derivation of problems and solutions. Requiring appropriate design documents—data flow diagrams, structure charts, structured flow charts, and the like—needs to be part of the specifications for subsystems that are to be developed independently.

Project managers may find analogies to the cattle range useful to help keep in mind an assortment of approaches for dealing with programming mavericks. Trail bosses had to ride herd on their charges, watching for strays that separated themselves too far from the group, gathering them in periodically. They kept close watch on their cowhands and the cattle they herded. They also left room for cowboys to let off steam on Saturday nights.

Cowboy Collectives

Meilir Page-Jones has developed a very practical schema for understanding the ages of software process maturity. Some groups operate in the *age of anarchy*, developing software without the benefit of any systematic approaches or even codified wisdom. Everything rests on the skill of the individual. The *age of folklore* is characterized by a culture of collective wisdom, accumulated knowledge that is often embodied in stories about successes and failures or rules of thumb extracted from past experiences. The *age of methods* is based in systematic, although not necessarily formal, approaches to software development that go beyond folklore. The *age of metrics* is based on measures for evaluating quality and productivity and organized feedback for improving the development process based on measurement. Finally, we reach the *age of engineering,* in which software development becomes a true engineering discipline, a process under continuous improvement using methods that are not based in folklore or armchair speculation but on theory validated through study and research, in which design decisions and trade-offs are systematic and derived from models and metrics that embody the results of a growing body of knowledge.

Engineering is what you get when mature individuals in mature organizations use mature methods. Anarchy is what you get when you simply throw a group of coding cowboys into the corral together and point them at a problem.

Unfortunately, when mavericks are put into groups they are prone to becoming oppositional. It is not uncommon for them to end up working at cross purposes. Without creative leadership, a whole group of coding cowboys is apt to lead to unmanageable chaos.

When teamed with other less contrary types, coding cowboys can have a tendency to undermine teamwork. Some may hold back and refuse to participate in group problem solving, others may take up most of the air time with their own favorite topics and approaches. Often they are critical of any ideas they did not generate and end up in conflict with the rest of the group.

In the worst cases, the contrarions end up being pushed into a corner and scapegoated for their negative attitudes. In turn, coding cowboys may come to view the rest of a team as a bunch of groupthink bozos who couldn't code their way out of a cardboard box and don't appreciate true genius when they see it.

Managers need to know how to head off such polarization for the sake of the team and the end product. Direct confrontation may not be the preferred style of management for handling coding cowboys. It can be risky to face down cowboys. They have deserved reputations for strong opinions, sensitive egos, and itchy trigger fingers. Managers are unlikely to be able to win such a face off and may only antagonize their cowboys into even more entrenched opposition.

The real challenge facing managers is what to do about the mavericks and strays. Some would argue that they need to be cut out of the herd and put out to pasture, but this option is not always available and may not serve the best interests of the organization. My boss says that the job of the manager is to get rid of the obstacles that keep others from doing their jobs well and from fulfilling their greatest potential. Lucky me. Part of the potential of well-managed mavericks is to bring their creative energy and critical abilities to the organization.

Some kinds of teams thrive on opposition, others cannot abide dissent. It depends on the basic model by which a team is organized (Constantine 1993c; Larson and LaFasto 1989). Project teams that are based on top-down management and work assignment, that rely on traditional authority for direction, or that are headed by highly directive leaders, will have greater problems with mavericks and coding cowboys. The work of such traditional tactical teams (see Chapter 11) can be hampered by opposition, and their controlled style of organization can push mavericks into rebellion.

A free-wheeling "breakthrough" team (Chapter 12), on the other hand, can be energized by mavericks, whose independent spirit and creative individuality are just what the group needs. The issue here is how to foster creativity rather than chaos. The key to getting useful work out of such a team is promoting high levels of mutual regard and respect for each other's competence. Teams where members see their teammates as skilled professionals with good ideas can engage in healthy competition without degenerating into a free-for-all.

Teams that work by building technical consensus (see Part I) can also be good settings for mavericks. A technical consensus is one in which the contributions of all team members are taken into account in arriving at a common decision that all members feel they can support, even if they do not necessarily agree on every detail.

Opposition or criticism should never be confused with disloyalty. In fact, critical feedback is often the most valuable information and the most important to hear. Healthy skepticism and critical perspectives should be encouraged, not disparaged. The quality of group problem solving has been shown to be critically dependent on this kind of "negative feedback." Groups that include a "resident critic" or "devil's advocate," or that exploit dialectical processes of opposing ideas and active critique, perform better (Constantine 1989; Priem and Price 1991).

Managers should remember that, just as authority tries to control opposition, opposition resists control and authority. So, instead of controlling, co-opt! One way to co-opt opposition and turn it to the advantage of the team is to institutionalize it. In one approach (Constantine 1989, 1991a), the critic or "devil's advocate" is regarded as a valued contributor whose role in the group is critical to success. Like the "grit in the oyster," critical monitoring of the work of the team is the necessary irritant that forms the basis for producing programming pearls (Thomsett 1990). As a team member, the maverick is formally charged with the responsibility to critique decisions, take alternative viewpoints, note exceptions, problems, and limitations, and make sure that the group considers alternatives and explores difficulties with proposed solutions.

Mavericks are often better at criticizing than being criticized. When they go off on their own, however, their work needs to be checked and reviewed, which they may resent as intrusive and distrusting. If critical feedback to the coding cowboy is needed, it is best rendered as impersonal as possible, appealing to the analytical and critical skills of mavericks, challenging them to be creative in solving whatever problems are uncovered.

It is not surprising that the biggest limitations on mavericks are self-imposed. They can get stuck in the need to be unique, to do things differently, even at the expense of practicality. Working alone also limits the size of what they can tackle. Mavericks can end up alienating coworkers.

Dissent and Diversity

We now know that diversity in teams promotes better problem solving and decision making. Several decades of research on group dynamics has demonstrated that heterogeneity beats homogeneity almost all the time. Teams of men and women solve problems better than single-sex teams. Groups that include varied specialties and training fare better. Diversity wins, whether it is diversity in personality, in interpersonal style, or in culture or ethnic background.

Clearly, then, we do not want to get rid of all the mavericks. We want teams in which a variety of leadership styles and responses to leadership are displayed—including resistance to leadership. We need movers and shakers on our teams, innovators who will generate ideas, and champions who will drive them forward. But we also need critics and skeptics who counter unbridled enthusiasm with cool doubt, who keep uncritical support from running away with unproved notions. Opposition to leadership can even serve the team by keeping leadership within bounds.

We are hampered in exploiting opposition by simplistic notions of teamwork that are based on ideals of perfect harmony and fantasies of cooperation without conflict. For the best collective performance, contention may be the most essential ingredient in a creative process that results in a quality product.

And what is a software sage? A software sage is someone who recognizes opposition as opportunity, and who sees flexibility in frustration. A software sage is the wise old ranch hand who has been through the range wars, has been there out on the lone prairie, and has returned to the homestead. A software sage may even be a reformed cowboy or cowgirl, one who has never lost respect for the individual but who has come to value cooperation.

Revised from *American Programmer*, July 1993.

III

Work Organization

Introduction

Although I started out in the computer field armed with a management degree from M.I.T., I was initially more interested in the technical side of programming. It was through my work on family systems that I first became seriously involved in issues of teamwork organization and organization development. Although my career in computers and software spans more than thirty years, I took a detour of some dozen years in the middle. I was lucky then to be an applied systems theorist moving into the family field at a time when family sociology and family therapy were moving toward systems theory (Whitchurch and Constantine 1992). Marriage and family studies, sociology, and social psychology had all begun to understand how groups of people function as systems and to apply general systems theory and systems thinking to making sense of human systems.

I had the very great fortune to study and work under psychologist David Kantor, one of the cleverest investigators and most creative thinkers in the field. Kantor had been studying families by direct observation, documenting and describing the delicate dance of daily living by which families coordinate and sustain their activities and relationships. Out of his extraordinarily rich observations came the recognition that even untroubled families were not all alike. He developed a framework for understanding the varied and quite distinct models under which families functioned. His book, *Inside the Family* (Kantor and Lehr 1975), one of the most inventive works of modern social science research, has become an influential classic.

David is a better researcher, but I think I am a better theorist, so I took up the challenge of refining and filling in some of the holes in his theoretical thinking. The result was an extension of the framework to cover the full array of human systems, from families to informal groups, from project teams to multinational organizations. Eventually, my own book on "family paradigms" (Constantine 1986) was completed, and to my surprise and delight it began to be used in graduate courses in management and organization development. Eventually a loose network of management consultants around the world developed around the application of David's and my work to the world of work. It was some of these who helped convince me there were exciting things going on in the computer field and that I ought to come back, bringing along what I'd learned from studying and working with families.

11

Traditional Tactics

Okay, people, time to get organized! The question is: how? If you work alone, you can work any darned way you please. You don't need to coordinate what you are doing with what anyone else is doing, and you don't have to get along with anyone. You can keep everything in its exact, obsessive-compulsive place and do things in the precise sequence of a standard software development life cycle model. Or you can leave everything spread out all over the office in utter chaos and code things as you get inspired or happen to think of them. However, once you have two or more people working together, the operant word is "together." The work they do and how they do it have to be coordinated.

This chapter begins an exploration of the organization and management of human work: how work is organized and how people who work together coordinate their activities (Constantine 1990a, 1991c, 1993c). Think of organization as the human equivalent of software architecture—with management corresponding to the dynamic control of program components. It's the old structure and dynamics thing again. Whether you are trying to organize a new software company or the next programming project, many of the same issues apply.

So how do you do it? How do you get a group of people—a project team or an entire corporation—to work together? How do you organize the group, structure the work, and manage the activity? What's the right way? Here it's time for one of those standard "consultant's answers": it depends!

Looking for the *right* way to organize projects is like looking for the *right* way to code a subroutine. It depends on what you are trying to accomplish (Constantine 1993c). The bread-and-butter work of producing yet another set of print drivers or another variant on a conventional screen generator may require a very different model for organization and management than what is needed for a team devising a breakthrough CASE tool to support concurrent software engineering and consensus design of object-oriented software. In an excellent little book on teamwork, Larson and LaFasto (1989) identified several major variants on project teamwork, each of which is better at some things than others. Here we'll look at four distinct and very different models for project teamwork organization, each having advantages in certain areas and each having its own particular weaknesses.

Getting Organized

So, let's get organized! The simplest and safest way to go is the tried and true of standard operating procedure. The traditional way to coordinate the work of more than one person is to put someone in charge, making them a supervisor. The function of the supervisor is to direct and oversee the work of others. This structure can be extended by recursion. The result is a hierarchy of managers in charge of others who manage still others. This is a simple, stable, and familiar form of organization: a traditional pyramid based on a hierarchy of authority. On software projects organized along this model, the hierarchy may not be many layers deep, but it is still a hierarchy. In principle, it can be amazingly efficient; in practice it can grow into a towering bureaucracy incapable of anything but sustaining its own bureaucratic inefficiency.

Such a model is more than merely a way of working; it can be a way of life. I was recently reorganizing my record collection to make room for the steadily multiplying CDs when I found a real treasure, a vintage recording of "Paean," selections from the IBM corporate songbook.* Listening to the Association of British Secretaries in America (indeed!) sing their stirring rendition of "The IBM Country Club Song," I started thinking about company culture and how the way we work shapes the way we view the world as much as the other way around.

---

* Released as a joke for one of the major computer conferences but not without its valid insight into corporate culture and politics.

The traditional view from the pyramid sees organization as the foundation of stable performance and sees control as the key to keeping it all together. Leadership depends on authority. Managers make decisions and subordinates are expected to implement them, to show loyalty, and to accept direction from their superiors. Predictable, reliable performance is achieved through standards and procedures, through rules of operation. Everyone has their job, their role, their responsibilities, their place in the hierarchy. Corporate or divisional or project interests come first and foremost; individuals are rewarded for faithfully carrying out their part of the larger job.

In basic form, this model is really very simple. Put somebody in charge who can start making decisions and giving orders, preferably someone who knows the ropes and has come up through the business. Decision making in traditional hierarchies is supposed to be strictly top down. It may take time for a given matter to reach the right person in charge, but once it does, decision making can be quite efficient. As fast as the leader can make up her or his mind, the decision is made. No one needs to be consulted; there is no need for discussion, debate, or exploration. Obviously, this can be a strength and a weakness. It means that a lot hinges on the one at the top. Bad decisions can be made as quickly as good ones, and a leader who is too slow or out of touch can bring the entire pyramid crumbling down in ruin.

Pyramid Power

When it comes to software projects and project teamwork, the traditional model is best at what can be called tactical work. In tactical projects, the territory is familiar and the parameters are known. The most important thing is to get the work out the door. I cut my programming teeth on tactical projects, producing routine business system applications, such as payroll, cost accounting, and personnel file maintenance. Once you have done a couple of payroll systems, they all begin to look alike. Even if they really aren't, seeing them that way helps you to simplify, making it easier to build and maintain standard ways of doing things. Eventually, you know all the steps and can do them in your sleep.

Clarity is the make-or-break issue for tactical teamwork—clear requirements, clear directions, clear roles. Within this world, development methods are more effective when they are well defined, with clear standards and guidelines. A detailed software development life cycle is specified within which successive phases are carried out. Work is expected to be accurate and efficient. The focus of the group in such a team is on the task at hand. Period. What team members need most is clear direction from project leaders and management. Team members are assigned specific portions of the well-understood work and do what they are supposed to do. Traditional hierarchy works. Many companies in our industry and countless software projects have been organized along these lines, including some of the biggest success stories in computing. Corporate songbooks extolling fearless leaders and loyal followers are the artifacts of some of the largest and best examples.

Such a well-defined and predictable environment can be comforting, but not everyone is comfortable fitting into that world. Those who do are likely to be loyal, committed, and action-oriented. They attach a sense of importance to the work they are doing more than to themselves, and they respond well to directions from leaders. They probably prefer to pay more attention to programs than people. Tactical teams are havens for conformists and obsessive-compulsives, for salt-of-the-earth basic programmers. Tactical teams work well for those who want to know what to do and just do it.

On the downside, any group organized as a traditional hierarchy can somewhat too easily get stuck in a rut, resisting useful innovation in the interests of maintaining stable authority, and ultimately spending more energy on rigidly enforcing standards and procedures than on solving problems or producing products. At their best, they are efficient and productive but not very innovative. To the extent that they do innovate, it is likely to be incremental improvements on established technology, evolution rather than revolution. Looking at the large industry leaders who rely on traditional hierarchy, we often find that their major innovations have come from acquisitions or from small internal spin-offs.

Companies and software groups organized along these lines are likely to have particular difficulty dealing with cowboy coders (Chapters 7, 8, and 10). Independent individualists and traditional hierarchy are an immiscible combination. Those who resist or question authority, who insist on going their own way or departing from standards, are likely to find themselves passed over for raises or on the short list for downsizing.

From the top of the pyramid or buried somewhere within, it may look like there is no other way to organize and manage. After all, somebody has to be in charge, right? Either you lead, you follow, or you get out of the way. Some people still don't see any alternative to hierarchy for human organizations. But then we once thought that nested subroutines topped by a control executive were the only way to modularize programs. Now we have communities of communicating objects and peer-to-peer networks with distributed databases.

And people are ever so much more flexible than programs. At least *some* people.

From *Software Development,* Volume 1, #3, March 1993.

12

Chaos Manners

I have some good news for all the coding "cowboys" and "cowgirls" out there. There is a kind of organization that not only tolerates but depends for its vitality on utilizing the talents of true independents.

It may come as a shock to some old-timers or young hard-liners, but neither hierarchy nor authority are necessary for groups of people to work together effectively. Indeed, a worldwide management revolution may be taking place, as more and more companies in numerous industries discover the advantages of self-directed teams, autonomous work groups, and managing without managers. One of the big problems with the traditional management pyramid is that it is so dense in the middle—in more than one sense of the phrase. All those layers of middle management cost, not only in terms of dollars but also in terms of responsiveness. The closer you try to dance along the precipitous leading edge of any technology, the more unwieldy the pyramid becomes. Genuine innovation requires an agility beyond the traditional tactics of top-down management.

Breaking Through

For real breakthroughs that push technology beyond the edge into unexplored regions, project teams are more likely to succeed by turning to the flexibility of independent action and the full force of individual creativity, unhampered by command-and-control. The trick is to bring out and capitalize on the inventive energy of independent thinkers, encouraging free exploration and individual initiative, to foster a kind of creative chaos that hovers on the supercharged edge of running completely amok, a sort of controlled insanity that breaks out of accepted modes of thinking and challenges assumptions about limits and possibilities. All these things run absolutely counter to the closed patterns of corporate pyramid power because they undermine authority and throw tradition to the winds—profoundly threatening to the traditional management mentality, but precisely what is needed to break new ground.

The key ingredients for a breakthrough initiative are, in fact, the exact antithesis of the tradition-bound hierarchical model. Instead of putting stability ahead of change, instability is promoted, becoming the driving force to overcome blindly accepted practices and unquestioned notions. Instead of putting corporate and collective interests above individual ones, individual freedom of expression and action come first. Where the traditional pyramid tries to rein in cantankerous coding "cowboys" and "cowgirls," breakthrough teams love them and let them run free. This free-wheeling atmosphere stimulates creativity and tends to promote the "personal best" performances that can generate breakthroughs.

Breakthrough teams actually depend on individual initiative to coordinate their activities. Decisions are not centralized but are made independently, close to the action, by whomever encounters the problems and has the know-how to resolve them. What keeps such a group on course is a kind of friendly competition; what keeps them from running off in every direction at once is their common interest in and love of the game and their mutual respect for each other as players.

You are most likely to find this model operating in smaller high-tech companies, entrepreneurial start-ups, and the research and development divisions of larger organizations. They can be remarkably successful. Indeed, many a muscle-bound corporate behemoth relies on an undisciplined "corporate skunkworks" for the new ideas and products that keep the collective engine primed and running.

Work and Play

Consider this scenario in an archetypal Pacific coast company drawn from real experience. You enter the lobby to find the phones being handled by a bearded, middle-aged guy who turns out to be the veep for R&D. You tell him you are a GUI consultant and he waves you down the hall to the left. Ducking a barely subsonic frisbee that sails past, you try to find someone in charge. No luck. Recognizing a screen on a workstation in one office, you approach someone who is browsing through a familiar class library and turns out to be the receptionist. But conversation becomes increasingly difficult as the pace of the hallway frisbee game picks up. A couple of programmers, who are busy debugging work-arounds to an operating system problem, holler for quiet but end up getting drawn into the melee of flying discs. Soon the entire department has adjourned to the adjacent parking lot for a furious five-frisbee tournament.

To a casual observer, it may look like bedlam or kindergarten, but during this particular frisbee game a couple of programmers get inspired by the pattern in which the group keeps multiple frisbees flying without interference. They devise from it a novel solution to a nagging problem in the groupware that the department has been developing. Was it dumb luck? Were they just fooling around on the job? Impossible to tell in such a group. Work is play and play is work. Is the receptionist a software engineer? You never know.

And what about the V.P. of R&D, is he part of the support staff? He is if he's any good. Effective managers of this kind of creative chaos know that their real job is to provide resources and support, run interference for the group, and stay out of the way. The best such managers and team leaders are also likely to be techies themselves, basically one of the bunch, but particularly respected for their own programming prowess or other technical talents.

Of course, it doesn't always work, and even when it is working, inventive nuttiness can have its downside. It can be darned difficult holding a planning meeting or a code walkthrough when staff are always coming and going and those in the room may be preparing e-mail on a laptop or playing chess on a pocket board. And communications within a breakthrough team can be haphazard at best, even when everyone is in the same room. Not that these creative independents are uncommunicative, just that information can too easily get lost in the chaos. ("Oh, yeah, the client did message us last week about a change in the interface protocol. The note got filed someplace. I think.")

The brilliant and decidedly independent psychologist David Kantor was among the first to observe that apparent randomness in human groups disguises an underlying, complexly patterned logic (Kantor and Lehr 1975). In this, his studies anticipated more recent work applying chaos theory to groups. Kantor recognized two variants of apparent randomness, one he called creative and the other chaotic, in the older and more traditional sense of chaos. The difference between "random creative" and "random chaotic" is crucial; it is the difference between success and failure in achieving a software breakthrough.

In extreme cases, a breakthrough team can become a *breakdown* team. Without the right ingredients, friendly competition can become unfriendly, unproductive, and even desperate. Would-be contributors work at cross purposes and fight for resources. Eventually, people may spin completely out of control, leaving the organization and project in shambles.

The first necessary ingredient to avoid chaotic collapse is good people, bolstered by good training and tools. Members of the team must have skills and abilities that are up to the challenge of the project and that are recognized by other members of the team. Mutual respect for technical competence and an implicit trust in the ability of other members to contribute to the effort are the essential glue holding the breakthrough team together.

The second necessary ingredient for success is sufficient, even abundant resources. The almost brownian motion of whole teams of innovators can lead to extraordinary solutions, but not typically with the greatest efficiency. New algorithms have to be tried out, novel data structures have to be implemented, and clever screen layouts have to be prototyped. The process of freely creating and trying out alternative ideas is essential; even dead ends that have to be abandoned are often an important part of the group learning process. Creativity comes at a cost and requires risk taking.

Opposing Charges

How do you lead a bunch of inventive independents? Not by taking charge. Leadership of breakthrough teams is a rather special role, radically different from management in traditional tactical teams. The most effective team and project leaders are peers who are highly respected as programmers and problem solvers, who are charismatic trend-setters to whom others naturally look. They lead by example rather than edict—which would almost certainly be resisted—and are able to foster an atmosphere of high mutual regard among team members. They are also good at getting needed resources—work stations, software, training, more time—for the team, keeping it well fueled and heading off any potential breakdown into counterproductive competition for scarce resources.

For success, breakthrough teams also need autonomy: freedom from interference, freedom to explore unanticipated angles and approaches. Good leaders of such teams say, "Let the games begin!" then stay out of the way. The best ones also make sure that nobody else gets in the way either.

A project team organized and managed for creative breakthrough can be a fun, interesting environment in which to work, but not everyone can work well in such a setting. People who need clear directions, well-defined goals, and straightforward expectations are likely to be more comfortable in a traditional hierarchy. The kinds of developers who perform best in breakthrough teams may be either artistic or intellectual, but they are sure to be seen as independent-minded. They are self-starters who don't wait for directions, but more than that, the best performers are also perversely persevering. Good tactical team members are often those who are especially responsive to direction from leaders, but good innovators are likely to be more individualistic, even resistant to authority and direction.

It probably would make little sense to turn an entire cadre of creative cowboys and cowgirls loose on a routine database application for the accounting department; the poor accountants might themselves be driven to stampede. On the other end of the scale, massive projects marked by countless components and complex interdependencies—the civilian space station software, for instance—are not the bailiwick of breakthrough teams, even when there is a clearly recognizable need for innovation. Teams of creative independents, for obvious reasons, fit better with smaller and simpler projects that do not require close coordination of too many highly interdependent parts.

The large-scale complexity of many modern software projects is better approached by other project models to be discussed in later chapters. In the meantime, the Nanomush Corporation and International Behemoth Management, Inc., types will have to continue to muddle their way through with their chaotic cowpokes and their megapyramids.

From *Software Development*, Volume 1, #5, May 1993.

13

Open Architects

Many folks believe that there are basically two kinds of people. The rest of us, of course, are different; we know better. So it is when it comes to work and organizations. There are those who think the choice is between orderly authority and unbridled anarchy—or between freedom and oppression—and that's it! The rest of us know it is never that simple. Whatever managers and management consultants may do to simplify the story, real people in real organizations defy the limitations of simple dichotomies and slip out of the one-dimensional conceptual boxes into which we try to stuff them.

On the one hand, we have the hierarchical model for work organization discussed in Chapter 11 and on the other, its exact opposite, the creative anarchy explored in Chapter 12. And in between the extremes of ordered traditionalism and freestyle innovation are scattered as many variations as there are projects and people to work on them.

Not every working group falls somewhere along this line, however. Some, quite far off in left field, do not see the basic issues of work organization as trade-offs. These are the people who think "both/and" rather than "either/or," who say, "We can work it out." Both traditionalists and their free-spirited competition tend to see an essential tension between "me" and "we." In the traditional hierarchy, the interests of individuals are subordinated to those of the team or group or organization; in innovative individualism, the individual reigns supreme and collective interests are moved backstage.

Others, however, believe there is no essential conflict between the whole and its parts, just as there is no need to choose between change and stability.

Their approach to working together, officially known as the "open paradigm," is a model for flexibility based on egalitarian cooperation and communication. In descriptive shorthand, we could call this model "adaptive collaboration," an open-ended architecture for human organization.

Hanging Loose, Hanging Together

Adaptive collaboration is tailored for technical problem solving. It values neither tradition and stability nor innovation and change in themselves. What is important in this view of projects and progress is the adaptive fit between how the team is working and what it is they are working on. Today we're designing independent programs, so we work separately; tomorrow we have to come up with a common communications protocol, so we meet as a group; everyone has something to say about database architecture, so let's get all the ideas out on the table.

The aim in such a group is to hang loose and talk things through so that competing goals can be integrated and alternative approaches can be synthesized. They are, in a sense, continually reinventing themselves, changing the way they work to fit the needs of the moment and the group's long-term goals. Who is "in charge" and how they are in charge depends on what the group is doing.

Development groups organized along these lines tend to be more of a flat circle than a pyramid. Team members work as colleagues with interchangeable roles. Unlike the free radicals of "breakthrough" teams, who may work quite independently and even competitively, these colleagues closely coordinate their efforts. Decisions are made collectively, through discussions, negotiation, and consensus building. This does not mean that everyone agrees on everything, but that they work on the basis of a technical consensus. A technical consensus is one in which all team members can support the group's actions and choices on all essential matters. This requires getting everyone's input on matters of importance. Technical consensus assures that co-workers "buy in" to the joint effort and feel pride of personal ownership in the collective product.

Because they talk things through together, these groups really shine on solving complex problems, especially where substantial quantities of information have to be exchanged and examined (which sounds suspiciously like a lot of software development). In fact, the more factors and facets and widgets and whatsits to the problem, the greater the relative advantage of open teams over tactical teams, where information may be too tightly controlled, and break-through teams, where information can get lost in the competition and chaos.

Breakthrough groups, putting a premium on free-thinking originality, may also come up with brilliant innovations that fall short of being completely practical. Their stolid counterparts in tactical teams may produce dependably routine programs but miss out on more creative possibilities in data structures or algorithms or user interfaces. Collaborative problem-solving teams are in the best position to pull together disparate ideas from all their members to produce solutions that are both practical and innovative.

Real collaboration requires the right kind of leadership, leadership that encourages free discussion and helps to build technical consensus. The best managers for open problem-solving projects tend to be working colleagues, competent professionals themselves who play an active technical role in analysis, design, and construction. Typically, they do not lead meetings or technical discussions themselves, because they don't want to bias the outcome. Instead, they let others facilitate the discussion, drawing out the best contributions of all members. This takes a certain act of faith, a belief that the group as a whole knows more and can come up with better solutions than any one member—including the manager! Managers who are convinced that they are the smartest and best and can lay out programs better than everyone else on the project put together are not likely to fare as well as collaborative colleagues. They might do better on their own or heading a traditional tactical team.

Not surprisingly, the strong suit of adaptive collaboration can also be a handicap. These people can talk up a storm. When an hour's discussion won't resolve an issue, they're ready to spend a couple more. Not only do they haggle over the technical issues, but the philosophy behind the issues; not only do they question the development methods, but the assumptions on which they are based. Even the way the group itself operates is grist for the mill, as they examine their own methods and structures and try to adapt them to fit the problem. ("Hey, guys, maybe we need to split up into subgroups on this part of the system, work for a few days, then reconvene to try to pull it together.")

There are ways to cut down on the wheel-spinning tendencies of problem-solving teams. Decisions can be time-boxed. If a technical consensus is not reached by a specific deadline, the issue may be set aside, or defaulted to some set solution, or put into the hands of the manager for arbitration. Although each of these options somewhat violates the rules of consensual decision making, as long as they remain uncommon exceptions, the payoffs in efficiency can offset some loss in the sense of ownership in the results.

But it depends; there is no simple formula. To remain open, each group has to find its own way, negotiating its own procedures and exceptions.

Keeping the Door Open

One of the best collaborative groups I ever knew was known as the Theory Construction Workshop, an independent working group loosely affiliated with a professional society. Members met as colleagues trying to advance a common enterprise of theory construction in an atmosphere of free discussion and mutual support. Its meetings were completely open to anyone who shared an interest in building better theory. The content and format of meetings were negotiable within the group's strong tradition of enhanced cooperation and communication. Inevitably, at almost every annual business meeting, some newcomer, flush with the excitement of joining in such a rare and wonderful interchange, would propose some form of institutionalization—incorporation, membership credentials, bylaws, printed proceedings, or the like. Every year we would dutifully discuss and debate these proposals; every year they would be defeated, the consensus being to stay open, informal, and flexible.

Then one year, without thinking it through, I arose with a radical proposal. Henceforth, to avoid wasting time deliberating these perennial proposals, all attempts to institute fixed and formal rules or structures would be banned. Even before I could finish my thought, I started laughing at my own self-contradictory suggestion. Our sincere and serious consideration of even the most ill-considered suggestions from the rankest newcomer were precisely what made the group process work. Everyone smiled, I sat down, and we went back to debating the latest plan for formal proceedings. To stay open, an open process must remain open to alternatives.

Steven Sondheim ends his brilliant theater piece, *Sunday in the Park with George*, in a wonderfully open-ended way with words attributed to Georges Seurat: "White, a blank page or canvas, his favorite: so many possibilities."

My favorite, too.

From *Software Development*, Volume 1, #6, June 1993

14

Synchronized Swimming

Want to see real rapid application development? Rent a video of the Harrison Ford movie, *Witness*, then fast forward to the scene where the Amish community builds a barn in a single day. The most remarkable thing about this particular project team is not their impressive efficiency but that there is really no leader, not even the need for leaders or leadership. They do not talk much and certainly don't have to debate over the design of the barn or negotiate who does what to build it; they just get right to work and continue to work rapidly and efficiently, in near perfect harmony, until the job is done.

This is a manager's dream come true, a kind of management utopia. "Utopia," of course, literally means "no place," and the scene from *Witness* actually happens with some regularity down in Lancaster County, Pennsylvania. "Eutopia," meaning "good place," is probably a better word. Eutopia is obviously where you want to be, an ideal. So we could call this model of project and work organization *eutopian teamwork*.

Being a software development manager in management eutopia is easy— so easy that you hardly have to lead at all. The people around you do whatever needs to be done on a software project without you looking over their shoulders or spelling things out for them. Things run so smoothly because the people who work for you and with you share your vision for the team—what you are doing and how you are going to do it. These are your kind of people; they think like you and see the world much as you do. You hardly have to say a word and they are off designing the next set of modules or coding the GUI extensions or doing whatever else is needed. Everything fits together—the people, the software, the programming—exactly as if you had worked it all out yourself, except you didn't have to figure it out. There is no conflict on the team and no insubordination. Like a synchronized swimming team, it's the very embodiment of precise perfection and harmony.

This eutopian fantasy is the last of our four basic models of project organization: the *synchronous paradigm*, a model for eutopian teamwork. Traditional tactical teams are coordinated by hierarchical authority, breakthrough teams by individual initiative, and problem-solving teams by collaborative communication. Eutopian teams depend on alignment; team members are aligned with the direction established by a shared vision and common values. Because they all understand and are in basic agreement with this common image of where the group is going and how they are going to get there, they are able to work cooperatively with almost invisible coordination. Although it is uncommon for visionary alignment to be the dominant unifying principle of an entire organization over extended periods of time, many groups, large and small, depend on some degree of alignment or function synchronously for shorter periods.

Where Nowhere Is

An incident that happened to a colleague of mine some years ago illustrates this mode of operation. An organization development consultant was meeting with clients in a hospital conference room when one leg of a massive oak conference table buckled. The table fell on her foot, twisting her leg and trapping her. Instantly, the others sprang into action. Two lifted the heavy table from her foot while another held her hand reassuringly. Someone else called ahead to x-ray while yet another slipped into the hall to get a gurney. Not a word passed among the members of this medical team. They all knew exactly what needed to be done and each simply started doing a part of it. No one had to take charge and no discussion or negotiation was necessary, yet they were not working at cross purposes.

There is nothing magical about this kind of synchronous operation. If you watched them closely enough, you would spot the communication going on, but it is largely nonverbal and relies heavily on tacit agreement and prior knowledge. As each member of the team sees what others are doing, they adjust their own actions to fit. That way everybody doesn't go for the phone at once and the gurney is available when needed.

Provided they understand the task well enough, eutopian teams can achieve high performance under demanding or critical conditions—like the situation in the hospital conference room—or for predictable and well-understood tasks of longer duration—such as the rural barn-raising. Their image and knowledge of the task and how it is best carried out is essential. Every worker in the Amish community had seen a barn-raising and probably participated in a number of them. Everyone in the hospital conference room had extensive experience with medical emergencies. It was almost certain that none of them had ever dealt with a falling conference table before, but that was unnecessary; their experience and training as medical professionals allowed them to quickly understand this new situation in a common way.

The key to effectiveness in eutopian teams is full commitment by all members to a sufficiently complex and well-articulated vision of the mission and methods of the group. If this alignment is weak or incomplete, or the vision itself is inadequate, the group will be unable to do the work without consultation or without conflict or will be unable to respond to the demands of changing conditions; they will either need tighter management or will run into more difficulties.

The first three of our basic team models and their underlying mechanisms are well understood by people who study management and organizations. Less is known about project teams that rely predominantly on alignment for coordination. Although purely synchronous groups may be relatively uncommon in the workplace, the combination of strong synchrony with traditional hierarchy is less rare. You are likely to find it in established companies doing business in mature industries with long traditions. Consultant Rob Thomsett and I found a number of quite synchronous software development groups within the British-modeled business of Australian banking. In Japan, where the corporate world holds conformity and uniformity in highest regard, even high-tech firms may rely heavily on synchronous alignment.

Smooth Waters

Eutopian teamwork is essentially the opposite of the collaborative model. Instead of talking and negotiation, the norm is not talking; after all, who needs to negotiate when people think so much alike that they are almost certain to agree from the start! The down side of such eutopian harmony is that under ordinary everyday operation all that peaceful cooperation can become somewhat dull. Since members of such a team get used to working with little or no discussion, they may not even communicate when they need to. When market conditions or underlying technology change radically or unexpectedly, they may not be able to respond or adapt as well as groups built on individual initiative or collaborative communication. At worst, they may continue on their contented way, oblivious to the world changing around them. If it is not a part of their shared vision, they may not see something as needing attention or response.

According to popular images, modern managers need to learn to survive in white water or to swim with the sharks and still succeed. While it is certainly possible to swim with sharks and survive, most swimmers would probably prefer warm, smooth waters. A synchronized swimming team would be well advised to stay out of white water altogether and far away from shark infested waters. Likewise, eutopian teams are better adapted to stable, consistent, and unhostile environments.

Even for teams built primarily on other models, though, a little synchrony can be useful. Closer alignment with a richer vision reduces the need for tight controls of any kind and increases the extent to which individual efforts reinforce and support rather than cancel out or interfere with each other.

Effective leaders of eutopian teams are charismatic gurus who can shape and share a sophisticated vision and draw others into committing to it. Especially important for the long haul is their ability to revise and expand this vision to fit new needs and reestablish alignment with the revision.

But, of course, I think you all know what I am talking about. You are my kind of people and we understand each other. Right? So there's no need to say anything more. (Say, this eutopian alignment is great!)

From *Software Development*, Volume 1, #17, July 1993.

15

Team Politics

The software project was an immense success. The programming team was stellar, churning out an amazing new system with enhanced features and a slick graphical interface. Then management killed the product.

No team is an island. Groups that work well as a team in the conference room may fail when it comes to the larger arena of corporate politics. Failure is failure. It's not enough to know the applications programming interface and the class library; it's not enough to know consensus and concurrent engineering processes. Unless you know how to play the game, you lose. The name of the game is "external environment."

Software teams need to manage their boundaries, protecting their territory but also building bridges. The new compiler is part of a suite of tools. The decision support system must interface with the accounting system, but it must also be used by executives to be useful for the business. A reputation as a bunch of unmanageable screw-ups can put a team on the short list for downsizing, but a rep as C++ super heroes could also lead to unreasonable expectations on the next object-oriented boondoggle launched by the president's son-in-law.

We've been looking at software teamwork in terms of models that shape internal styles of working, but Deborah Ancona at M.I.T.'s Sloan School of Management has been looking at how teams function in the larger environment of corporate realities, how their external strategies and styles affect performance (Ancona and Caldwell 1992). She studied consulting and new product teams, as

well as sales and management teams. What she has learned over the years fits
with my experience with programming teams.

Through the Dimensions

The external strategies of teams are a complex matter. The team leader or
project manager may play a key role in managing outside relations, but there's
more to it than just your boss dealing with her boss. Teams need to manage various interfaces and interconnections with numerous parts of the organization.
These interactions really take place in several dimensions: the power structure,
the task structure, and the information structure.

Think of the power dimension as vertical. The important external connections in this dimension are upward. Few teams achieve real high performance without learning how to "manage up." They need "ambassadors,"
politicians who know how to play organizational politics and work the power
structure, effectively marketing the project and the team, as well as building
and maintaining a good group reputation through how they represent the team
and its interests to others. Public relations can have a lot to do with team success, since a team's reputation can become a self-fulfilling prophecy. "Good"
teams get the pick of projects and priority access to new software and
machines. A lot of success can be a matter of taking on the doable challenges
and passing on the boring and the impossible.

The most important political issue for teams is probably the need to
identify and secure effective sponsorship within upper management. Well-
placed sponsors or mentors can do more for a development team than all the
CASE tools and work stations in Silicon Valley. Good politicians, well connected and fast on their feet, can also buffer for a software team, protecting it
from the shifting winds of influence and interests as divisions are sold and
companies are acquired, as middle managers move or CIOs come and go.

Task coordination is essentially a horizontal matter, involving lateral
connections across functions, managing a team's working interdependence
with other organizational units. Good coordinators bargain with other groups,
trading services or essential resources, getting feedback on progress in other
parts of the project that may have to function with the team's product. They
keep the work flowing in and out of the team, making sure that component
libraries are available, passing on specs to the people generating test suites, or
clearing screen layouts with the human factors group.

The information dimension is also largely lateral. Liaison here involves
investigating, gathering information needed for project success, sharing

selected data with others. The team researchers effectively act as gatekeepers for information, screening it so that other developers don't have to wade through piles of documentation, chasing down missing pieces so that data is available when needed.

Just as teams develop distinct styles of working internally, specializing in different things, they also seem to develop characteristic ways of managing their boundaries and interacting with the rest of an organization. Among the teams that Ancona studied were four variants, which we'll call the politicians, the researchers, the isolationists, and the generalists.

Political teams specialized in "working vertically," concentrating their efforts on good relations with the higher-ups. Researcher teams were specialists in scouting out and gathering in information. Isolationist teams, on the other hand, kept themselves apart, protecting and patrolling their tightly closed boundaries. They were not very well connected in terms of power, task, or information.

The generalist teams did it all. They were well integrated into the organization through a mix of interface management activities. They were plugged into the information network through "research" and "scouting" activities, coordinated with other teams and functions through the work-flow network, and politically connected and protected in terms of the power structure.

How did these various kinds of teams fare in the real world? Team performance can be looked at from the inside or from the outside, as team members see it or as the larger organization sees it. Members of the political and the isolated teams alike thought they were the greatest, but top management saw things a little differently. In early evaluations they tended to rate the politicians and the generalists as top performers, both of these types being better tapped into the power structure.

Final Scores

A different picture emerges over the long haul. When teams were evaluated a year and a half later, the politicians had fallen from grace, earning the lowest performance ratings. Apparently these were teams that talked a good line but failed to produce. (Sounds like politicians everywhere, doesn't it?)

Researchers, who sometimes never got beyond information gathering, often ended up being disbanded by management. Isolationist teams turned out to be a mixed bag. Most of these self-contained groups failed miserably, but a few were outstanding successes. Keeping your team of crack coders insulated from the rest of the company may look like a good way to concentrate on the end product, but it could be one of those high-risk, high-payoff maneuvers.

The generalist teams, with their well-orchestrated and diversified external strategies, came out the corporate winners. Such teams seem to balance internal performance with external demands. They get the information they need but don't get stuck in perpetual research. They work the system in terms of the power structure and work flow in order to reach their goals. In other words, high-performance project teamwork is more than working well together. It's also working well with others.

So, ask not for whom the gong sounds. If you have to ask, your team has an ineffective external strategy. It sounds for thee.

From *Software Development*, Volume 1, #8, August 1993.

16

Having It All

No team is all things to all projects. Some teams will be better at routine development, some will excel on the most intricate applications, still others are best at breaking new ground. In part, it depends on how the team is organized and coordinated. Set up your team with fixed job assignments and run it from the top down with tight controls and close supervision and you are not likely to see much in the way of innovation. Loosely run teams that foster independent initiative are more able to chart new territory; traditional teams with fixed roles are better on well-understood applications. Teams that promote open discussion and consensus building do better on really complex problems. Depending on the nature of the problem you are facing and the technical objectives of the project, one kind of teamwork organization or another will increase your chances of success.

But you knew all that. Unfortunately, the work you do doesn't fit nicely into one of the standard boxes. Your software projects are neither without precedent nor strictly routine. The problems are complex and multifaceted, yet, to deliver on time and meet requirements, high levels of dependable development performance must be seasoned with some clever invention. You might even be tempted to give some form of creative collaboration a try, but the boss doesn't understand this touchy-feely team stuff anyway and is going to hold you and you alone accountable.

This is the way of the world, at least the world of software. None of the more or less clean teamwork models discussed in Chapters 11 through 14 quite fits the bill for the typical software project. What is needed is a more or less dirty combination tailored to the grimy details of software reality.

Management Models

Actually, real programming groups provide an abundance of messy mixtures and mongrel models, but, although some of them are more successful than others, most are either trial-and-error patchworks or are based on management models from other fields. We would like to have a project teamwork model tailored to software development, one in which the predictability of organized and established procedures and the simple accountability you get when one person is in charge are combined with the high visibility and potential for creative consensus of free-wheeling collaboration.

Coming from different points of view and working independently on different continents, Australian consultant Rob Thomsett and I both tackled this problem and designed similar solutions (Thomsett 1990; Constantine 1989, 1991a). Software teams may work best when they are carefully structured to make open collaboration and consensus engineering more efficient and manageable. This "structured open" approach combines elements of the traditional closed and collaborative open teamwork models. The team is a traditional hierarchy as viewed from outside—a single project leader is held accountable—but internally it functions as a collaborative community of peers. There are well-defined roles within the team, but these are rotated among members. There are rules and formal procedures, but these are devised to promote free exploration and consensus building. Every aspect of this approach has been designed to offset shortcomings of one model with features borrowed from the other. Nothing is fundamentally new in the Constantine-Thomsett model, but the combination is interesting in its own right.

To begin with, the project leader, who is ultimately accountable for the outcome, is expected to be an active participant in the discussions and work of the team without dominating. In particular, the project leader never leads working sessions; instead, these are led by a neutral facilitator. Open-style consensus engineering can be dramatically more efficient if discussions are facilitated by neutral discussion leaders rather than by project managers (see chapters 1 through 3). On the other hand, collaborative problem solving can too easily get bogged down in distracting side issues or fruitless debate. These are best terminated by the accountable project leader, who can set the topic aside temporarily or, on rare occasions, act as final arbiter when the group is hopelessly deadlocked.

Keeping a visible, permanent record of the twists and turns of group development work also makes the process more reliable and manageable. A structured "group memory" can keep track of decisions, rationales, work products, deferred decisions, things to do and find out, and even rejected approaches. The group memory enhances traceability and makes discussions more efficient. Key information and conclusions remain available and arguments are less likely to be forgotten and repeated. The group memory can also simplify and speed discussions by providing a convenient place to record things that become distractions or can't be resolved right away.

Both facilitators and recorders need to stay on the sidelines of technical debates if the group is to do the best job. Because typical software groups can't afford and don't have access to trained outside facilitators and recorders, these functions are turned into rotating roles instead of job descriptions. The person facilitating discussion changes with the changing course of meetings, and the structured group memory becomes the responsibility of the entire team, rotating the role of "information manager" (the "lowly and exalted scribe" of Chapter 4) among members.

Meeting Management

Structured open teams do much of their work face-to-face. This does not mean wasting time in meetings; it means working sessions, collaborating as a group on defining functionality and requirements, analyzing problems, laying out system architecture, reviewing designs, even coding critical sections. The idea is to lower defects and improve quality by increasing the visibility of work (see Chapter 26) and by taking advantage of the varied skills and perspectives that team members bring to a project.

Other functional roles may be shared by the team and rotated among members. These include maintaining access to applications expertise, especially important in object-oriented development and for user interface design, and providing liaison with the larger organization (the "team politics" discussed in the preceding chapter). Recognizing that critical feedback is an essential ingredient in improving software quality, the role of "resident critic" is formally recognized as an official part of the team. The resident critic is responsible for such things as pointing out problems and alternatives, keeping the group from closing in too quickly on an easy but inferior solution. But no team member gets to be permanent curmudgeon; it's a temporary role that is rotated. For awhile you get to be the skeptical critic, then it's my turn.

The main features of the structured open model—facilitated working sessions, structured group memory, rotating team roles—are optimized for software and applications development. By striking a creative balance between structure and flexibility, the model makes technical consensus more efficient and tactical performance more flexible.

Okay, those of you who remember your Heinlein are thinking "tanstaafl,"* and, indeed, this model has its down side, too. It takes extra training and practice to get up to speed. Not all managers are comfortable with abdicating part of their control to function as peers within a team. Formal role assignments and strict rotation can be too cumbersome for smaller teams. It's silly for one person to facilitate and another to record while the one remaining programmer engages in a lively monologue on icon design. Very small teams either have to make major compromises or use a different model.

Anyway, in the spirit of the model, I'm open to ideas for improved structure.

From *Software Development*, Volume 1 #9, September 1993.

---

* For those who missed the classic Robert A. Heinlein novel, *The Moon is a Harsh Mistress,* "There ain't no such thing as a free lunch!"

17

Contrarion Conspiracy

New England is famed for its winters and its roads. We have colorful regional habits when it comes to marking our streets and byways. For example, New England street signs typically identify only cross streets, not the main thoroughfares. After all, so the Yankee logic goes, everyone should know Main Street or Massachusetts Avenue. What would be the point of marking them? A sign on an interstate may warn you that the exit for Middleboro is coming up in one mile, but at the exit it's labeled "Sherwood and Beanville Exit." Then, at the bottom of the off ramp you are offered the choice of left to Merton or right to Chester! If you don't know where to turn, perhaps you have no business being there. I am convinced this logic is also followed by certain software developers, who use one term in the manual, another in the on-line help, and an unrelated icon on the button bar. Navigating their menus and dialogue boxes is like getting to Freeport from West Roxbury via Providence. As they say Down East, "You can't get there from here."

Some of our expressway interchanges are works of art. We don't quite have the traffic volume of, say, an LA, but we make up for it with the most convoluted highway interchanges in the world. These asphalt pretzels are capable of turning even light traffic into a snarl. A few cars with out-of-state license plates or one stalled vehicle anytime after three on a weekday and it's parking lot city.

The most mind-boggling of the elaborate interchanges in the Greater Boston area were, I have become convinced, designed by specialized contractors. Such monuments to creative complexification require engineering genius and a commitment to perversity. For example, a westbound vehicle leaving a toll road for a northbound alternate might have to make a left exit, crossing under the eastbound traffic, then enter rotary traffic for three-quarters of the circle, bear right, stop for tolls, next cross under both original eastbound and westbound lanes, then over entering street-level traffic, then onto the northbound on-ramp, merging with another on-ramp for one-half mile before finally squeezing left into traffic. Got that? Remind you of a favorite Windows program?

The best of Massachusetts's macadam monstrosities could never have been developed by any conventional notion of teamwork. Traditional teams are incapable of such heights of multileveled mania. No, these require a model of project organization that must certainly have counterparts in software development. They must have been designed and built by a group modeled on a fundamentally different paradigm: the Contrarion Conspiracy!

The Contrarion Conspiracy is an international cabal of engineers, technicians, and managers in numerous fields. Their secret icon is the Knot of Gordius, their avowed purpose, the ultimate complexification of everything. They are guided by the Contrarion Credo: Different or dead. What matters is not that a system be usable or even reasonable, only that it be different, that it have more doodads. Look-and-feel *über alles*.

Use It or Lose It

The ghost of Cyril Northcote Parkinson is the god of the conspiracy. Their most sacred operating principle is to let no resource go unused. For every off-ramp there must be an overpass. For every obscure API call there must be a use, and a truly good program uses them all. A system that does not ship compressed on at least 10 high-density disks or, better yet, CD-ROM, can hardly be worth what you paid for it. The installed footprint must be at least 25 megabytes. Installation should create numerous new directories, at least some of which are subdirectories to \WINDOWS, into which various obscurely named files will also be plunked along with the new product's own .INI files. And, of course, installation can hardly be said to be robust unless WIN.INI, CONFIG.SYS, AUTOEXEC.BAT, and even SYSTEM.INI are extensively doctored. Otherwise some unhappy user might be able to remove the software just by deleting a few files and directories.

The Contrarion Conspiracy has roots in civil engineering and municipal contracting, where the name of the game is to use as much brick and mortar as possible, since cousin Bert owns the kiln and nephew Phineas has the cement works. In programming, someone has to find a way to use up all those megabytes of RAM and gigabytes of hard disk. We would hate to see the power of the Pentium go unused.

End users may actually be hindered by too much real computational power anyway. They are blinded by blinding speed. What they really want is to see things happening; they want scintillating screens, prancing pictographs, and flickering flames. The appearance of action is more important than accomplishment, and, by golly, the Contrarion Conspiracy stands ready to see that Parkinson's Law is honored by seeking sophisticated solutions, which means unnecessarily complex ones. Project groups are deliberately organized to work at cross purposes, because this guarantees redundant features and internal incompatibilities, ensuring a high degree of needless complexity.

Dear reader, do not doubt me. Do not dismiss this as the paranoid palaver of a mad methodologist! The proof of this diabolism is right in front of you. On the very windows of your wondrous machines are splattered the cabalistic symbols of their programmatic perversion, in the chevrons of maximization and minimization, in the bars of control, in the windmills of waiting states.

Devil You Say

Proof you ask for, proof you get. My office mate and I have been checking out Windows-based Personal Information Managers. One in particular is so fiendishly clever, with its cutesy DayTimer™ simulation and profligate use of screen real estate, that only a Contrarion Conspiracy could have produced it.

Deletion is the definitively damning datum: you delete an item from your notebook by dragging it to a wire wastebasket icon. (Yes, *wire!*) Then the wastebasket bursts into flames! Iconic immolation! Major programming resources were wasted on this software basket case. But it is so *cute!* It really impresses upper management, purchasing agents, and other mental defectives. Few, however, have discovered that, on a fast 486 with an accelerated video board and a large-screen monitor, the fast flickering flames are seen to form the perfect likeness of the late Lawrence Welk! Need I say more?

The software development methods of the conspiracy reflect and serve its goals. The best practitioners announce a product, then design the box, then begin coding. Flow charting is tough. Flow charts are much easier to draw from existing code, so contrarion project teams start by coding low-level routines, such as display drivers and flaming icons, around which they organize everything else and from which they derive flow charts for the overall processing. Once the software is in beta test, the system requirements can be written as the foreword to the manual.

Beware, because a Contrarion Conspiracy may masquerade as an ordinary R&D group or project team, but in clandestine meetings held after 10 P.M. they plan their deviant development scenarios. Have you ever wondered about some of your programming buddies who work so late? Odds are they have been inducted into the secret rites of the Contrarion Conspiracy, which celebrates its 666th anniversary on the first of April 1993.*

From *Software Development*, Volume 1, #4, April 1993.

* From the email responses I got, not all readers took into account the April Fools' Day dateline of this piece when it was originally published.

IV

Tools, Models, and Methods

Introduction

Our distant ancestors were dubbed *homo habilis*, "man, the tool maker." Human beings are not nature's only tool makers, but it is certainly an essential expression of our relation to the world around us. We extend our reach through tools. We see the un-seeable, move the unmovable, manipulate the microscopic, and construct the gargantuan. We write programs, which are at once invisible and enormous. Many common trades and activities would be all but impossible in their modern form were it not for good tools. Carpentry, mechanics, civil engineering, aeronautics, electronics, cooking—all have their kits of essential tools and their methods of application.

The tools of many trades include not only those tools that you can hold in your hand but also those that you hold in your head. These are the ways of thinking and of representing thoughts that define the profession and the professional. Models and model-building are conceptual tools that give software developers intellectual leverage as surely as a crowbar gives mechanical leverage to construction crews. Just as the carpenter must learn how and when to use a crosscut saw, a software engineer must understand the appropriate methods for applying the conceptual and other tools of software development.

Tools and trades alike evolve over time with changes in practice and materials. There was a time when you could recognize an engineer coming toward you by the ubiquitous slide rule hanging in its belt case. When I started programming the standard tools were a coding sheet, a plastic flowcharting template, and a core dump. We wrote in FORTRAN or assembler and never laid hands on the computer itself. A big program was a tray of cards: 4,000 lines of code. You could, if you were good, hold it in your head. Elaborate tools for modeling, design, and debugging were neither available nor needed.

As applications have grown, so have the tools and techniques needed by software developers. The typical contemporary developer may have an assortment of favorite tools, methods, and models for every phase of development—from conception through debugging and installation. This section explores some aspects of the relationship between developers and their tools and between programming tools and the methods by which they are used. Included (in Chapter 22) is a reprint of the first published account of essential use cases, a conceptual tool of increasing importance in modern software engineering practice and the subject of more detailed discussion in Section VII.

18

CASE and Cognition

Computer-Aided Software Engineering, CASE, is no longer the hottest topic in software and applications development. Even the vendors of CASE tools are retitling their products, calling them "integrated development environments" or just "tool suites." Whatever they are called, the development tools we use or fail to use can have a lot to do with what we accomplish as developers.

I happen to be a strong proponent of tools. Admittedly, many of those available today are relatively primitive, often misconceived systems produced by misguided tool vendors who neither understand nor use the software engineering methodologies their tools support. Still, they can be effective tools in much the same way that a stone ax beats bare hands for felling trees.

Not surprisingly, you often hear something like this: "We don't have time to use CASE; we have a deadline to meet." Some of these protesters are the same programmers, now balding or graying, who resisted higher level languages. They probably never flow chart or draw a data flow diagram and will insist that they, unlike us ordinary mortals, can keep track of everything in their heads. On the other hand, many critics of CASE tools really do try to practice some kind of reasonable design and development discipline. Unfortunately, many of the CASE tools, rather than helping the process of methodical problem solving or creative engineering, actually hinder it.

What's wrong with this picture? You see a high-salary software engineer, in an office with a six-thousand-dollar workstation, running a twelve-thousand-dollar CASE tool, and he's drawing on his desk pad, making notes on a yellow tablet of recycled notepaper. Finally, after much crossing out, erasing, and redrawing, he puts mitt to mouse and begins to enter what he's worked out, effectively reducing the sophisticated tool suite on his workstation to an elaborate electronic drafting board.

What's wrong is this: Rather than working with the software engineer and how engineers think, the tool is probably working against him. Instead of supporting natural ability and the habits sharpened through training, the CASE tool is interfering with them. To understand the exact nature of this failure, we need to look at how people, especially engineer-type people, solve problems.

Sketching

We know, for example, that many of the better software engineers, analysts, and designers do their finest work by sketching out a broad-brushed picture of what they want to do, then going back to fill in details or elaborate. Look over the shoulder of such a problem solver and watch what she does. She might start a design by drawing a whole collection of component symbols. Then she begins to fill in the relationships among some of these blank boxes, drawing lines and arrows among them. Finally, she labels the components and specifies some details of the interconnections.

What about typical CASE tools? In many of them, you select a diagram symbol with the mouse from a collection of icons, position the cursor, again with the mouse, where you want the symbol to appear in the diagram being developed, and then click to drop the symbol in place. At this point, a dialogue box opens up and asks you to name the thing, which you must do in compliance with whatever general and corporate standards are being enforced for the naming of such symbols. Next you are called on to describe it, specify its interfaces, and maybe choose among several variants. Only after all this is completed in conformance with the syntax checking in force are you allowed to return to the drawing. By this time you have probably forgotten what you earlier knew you were going to do next. Worse, the general conception of the content and structure of the problem that seemed so clear when you reached for the mouse is now lost, erased from your mental map by the CASE tool's preoccupation with distracting details.

Alternatives and Alternative Views

All engineering is trade-offs. There is research going back over thirty years showing that more effective engineers typically compare two or more alternative approaches to each significant design problem. This strategy applies just as well to software engineering as to our older sister professions. (My thesis at M.I.T. was on just this subject.) The comparison between alternative approaches may be quick and mostly mental, or it may involve elaborate description and modeling of each alternative, with careful analysis and evaluation of the consequences. A clear winning strategy may emerge, but sometimes what is chosen is a creative synthesis of more than one alternative, sometimes a compromise. The essential part of the process is the weighing of alternatives, being able to eyeball two designs or interpretations side-by-side. Current CASE tools do not, for the most part, support having two versions of the same system, diagram, or model simultaneously active and accessible, certainly not for side-by-side comparisons.

I've seen some pretty clever subterfuges used to get around this limitation of CASE tools. At one firm, a systems analyst had two workstations in his office, one processing a dummy project record, so that he could keep two full-fledged versions of the same systems design in front of him to analyze their advantages and disadvantages. More commonly, one of the alternatives is on paper, the other in the CASE repository.

Here's a scenario you may have seen or acted out yourself. The software engineer using a CASE tool tells the tool to print or plot one model of the system being designed, perhaps a data flow diagram, runs down the hall to the print server and retrieves the output, then returns to the office to call up another model of the same system, maybe a structure chart. The software engineer then keeps going back and forth between the model on the screen and the one on the paper.

Even the so-called "integrated" CASE "tool suites" do not generally support simple, rapid shifting among alternative views or models of the same system-in-progress. It should be at most a keystroke between views. Better yet would be true, side-by-side comparison. And windows just don't quite cut it. By the time you have two windows up in a CASE tool that operates in a windowed mode or environment, there isn't enough screen left to actually see anything useful. Either you get a little peek at a small part of each diagram, or you get an overview of tiny, unreadable symbols and text. Hardly a computer aid to software engineering!

Creation and Evaluation

Among the worst offenders in interfering with the thought processes of software developers are some of the more advanced tools, such as the context-sensitive program editors that do syntax checking on entry, or the CASE tools that support and enforce a software development "methodology" by constraining the CASE user to entering only proper diagrams and descriptions in precisely the order defined by some definitive text by some definitive methodology guru.

In the early days of computer-supported word processing, spell-checkers were separate programs, so slow and inefficient that you never checked a document more than absolutely necessary, and often you "forgot." But, the computers and the search techniques got faster. Spell-checkers were integrated with the word processors. Pretty soon some programmer with time on his hands thought of doing spell-checking "on-the-fly," as words were actually being entered. After all, during text entry, the processor is idle most of the time anyway, and the lookup can proceed, letter by letter, between keystrokes. Clever idea, right? Wrong!

If you have ever used a word processor or electronic typewriter with a real-time spell-checker, you know. The little gremlin is constantly interrupting to tell you about some alleged misspelling, popping up like an over-eager puppy or beeping liking a bar-code scanner at the grocery checkout. Even when it is right and you're wrong, you don't care, you just want to get your thoughts on paper without being interrupted by the mishuganah spell-checking smarty.

One of the rules of the simple but powerful technique of brainstorming is that no one is allowed to criticize or comment on any idea until the entire process is completed and all ideas are on the table. Separating the process of creation from the process of evaluation improves problem solving.

A CASE tool that fits with how people think would not criticize while you are creating. In fact, it would allow you to draw and specify all sorts of things that "aren't proper" because these "framebreaking" departures from the rules are often crucial steps along the way to finding better solutions. And it would allow you to depart from the prescribed sequence for entering things, because the "methodologies" in the books are not necessarily the last word on software engineering. (In fact, many methodologies are really quite wrong in terms of human problem solving, but that's another subject.)

Should we abandon hope and leave the CASE tools on the shelf? No, there's still hope. Present-day CASE tools are the primitive precursors of the tools we really need. They'll evolve.

It's a little like the early word processing programs, such as Electric Pencil or the first versions of WordStar. By today's standards of functionality and convenience, they were not much. You had to wait for minutes to go between one end of a document and another, the keystrokes to accomplish common tasks were obscure and complicated, and format control was limited, but they were so very much better than handwriting on foolscap or typing and retyping and retyping.

Besides, some of those who create CASE tools may be listening.

From *Computer Language Magazine*, Volume 9, #1, January 1992.

19

Modeling Matters

"A good development tool is one that doesn't slow me down." The programmer looked warily at the eighty-pound box holding the latest and greatest in C++ development environments. "What I really want is one that lets me just get on with programming the way I want to, then it takes the code and generates those stupid diagrams that my boss insists on having." As I watch, I'm thinking that maybe it's time we talked about those stupid diagrams.

Many developers, especially those who cut their coding teeth on microcomputers and workstations, take a pretty dim view of structure charts, object communication diagrams, data flow diagrams, and flow charts. Quite a few of them have never drawn a functional hierarchy and wouldn't know what to do with one if it was lying on the desk. To them, a Booch-gram is bad news delivered on yellow paper by a courier from Booch Telecommunications.

To many of today's software wizards, those boxes and bubbles and clouds and arrows look like the hieroglyphics of a vanished priesthood, the legacy of moribund methods, like structured analysis and design, that have been superseded by streamlined object-oriented rapid prototyping. Charts and diagrams have no place in the fast-paced world of hack-and-backslash micro applications and software development using visual programming and rapid application development. "We don't have time to draw pictures; we have a release date to meet!" "Why would anyone ever draw diagrams when they could be cutting code?" It's a good question. Why does anyone do those drawings?

Of course, structure charts and other classic design and analysis models were not developed to slow down programming, any more than they were created to satisfy fussy customers or to keep meddling managers happy. Most were developed by developers for their own use in order to simplify and speed up their work. Time spent thinking about programs through models is time saved programming and debugging. By allowing the software developer to model programs without having to code them, by making it easier to lay out the organization of intricate solutions for complex problems, analysis and design models shorten development time. All this is well established and well known. Good design cuts development time; good design models simplify design.

Not all graphical models work this way in practice. Some, like IBM's HIPO charts and its companion methods, have died a well-deserved death. Others were impeded by the clumsiness or complexity of the notation or the mechanics of drawing them. CASE tools first arrived on the scene primarily as specialized drawing tools to make the drafting of diagrams easier. Over time they evolved into more comprehensive aids to software engineering.

Picture This

Software developers draw pictures when they could be writing real programs for much the same reasons that architects draw floor plans and elevations before building a house. Buildings were not always built from plans and drawings, though. If a building is simple enough and familiar enough, crews can work without models, figuring out the design as they go along. The turn-of-the-century rural community didn't need blueprints to raise a barn. Those old barns were simple designs and used simplified construction methods. Everyone knew what a barn looked like, how it was constructed, and what was needed to build it. Most of the community had done it before, and any first-timers could learn just by paying attention and doing what they saw others do. But when you go from yerts and barns to four-bedroom garrison colonials or high-rise apartment complexes, things get more complex.

And so it is with computer programs. Back when 64K of RAM was the limit and CP/M was the operating environment, keeping an entire program in your head may have been possible and sensible. But anyone who says they can keep track of and make sense of the details in a hundred thousand lines of C code is lying—if not to you, then to themselves. This is where design models come in.

Note that we are talking about models, not diagrams, about design, not documentation. To many software developers, those odd little pictures are ends in themselves, at best only another form of documentation, something to be stored in a binder because the contract requires it. Design models can indeed be useful as documentation. The blueprints for your house not only guided the contractors but can help show where to cut into a wall to find—or avoid—a hot water pipe. Structure charts and block communication diagrams can tell you where to look for particular procedures or to trace the flow of information or to understand how a completed system was laid out. But the main purpose of design models is to help in design.

Managing Complexity

A model, at least any reasonable model, is simpler than the thing it models. Using a good modeling notation, the important features and characteristics of a very complex system can be represented in a relatively small and simple diagram.

Modeling gives mental leverage. If you know the symbols and the language, the model can be a way of picturing and then thinking about complex problems, especially in terms of the relationships among pieces. In code or text, relationships are implicit; a word or label here refers to a thing that is elsewhere. In most graphical models, relationships are explicit, visible as those lines and arrows connecting parts of the diagram. Good graphical models can also offer a meaningful overview of a system that would be impossible to get from reading—or writing—page after page of code.

Of course, many people create purely mental models of problems they are working on. Some experienced developers may even visualize systems through structural diagrams they keep in their heads. Diagrams on paper or on a screen still have advantages because they externalize the internal mental models. External models become stable and can be reflected upon or compared to other models. An externalized model can be set aside and re-examined later from a fresh perspective. Often times, seeing something committed to lines and boxes changes how you think about it, suggesting other possibilities or causing mistakes or oversights to become more obvious. And no one else can see the model you have in your head, but an entire project team can study and work on the model on the wall or in the CASE tool repository.

Good modeling tools also allow for a kind of sketching that is difficult in code. Programming languages are precise and detailed and compilers stubbornly insist on exact syntax and completed constructs. A whiteboard has no such constraints. A developer or group can gather around and play with the pictures, moving things around and tracing out complex paths over widely separated regions of the system. In short, design models allow software engineers to act more like real engineers, trying out and comparing alternative ways to organize software without having to reduce ideas to code.

Almost any aspect of software can be modeled graphically: algorithm, data structure, communication, composition, dynamics. For each of these and others there may be dozens of competing notations and conventions. But one model is not necessarily as good as another. Notations vary tremendously in their ability to carry meaning. It matters what shape the blobs are and which way the arrows point.

How do you tell the good from the bad from the ugly? Stay tuned.

From *Software Development,* Volume 2, #2, February 1994.

20

Mirror, Mirror

Mirror, mirror, on the wall, who's the fairest of them all? The wicked queen in *Snow White* had only to look in her mirror to get the true picture. Software engineers should be so lucky. They need good mirrors that simply and accurately reflect the software being engineered. The wicked queen may have been displeased by what she learned, but at least her mirror gave a true image with no difficulty in interpretation.

That's what a good modeling notation offers: a clear image of software—unambiguous and easy to interpret. Unlike a looking glass, a useful modeling notation cannot simply reflect a detailed picture with a one-to-one correspondence to code. A good model is an accurate but selective embodiment of software, a necessarily simplified picture. The effectiveness of a modeling notation for expressing problems and their software solutions depends on how this simplification is achieved. The precise nature of the translation between the medium of the programming language and the medium of the modeling notation should be simple, straightforward, logical, and easy to learn.

Unfortunately, many of today's proliferating program analysis and design notations fail in these fundamental requirements. They are overly complex, arbitrary, ambiguous, difficult to learn, and difficult to interpret. And, of course, there are far too many of them.

Complete modeling of software is complicated, involving numerous views of static and dynamic aspects: the structure and composition of information, the nature of the algorithms and their realization as procedures, factoring into component parts, and communication among parts. If the data model, procedural model, communication model, state model, and functional composition of software are all conflated into a single diagram in one comprehensive notation, the result is baroque, visually cluttered, and hard to understand.

Getting the Picture

Software engineering models serve much the same purposes as the wicked queen's mirror. Notations should make clear the difference between the fairest of solutions and those that are only fair. Developers need to be able to tell by looking at a model whether the design is sound or stupid. A software design model is not merely a holding place for as-yet-unbuilt software ideas. It allows developers to spot problems and shortcomings in the design and to compare approaches to see which is superior. Ultimately this is why good developers draw pictures before they code—it's cheaper to build paper models than to build software, and good models make it easier to see how to do things well.

Good notation allows for simple, direct, and unambiguous translation between model and code: to develop code from a model and to model existing code. Sloppy, obscure, or imprecise notation makes for sloppy, obscure, and imprecise translation. Every visual element in the notation should correspond with some specific and relevant aspect of the software being modeled; every important feature in the code should be expressible in the notation.

A good notation produces pictures that can be interpreted analytically, through a thorough study of details, and understood intuitively as a gestalt—a whole representing the overall character of a system. Complicated designs should look more complicated than simple ones, good architecture should be more visually appealing than bad design. In other words, a good notation allows developers to use both sides of the brain; it helps them think both logically and intuitively about the system being designed.

To accurately mirror software, yet present a substantially simplified view, good notation highlights things that are important and hides or suppresses those that are not. Dominant features and major components are writ large, while minor details are annotations or disappear from view.

The picture is kept simple by not showing internal details. A software component that is basically a black box becomes a simple box drawn on screen or paper; internal details are invisible. Lines pointing to these graphical boxes suggest programming references to software boxes, not to their internal features.

Ideally, we want the kind of selective control over visibility only possible in a computerized tool. We would like, for instance, to browse through an object communication diagram, skimming over a landscape of tiny objects, then zoom in to study relationships in one region. We might close in on one object to see what methods it supports. We double-click and are looking at the C++ code defining one method. Or we might flip to a view that superimposes user interaction scenarios on the communication diagram, highlighting or coloring objects participating in one scenario.

Notation and Usability

It's easy to develop your own notation; all too many people do. It's hard to do it well, and many notations that fill our journals and magazines are not very good as modeling tools.

Designing a good notation is like designing a good user interface. The goal is to reduce human memory load. The Great Law of Usability says a system should be usable—without training, assistance, or manuals—by someone who knows the application but not the software (Constantine 1991b). A really good notation, then, is one that an experienced software engineer who knows how to design and build software can interpret directly and intuitively without a week-long class or a complicated cheat-sheet. You shouldn't have to remember arbitrary things like a double-barred box as a dynamic object or one with a flag in the corner as a reused library component.

Things should look like what they are. Symbol shapes and line styles cannot be arbitrary or counter-intuitive. For instance, the basic foundation upon which other components are built through inheritance and reuse should look like solid and well-defined elements, not ephemeral clouds.

Strong connections between parts should look strong; weaker ones should look more tenuous. Stable objects should appear solid, dynamic ones should convey some sense of activity or changeability. For example, inheritance by one class of the features and characteristics of another means that the subclass is strongly dependent on the superclass, just as a child's genetic characteristics are strongly dependent on those of both parents. To accurately reflect the characteristics of software using it, inheritance should be shown in a way that looks stronger than message passing or reference to an object as an attribute (Page-Jones, Constantine, and Weiss 1990).

What makes a notation intuitive and easy to learn can be a matter of small and subtle details. In Jacobson's notation for object-oriented software (Jacobson et al. 1992), objects that interface with the outside have a "lazy-tee"

(⊢) on one side as a visual reminder of the interface. Dynamic objects that control sequences of interaction have an arrowhead imbedded in the border, suggesting a loop or iteration. In several notations, internal features of components that are externally accessible are shown straddling the border of the component.

A good notation also builds on and uses what software engineers already know, especially what they know about notations. That means not using new symbols for old concepts and not recycling the same pictures for new and incompatible ideas. In fact, we probably don't need any new notations. Our efforts would be better spent standardizing and consolidating what we already have, applying sound principles of modeling and human thought.

Think about it.

From *Software Development,* Volume 2, #3, March 1994.

21

Methodical Madness

As if all those dumb diagrams were not enough to bury the busy programmer, every model seems to come with its own method attached. Structured methods may no longer be cool beans, but there seems to be no shortage of newcomers to fill bookshelves and journals and conference programs. These latest and greatest methods may be rapid and reuse objects for prototypes, but there is much that is vaguely familiar about even the most radical of the new development methods.

There's no real mystery to software methods. You, too, can be a software methodologist, without even taking a correspondence course. Whether it's called structured analysis and design, information engineering, or round-trip gestalt, whether it's object-oriented or just plain vanilla procedural programming, behind all the books and the babble, it all boils down to systematic problem solving. By furnishing a framework for orderly use of models and tools, methods can make the software development process more repeatable, which means easier to learn and easier to refine and improve.

Underlying all major software analysis and design methods is a very small set of basic principles, repeatedly rediscovered and recast in ever fresh vocabulary, but still just the same old shinola. It's all based on how human beings solve complex problems. The five principles underlying all software engineering methods are: (1) orderly progression, (2) solution by subdivision, (3) component independence, (4) component integrity, and (5) structural fit.

Step One

The important thing in getting a big job done is to start someplace, do something, then do something else. Methods give you a place to start and someplace to go next. Each step in the process takes you, with hope in your heart and code in your head, one step closer to a finished software solution.

All methods give you some kind of orderly recipe that outlines all the things you will have to do to complete the work and deliver the software. They serve as a reminder of the various matters that must be considered and understood in order to develop systems. Good methods put first things first and defer the deferrable. This is the principle of orderly progression at work: do this, then that, then this.

Subdivide

All *real* software problems, the sort that programming professionals confront daily in their jobs, are too big and complicated to solve. The only completely solvable programming problems are those toy applications and academic exercises found in textbooks and taught in all-day tutorials. This is one reason why academic computer scientists can waste entire careers on elegant mathematics and methods of formal proof that are hopelessly inadequate to everyday programming problems. They never see real problems.

We do. When confronted by unmanageable complexity, what do we do? The same thing our primitive ancestors did when faced with a haunch of mastodon too big to swallow: we bite off a chunk and start chewing. We tackle big problems by breaking them up into little ones. It's a bit of mental magic, hand waving that does not really make the true enormity of software problems go away. But it often works anyway, giving the overloaded developer the illusion that big, complex systems can be built out of lots of small, simple pieces of code.

Sometimes, like the hapless little apprentice sorcerer, we find that chopping up one big problem only compounds our problems. Big problems become smaller when chopped up only to the extent that the little pieces don't have much to do with each other and can be approached more or less independently, each designed and programmed as a manageable little software exercise in itself. All effective software engineering methods include some form of rules or guidance that tells you to make clean cuts when you carve up the problem, separating the total into independent bits, each of which makes sense as a distinct subproblem.

There are really two problem-solving principles rolled up into one here. The principle of component independence says you should subdivide the problem into loosely related subproblems. The principle of component integrity says each of the pieces should make sense as an integral whole.

In traditional structured design, these principles are embodied in the venerable concepts of coupling and cohesion. Coupling is a measure of the degree of interaction and interdependence between software components; cohesion is a measure of the degree to which a component comprises a well-defined functional whole. These old concepts have been rediscovered in the fresh world of object technology. Good object-oriented methods remind programmers to reduce object coupling and to raise the cohesion of methods by encapsulating all the right goodies in each object basket (Henderson-Sellers and Constantine, 1996). Otherwise you end up with a tortuous tangle of interwoven objects that defy analysis and resist reuse.

Structural Fit

These first principles of complex problem solving are all concerned with individual pieces of software, but do not say much about how these parts are best organized into a working whole. Most methods tell us in one form or another to look to the real world, to emulate the structure of the problem in the structure of our solution. In other words, the software should be organized along the same lines as the "real-world" problem it is supposed to solve. This is the principle of structural fit, software engineering's version of the Bauhaus dictum that form should follow from function.

This principle gets its most radical realization in the more simplistic methods of object technology that say all you have to do is look at the real world and construct object classes for whatever you see "out there." Here's a chair, there's a chair—tada! We create class chair, with superclass furniture. Following this advice too blindly leads to clumsy translations of physical systems into klutzy software. And then there's the problem that your reality and mine may have little overlap.

Still, the basic premise is sound. Reflecting the "natural" structure of the problem domain in software saves us from solving problems that don't need solving. Instead of inventing whole new architectures, we use the serviceable ones that already exist "out there." By sticking to the structure of the problem domain, maintenance, expansion, and reuse are all made easier because the software is simply structured the way people already think about the problem.

That's it. Methods are the frameworks for using models to solve software problems.

Of course, it takes a lot more to have a real method and justify calling yourself a real methodologist. You have to be good at making up words. You need a lot of new vocabulary or people will think they already know what you are trying to teach. And you have to be able to stretch a few good ideas into 700 pages of textbook. And don't forget the notation, those clever little shapes that make your method recognizable among its many competitors. But be careful not to make the pictures too simple or the principles too transparent, or you won't be able to justify those training and consulting fees!

From *Software Development*, Volume 2, #5, May 1994.

22

Essentially Speaking

Moving home and office 11,000 miles can really get one thinking about what is essential. Packing everything for a year abroad into suitcases and cartons certainly highlights the difference between "needs" and "wants," a distinction made sharper by excess baggage charges of over $90 per bag. In software and applications development it is also important to get down to essentials, to distinguish the essential heart of what you need to program from the inessential wants and the unnecessary what-ifs.

Essential modeling is a conceptual tool for focusing the developer's mind on what matters. An essential model is a representation of the core of an application, a problem stripped down to its bare essentials, stripped, that is, of all unnecessary or constraining assumptions.

The notion of essential modeling in software traces back at least to the origins of structured design. Data flow diagrams were intended as a nonprocedural model of computation, one that separated the essence of what the computer was to do from how it was to be accomplished through any particular algorithm or procedure. By designing the modular structure to fit this essential definition of the problem, it became possible to build more robust software whose basic form could survive changes in processing details. Or so the reasoning went. In practice, dataflow diagrams were often turned into little more than flowcharts with funny figures, a corruption encouraged by later enhancements, such as data stores and control flows, that implicitly invited procedural thinking. Essential models finally came into their own with the now-classic book *Essential Systems Analysis* (McMenamin and Palmer 1984), which made them the cornerstone of a revised and refurbished structured analysis.

In the broadest sense, essential models capture the essence of systems: a technology-free, idealized, and abstract picture grounded in the intentions of users and the fundamental purposes of the system that supports them. The best essential models are simplified and generalized through repeated refinement. They capture the nonphysical spirit of an application, not the physical embodiment in real code on real equipment.

An essential model is based on perfect technology—infinitely fast computers, arbitrarily large displays, keyless input from users—whatever would be needed to most expeditiously realize necessary functions. This flight into technical fantasy is not intended to indulge the imagination but to assure that the model is as independent of current technology as possible. Technology changes much faster than either business practices or people; solutions that are intimately wedded to any particular technology are ultimately less enduring, less flexible.

Essential Interfaces

User interface design is one promising application of essential models. Essential use case modeling is an approach that extends Jacobson's object-oriented use cases (Jacobson et al. 1992) to apply to user interface design. An essential use case is an abstract scenario for one complete and intrinsically useful interaction with a system as understood from the perspective of the user's intentions or purpose. It is a generalized description of a kind or class of use to which a system may be put, conveying the user actions and system responses[*] in simplified and generalized form. The idea is to design interfaces to fit intentions— what users want to accomplish—with a minimum of presuppositions about technology, such as the shape of visual widgets or even the devices to be used for interaction.

For example, consider the task of withdrawing cash from an automatic teller machine. A physical model might take this form: customer inserts card; system reads magnetic stripe, requests PIN; user types PIN; system confirms PIN, offers menu of transactions; user keys in selection; system offers menu of accounts; user keys in selection; system requests amount; user keys in amount

---

[*] These two sides of the model are probably even better characterized as *user intentions* and *system responsibilities,* which is precisely what they are called in usage-centered design, an approach based on essential use cases (Constantine and Lockwood 1999).

and presses confirmation button; system spits out cash; user takes the money and runs. What could be simpler?

Magnetic Strips

Stripped of physical detail and technological assumptions, the essential use case for this task presents a simpler process: customer identifies self, system offers choices, user selects, system gives money, and user takes it. This description covers a lot more possibilities for the user interface design. It opens the way to a variety of media for offering choices to the user and for user selection, including touch-screen or voice response. It highlights that the ATM card and PIN are nonessential; their essential purpose is simply to identify the user. Thumbprints, iris scans, voice recognition, and badge readers might be workable alternatives in some cases. The essential model leaves open more possibilities, making it more likely that portions of any resulting design will be reusable when assumptions and conditions change.

This essential use case also paves the way to simpler interfaces by highlighting the real heart of the matter to the user: getting the cash, the most common ATM transaction. Most users habitually take the same amount from the same account time after time. The first choice offered by the system could be this user's default, culled from past history: "The usual $250.00 from Regular Checking, Mr. Chatworth?" Or whatever.

The essential model presents an idealized design target. A well-designed user interface requires only as many steps or as much information as is spelled out in the essential use case. The bank customer wants to be able to say, "It's me. The usual. Thanks!" and be off. We spell out the ideal case because if we don't model it, we can't design to it. If we don't design to the ideal, we can't see where technology or technical assumptions are limiting us, and we may miss completely the opportunity for alternative approaches.

Re: Redesign

Another area in which essential models can be useful is in process reengineering. When it is not just another euphemism for layoffs or downsizing, business process reengineering can be an opportunity to make business processes more efficient and effective. In order to reengineer a process successfully, you must know what the process is intended to accomplish—what fundamental business or organizational purpose it serves. The single most essential issue in any process or system is the teleological question: Why does this exist? Why should it exist? What is it really for?

Consider the process of exchanging foreign currency at a bank. In some banks, in some countries, this can require queuing up twice or even three times, with multipart forms, repeated calculation of amounts, and sign-offs by multiple tellers and clerks. From the standpoint of the bank customer, such a transaction is ultrasimple: give money in one currency, get an equivalent amount in another. The bank has an interest in assuring that the exchange rates and amounts are correct and in making a small profit on the exchange, but has no real interest in generating paper or keeping clerks busy—not if the goal is process reengineering.

There is no essential need for a customer or clerk to fill out triplicate forms with names and addresses and signatures and amounts in numerals and text. Exchange rates need not be manually verified if they are derived from one central database; a display facing the customer, as used in many grocery-store checkouts, would serve to validate the incoming amount; a printout of the transaction satisfies the customer's need for a record; the transaction record into the repository gives the bank its audit trail. Indeed, I've used automatic cash machines in Europe that offer precisely this streamlined implementation.

Trance Actions

Unfortunately, many professionals have trouble seeing the essence of their transactions. Not everyone is good at the sort of abstract thinking required for essential modeling. Thinking in terms of essentials can require setting aside the technical blinders that prevent us from seeing things in a fresh light. Meilir Page-Jones refers to this as "dereferencing," mentally stepping out of the frame of conventional assumptions. It is something at which gifted comedians and talented designers are especially good.

I remember once motoring along the Rhein River with Meilir as he translated the German signs we passed. One pictograph showed only a black mass sloping down to the left to meet a stack of wavy lines. Canted in midair between the representations of the river embankment and the river was an iconic car.

Without hesitation, Meilir translated. "Beware of cars leaping from water on left," he said.

Dereferencing. Try it. And think essentially.

23

Shapes to Come

Is CASE dead? Various among the pontiffs of programming have declared the death, but for every mourner there is an optimistic resurrectionist, for every detractor, a jubilant convert. Guided by this zeitgeist, in 1994 the Australian Computer Society assembled in Melbourne two stellar teams of Aussie consultants and practitioners led by supporter Graeme Simsion and skeptic Rob Thomsett. "The great CASE debate," as it was styled, argued the pros and cons of the question "Is there a case for CASE in Australia?" The debate proved to be a big event for the Victorian ACS, outdrawing the book launching by a former prime minister held in the same hall earlier that day. For reasons unknown, I had been recruited to round out the negative team. Thomsett, described by Simsion as Australia's most feral consultant, guided our team to victory, although both sides finished on notes of suspiciously similar pitch.

Rumors of the imminent interment of CASE are disturbing indeed, since CASE is no more than computer-aided software engineering. Is it that computers have ceased their aid? Or is it software engineering that has died? Neither, we hope. CASE is not dead and not doomed, although it may be distinctly déclassé. In the never-ending propensity of industry pundits to euphemize or eulogize what they once elevated to sainthood, CASE is out and "integrated development environments" are in. Or at least they were last month.

Certainly part of the problem has been unreasonable expectations sparked by the hype of software vendors mixed with the hopes of wishful thinkers. With nearly everyone in our business forever in search of a code-cutting Excalibur, the keenest of real tools will always disappoint. Part of the problem is that the developers and vendors of CASE tools have often understood neither models and modeling nor the methods their tools purport to support. Even more to the point, CASE tools are simply not what is really needed to speed and refine development. What is needed is both more and less than what most CASE tools provide. We need to look to visual development environments to understand what CASE should have been and may yet become.

Visual development environments comprise one of the most colorful and energetic strands in the skein of contemporary development practices and products. Visual development refers to a variety of tools and approaches that allow developers to generate code by direct manipulation of visual objects on a graphical user interface. The oldest and best known of this genre is Microsoft's Visual Basic. Later products, for example, IBM's VisualAge and Borland's Delphi, began to hint at the full potential of what visual development could someday become. Although most such products were originally aimed principally at applications developers, the visual development paradigm may be in everybody's future.

Visual development software is just technology, but technology that could dramatically alter how software developers work. In its purest form, visual development allows you to create complete working systems largely or exclusively by moving visible objects around on your monitor screen. Direct manipulation of graphical elements is an obvious approach for designing GUIs, and that is just where visual development began—with so-called GUI builders. The problem with many of the earliest tools was that once you dropped beneath the slick GUI surface, what you ran into was some of the ugliest Basic or messiest C++ ever conceived, all spread around in an undisciplined clutter behind the screen. You had to wallow around a lot in this muck to get anything significant to actually work.

Between GUI and Grit

When the systems under construction become really complex, developers begin to long for the ability to build models at higher levels of abstraction, to represent and review the architecture of the system, not just the actual construction and not just the surface manifestations at the user interface. What you want is to make the programming units and their relationships visual as well. You want to be able to see the modules, the classes and objects, and the messages and references that interconnect them. You want to be able to see the structure of your code based on familiar notation and move through it using what J. D. Hildebrand has called a visual browser (Hildebrand 1994). You want to be able to send a message from here to there by drawing a line or to be able to move a method from one class to another by a drag-and-drop. In effect, you want a continuously active CASE tool with code conversion built in dynamically so that whatever you do in pictures is immediately reflected in code. And vice versa.

In other words, you want a truly integrated visual development environment, the convergence of CASE and WYSIWYG applications builders resulting from the continued addition of CASE-like capability to application development environments and from the tighter integration of GUI building and code generation within CASE tools. VisualAge represents the trend toward direct modeling in application builders, already allowing you to draw lines to interconnect GUI objects as well as nonvisible objects that lurk behind the scenes. On the more vanilla CASE side of things, tools like Together C++ keep the implementation model—the code—and the design models—the diagrams—in synch.

Instead of code-generation as something apart from model building and graphics design, a true visual development environment would maintain the visible features of a system (the GUI), the visualized architecture (the analysis and design diagrams), and the underlying code in perfect synch, so that the developer can move smoothly back and forth between design and implementation models, speaking in code or in pictures as fits the problem and priorities or the mood of the moment. This would carry development tools a lot closer to how humans solve problems. People typically think in both words and pictures and bounce back and forth between the clarity of higher-level abstractions and the dirty grit of solution details. (See also Chapter 18.)

Visual development in this fullest form is a significant new paradigm for the relationship between programmers and computers. Potentially it allows analysts and designers to use the same mental and manual skills to describe a problem, design a solution, and construct the system. That may sound like a return to yesteryear, when code was designed by writing code, but in this case, designs could become coded simply by designing. The real difference in the newer paradigm is that visual development allows the creation and manipulation to take place at a higher level, in bigger chunks, with more visible connections and consequences. It can literally allow you to see where you are, what you are doing, and how it all fits into the larger scheme of the system under construction.

Dual Processors

Visual development allows thinking to take place in two modes simultaneously—one being the analytical, sequential reasoning mode that goes with using language and expressing processes in code, the other being the visual-spatial mode that is invoked when we draw pictures or build things with Legos or try to figure out a diagram. Visual programming is, thus, like a CPU upgrade to your brain, increasing your mental processing power and allowing you to tackle larger problems or build systems faster.

Visual development environments also hold the potential for changing how development proceeds. Promoters of object technology say it enables a "seamless" development process, in large part because the same concepts and vocabulary that are used to describe a problem and to interact with users and clients are also used to design and to express the software solution. It's all just objects. Delivery on this promise is another matter, however, and traditional object-oriented development tools have not in themselves been all that seamless. The combination of visual development with object-oriented design and programming may finally turn the trick. Not only do you get to accomplish the whole task through direct manipulation of objects, but the coming generation of tools may allow you to restructure and extend the tools themselves using the same visual programming methods you use to build applications.

Instead of seeing CASE in a coffin, maybe it's a matter of visualizing development.

From *Software Development,* Volume 3, #5, May 1995.

24

Software Objectives

A programmer who snoozed through the better part of the last decade or two might not know about object-oriented programming. The rest of us have had it up to our tushies in objects. I am actually somewhat sympathetic toward the van Winkles of the industry, because in 1986, when I stumbled back into the computer field, object technology was a star on a meteoric rise, while a decade earlier, when I had last absented myself, object-oriented programming was an obscure brown dwarf hidden away in the cosmos of nebulous computing techniques. Trend spotting is surprisingly easy when you peek once a decade or so.

Not that object-orientation is particularly new. Although some writers have credited the failure of structured methods for the genesis of object-orientation, in truth, structured programming and design arose right alongside objects, slithering out of the same primordial swamp of unstructured methods. Dijkstra, Constantine, Kaye, Dahl, and Sutherland were all working in parallel in the late 1960s and early 1970s, devising and dispersing the core concepts of these new ways of thinking about programs and programming.

By the mid-1980s, the concepts of object-orientation were well established, although not necessarily well understood. Of course, there was no shortage of skilled early adopters who could OOP their way through any problem. There was just a shortage of people who could give clear explanations. According to the rhetoric of the time, you had to live objects to learn to think and design in terms of them.

"How does an object compare to an information cluster or a module with informational cohesion?" asks the earnest student.

"Look," responds the impatient instructor, "I told you to forget about that old structured stuff. It didn't work. Unless you cleanse your cortex of these things, you'll stay confused." (Meaning, of course, that the teacher didn't know what the student was talking about, so shut up and listen!)

Many of the early pedagogues and demagogues of OO preached that the only route to objective effectiveness was to give up the ways of the past, to forget everything you ever knew or thought you knew about software engineering and learn a whole new paradigm. You had to start over, with a blank mental slate.

As if that were possible. What they advocated had more the ring of religious conversion than of learning new technical skills and concepts. Some gurus of objects still preach that way. Get them while they're young and untainted by procedures and you can make them true believers. Or so the evangelists claim.

Of course, as I quickly learned when I first took up the OO cause, many of those early proponents had to take this evangelical stance. Knowing nothing about structured methods or relational data models, they could not comment intelligently on the relationship of these concepts to OO and so could not risk getting probing questions from their more experienced students. When they did speak of the then-current software engineering practices, it was to attack them, playing an easy sport of shooting at targets that were carefully constructed of structured straw.

A certain fuzziness of definitions and a glaring lack of consensus on what constituted the core concepts of OO did not improve the plight of the poor pilgrim seeking object-oriented enlightenment. With time, though, things jelled, so that today there is fairly widespread agreement on the essential vocabulary and concepts of object-orientation.

Packaging

Object-orientation is a lot of things. For some it is a way of making a living, for some it is a way of life. To understand object-orientation in its full glory you need to appreciate not only encapsulation and implementation hiding, but inheritance, delegation, genericity, dynamic binding, and polymorphism. (And people say the structural revolution foisted too many new terms on the field!) All of these concepts represent important aspects of the paradigm and its practice, but the real reason that objects have a secure future in software development is much simpler.

Not too much of the subtlety of object-orientation can be captured in a short essay, but the real peopleware issues are actually quite simple. (Even as I wrote this, I could hear the click of keyboards preparing the protesting email that would soon flood my in-box.)

Forget the hype of the true believers who tell you that OO is a new paradigm for thinking about problems. It's just like a "new, improved" breakfast cereal—it's all about better packaging. Classes, which are the essential component of object-oriented programming, are just improved containers for code. Object classes have a number of advantages over functions and subroutines. First, classes are large, economy-size containers, and bigger boxes means bigger systems can be built from a given number of components. Even though object classes are bigger, they look smaller and simpler because, cleverly, they tightly pack all the things about a single idea, such as ComputerCustomer or LaserPrinter, into one neat bundle that is easy to recognize and haul around. Yes, you do throw data and procedure into the same box, but it's the right data and procedure, the stuff that belongs together in the same box.

The box even bears a comforting label that sounds a lot like the real world of clients and users, which is the second major advantage of objects. All else is bonus goodies in the bottom of the cereal box. As OO pioneer Brad Cox was wont to say to anyone who looked in his direction with the vaguest hint of interest, the OO revolution in packaging is exactly like the transition from discrete electronics to integrated circuits, that is, from transistors to chips. It's a small difference that makes a big difference

I'll leave the rest of the details to Roland Racko, Meilir Page-Jones, and other real OO gurus who can demonstrate in their columns and books that even OO in all its glory doesn't have to be difficult, even for rusty old minds thoroughly tainted by structured methods.

Subjective Programming

The bottom line on object-orientation is that it is such a rousing good idea at its heart that eventually it will be virtually the only way serious software is developed. So, unless you only develop silly or stupid software, sooner or later you will get oriented. Good sources of object-oriented advice and knowledge abound.

If you are a programmer at heart, you will want, as is your bent, to cut some code. In the right language, this can be very instructive. The right language could be almost anything, but it's probably Eiffel, a language that deserves to be more widely known and more commercially successful than it is. Arguably one of the best-designed languages ever developed for engineering software, Eiffel is the virtual antithesis of the far more popular C++. Eiffel makes it easy to learn to think and build with objects while C++ makes it easy to fool yourself into thinking you've changed even while you're serving up the same old Shinola. Eiffel is clean and compact, C++ is another story. Within Eiffel, it is easier to program well and harder to do dumb things. Granted, Eiffel should be available from more vendors on more platforms, it could benefit from a viable and versatile visual development environment, and its tools should support established methods and notations. Native code compilation would probably help, and it wouldn't hurt if some of its supporters were less bristly. Smalltalk is bigger, Java is the brew of the day, but still, Eiffel is a language with a lot of friends. (*Je suis ton ami*, Bertrand.)

For years, my recommended OO primer for programmers was from the man who finally made structured design accessible to mere mortals. *What Every Programmer Should Know About Object-Oriented Design* (Page-Jones 1995) was not the first book on the subject, but it is never too late for someone to write clearly and well about a complex subject. (Now, that book has been superceded by an equally good tome from the same author, *Fundamentals of Object-Oriented Design* (Page-Jones 2000)).

So, get oriented.

From *Software Development,* Volume 3, #6, June 1995.

25

The Seams Are Showing

Now and then, in a few of the old schlock science-fiction films, one will catch a glimpse of stitches or a zipper running down the back of an alien mutant's supposed skin. In object-oriented software development, despite frequent claims to the contrary, the seams are often no less visible than on the shoddily costumed bug-eyed denizens of a cheap sci-fi flick. If we judge the process by the end product, the promise of seamless object-oriented development remains largely unfulfilled.

Seamless development, according to the modern mythology of object technology, delivers better software through a simpler process. How? One common and consistent set of constructs—the concepts of the application domain as construed by real users dwelling in that fabled land of the real world—are carried throughout the entire development process, informing the models through which developers analyze and resolve their problems and ultimately becoming embodied in the very structure of the code itself. By thinking in objects, recirculating a single set of ideas through all activities of the process, developers simplify their work. So the public relations go.

However, developers are not the only ones who would stand to gain from a seamless development process were it ever to materialize on this planet. Much of my work focuses on improving the lot of users, saving them from suffering and humiliation at the hands of bad software with incomprehensibly alien user interfaces. Users have a stake in the fruits of seamless development. The constructs of the application domain that inform the classes and objects of the software can be, in turn, reflected back to the user in a user interface that is itself organized from those very terms. Mirabile dictu, the product of a seamless development process oriented by the objects of the user's world is a product that speaks the user's language and presents itself as a recognizable extension of the world within which the user works. It collects together those things that are thought of together or employed together by the user. (See Chapters 24 and 48.)

Users and developers alike have a stake in software that is easier to master and requires less ongoing technical support, but many organizations have found it hard to improve the usability of their products. Organizations fail to deliver usability to their users and customers for many reasons, but there are common barriers to success in this realm. In some cases, the organization itself is the problem, in others, the methods are ineffective, and sometimes the tools are to blame.

Some organizations fall victim to their own lack of real resolve. As long as an idea does not cost anything or take any time, these organizations are as ready as any of their competitors to hearken to the voice of the customer or to fit the interface to the user. Such groups may talk the talk, advocating intelligent user interfaces or user-friendly software, but, lacking a consistent and appropriately focused organizational commitment to usability, they never quite walk the walk. Increasingly, I also encounter organizations where the developers are more committed to improving software usability than their management. Management will not invest in training. They do not consider usability part of the job of software developers. They prefer more features to more usable software.

Other development groups, though fully committed to enhancing software usability, can be hampered by inadequate methods, relying, for example, on testing to discover usability defects instead of on good design to avoid them in the first place. They may be prepared to invest in usability, but are uncertain about where to invest. In some ways, these are the easiest groups to help, because they already have the will to proceed and the willingness to commit resources. They need only to be shown the way. Once they learn how to apply effective models, they can achieve dramatic gains in end-product usability.

Tool Time

Even a full and focused commitment to usability and a well-structured process may not be enough, however. Often, modern development tools are themselves impediments to delivering on the paired promises of software usability and seamless development. The tools not only do not support a truly seamless development process, some of them make it difficult to pursue a systematic, model-driven approach to usability engineering.

Software development tools continue to improve dramatically, particularly in the form of visual development tools. Visual development tools—from Visual Basic and Delphi to Visual C++ and J-Builder—represent a major advancement in software and applications development, not just as technology but also in terms of how such tools fit with the way human beings solve problems. The best of these tools make it easy for developers to move back and forth between the visual representation of the software on the user interface and the underlying code, to think in visible objects or in invisible code as suits the problem at hand.

Where the seams in the tools begin to show is between the user interface and the models by which developers represent objects, communication, and tasks. The promise of full and complete integration, raised in Chapter 23, is not materializing. Modeling tools are still just modeling tools and development tools are just development tools. Even where they can import each other's files or share information through an API, the zippers and stitches are often painfully obvious. Even worse, key connections and relationships fail to be recognized by the tools. For example, use cases are widely acknowledged as an important model for object-oriented development and are supported by some modeling tools, but the connection of use cases to the user interface is unrecognized by most such tools and remains solely in the minds of developers.

What, then, do we need from our tools in order to produce highly usable software through a seamless development process? We need the tool vendors to think outside their traditional boxes. We need them to understand view-based development, an idea that has been waiting a long time to be recognized (see Chapter 18).

Views

A software system can be viewed from different perspectives. Each view or perspective highlights certain features or aspects of the system, while ignoring or de-emphasizing others. A process model, such as the venerable flowchart, handily conveys the structure of algorithms but shows little or nothing of data. A domain model effectively represents object classes and their relationships but is useless for screen layout. That the common models employed in software engineering are so focused on specific aspects is not a failing but a strength. Each view simplifies the system for some purposes, making it easier for developers to talk about and think about a particular issue or kind of problem in the course of producing the software.

The user interface itself is just one view of software, representing the software as actually seen by end users. A content model provides another view of the user interface as seen from the designer's point of view, modeling its contents apart from their visual appearance or manifestation within any actual graphical user interface (Constantine 1998). A context navigation map provides a representation of all the component parts of the user interface along with their interrelationships. (For more about content and navigation models, see Chapter 44.)

Even help files and documentation are really just alternative views of the underlying software. Although these views are often thought of by developers as an ancillary annoyance, both are actually parts of the user interface, since they mediate between users and the system. In practice, the ultimate usability of software depends not only on the quality of screen layout and of dialog design, but also on the quality of help files and manuals.

Of course, all of the models or views of a given system are intimately interrelated. After all, they describe a single system. Visual objects on the user interface are linked to internal objects and their methods, for example, and abstract components in a content model are manifest as particular user interface widgets. Various interaction contexts—windows, forms, dialog boxes, and the like—are linked by transitions that are achieved through selection of specific user interface widgets. Use cases not only model the interaction between users and the system but also imply interaction among communicating software objects.

In the rare case where online and offline documentation are current and accurate, these, too, are tightly tied to other views. They describe the visible and nonvisible features of the system using that same common vocabulary employed in the object model and reflected in the user interface design. They inform users of the use cases that they can accomplish through the software.

In a view-based perspective on software development, the objective of the developer is to build the software by completing the various views that describe and specify it. The objective of the development tools should be to support creating the underlying software while maintaining consistency between the code—one view—and all other views. At every moment, any view is a valid way of examining and modifying the system. Change the code and the represented interface changes. Alter a model and the code changes. Create a new content model and an empty form appears in the interface view. Add a use case and another entry is created in the help file. The developer who is stymied in one view can instantly shift to another and proceed.

Traces

One of the payoffs of a view-based development process supported by adequate tools is enhanced traceability. Everything in the software being developed is interconnected with the models and documentation describing it, right back to the original requirements.

While the developer is laying out the widgets of a particular form or dialog box, the use cases to be supported within that interaction context should be visible. In fact, the connection between each step in a use case and the widget or widgets used to enact the use case should be known to the system. If a content model has been created as an abstract view intermediate between the use case model and the user interface as implemented, it should be available to the developer while the user interface is being laid out with the visual development tool.

In general, it should be possible, from moment to moment, to move from one view to another, through linkages that are visible to the developer and known to the system. The developer should be able to see all the use cases supported by some interaction context within the user interface by no more than a click or a selection. Conversely, it should be possible to point to a step in a use case and get to the visual component or components that realize it or to drill down into the object model to see how it is implemented by objects.

In the course of solving a problem in one view, the developer may find it convenient to switch to another view that is more conducive to working out a solution. The developer should not have to generate code to see the working results nor reverse engineer a program to see the models. It should not be necessary to export models in one tool and import them in the next. All views need to be maintained in complete synchrony by an integrated development environment.

Many analysts have begun employing use cases as a core model for defining requirements. In an appropriate development environment and process, use cases support end-to-end requirements tracing. The use case model links most of the other views of interest in the development process. It ties back to the model of user roles on which it ultimately rests. It connects to the content and navigation models representing the abstract structure of the user interface, and, of course to the user interface itself. It is linked to the object class model or data model in its vocabulary and to the object communication model for software internals. It maps to the help that documents for the user the available use cases and how they are enacted. It is connected with test cases for regression testing and acceptance testing, as well as the scenarios for usability testing.

True, some software development tools support parts of this view-based development approach, but all fall down at one point or another, most particularly in bridging between use cases and object models on the one hand and the visual design of the user interface on the other. This is the crucial seam when it comes to producing highly usable software. It is time we ironed it out.

From *Object Magazine,* December 1997.

V

Process Improvements

Introduction

Producing software is a process. Applications do not just happen, programs do not simply spring full-blown from the brains of programmers. This is a good thing, since one of the basic principles of the modern "quality" movement is that processes can be improved. Indeed, the goal in the so-called "total quality" movement and its various incarnations in the software world is not just improvements in steps or fits or bursts, but continuous process improvement. The most advanced organizations not only study the processes by which software and applications are produced, but have instituted programs for feeding their findings back into the process in a closed loop that refines their systems and procedures continuously.

Achieving this somewhat utopian ideal of nonstop improvement can take a major corporate commitment. Companies that embark on this journey toward software engineering enlightenment often start with an expensive and elaborate appraisal of their current culture and practices. They may hire consultants to evaluate their organization using something like the Capability Maturity Model developed by the Software Engineering Institute, an elaborate rating that boils down to a number from 1 to 5. If all you want to do is find out how mature your organization is, you can save your money. Probably you are at Level 1, meaning your processes are lousy and unreliable but you don't even know quite how lousy or unreliable because you don't measure anything. Almost everyone is at Level 1, so this is a fairly safe bet. (If you want, I'll come visit and send you a bill before announcing the foregone conclusion.)

The real reason for going through the pain and expense of a more elaborate and formal assessment is not to find out a number but to learn in some detail where and how things are going wrong and where you can start creating institutionalized practices that will make things better. Maybe after some years of effort—and more money to consultants—you will reach Level 3. Rumors of a rare Level 5 software engineering group being spotted in the wilds of rural Virginia are frequently referenced but remain unconfirmed. Do not misinterpret my casual stance. I am not knocking consultants—I am one myself, after all—nor am I questioning the potential payoffs of thorough organizational assessments; in fact, my firm does such assessments for clients. And I am most emphatically *not* opposed to software developers being prepared to invest substantial sums and resources in process improvement. But I do want to make clear that I think there may be other ways to create improved processes, ways that are not as dramatic, do not cost as much, and are not quite so high profile.

This section will look at some of these simple ideas and modest proposals for improving software quality through better development processes. There are no major social programs here, nothing that could justify astronomical consulting fees for business process re-engineering, just things that small groups and even individual developers and managers can do to do a better job.

The Benefits of Visibility

I remember writing my first program, a FORTRAN exercise for a course known as 6.41. Everything went by the numbers at M.I.T. in those days, and so did my program. It was a breeze to write, it just didn't compile the first time. Or the second. I was devastated and dumbfounded. When I finally did get it to compile, I was utterly shocked to find out it didn't work. I couldn't see why; it looked right to me. I showed it to my roommate. Marshall was a math major. I think he was writing algorithms before there were computers to run them on.

"I can't figure out what's wrong with this program, see, it's supposed to…" He grabbed the print-out, what we affectionately called an 80-80 listing, for reasons that only those who remember punched cards will know.

"What's that?" He jabbed with his stubby Brooklyn finger.

"Looks like a C."

"You don't want it there." He was right. The statement still compiled, but the computer wasn't reading it the way I had intended. Marshall went back to something having to do with gradients and del operators, all the while polishing his interpretation of Marlon Brando in *A Streetcar Named Desire*. What I learned from this was never to show Marshall anything I ever wrote, especially code. He would always find something wrong with it, and I had yet to reach the point where I could regard this as a favor. Besides, it invariably seemed to inspire another bout of his bellowing out, "Stella, Stella!" There was a lesson lurking here, but I wasn't ready for it. Eventually, of course, I caught on to the fact that running a problem past a fellow programmer was often the most efficient way to find some elusive bug or to work out some tricky algorithm. In fact, most of us learn that talking out our ideas, using a colleague as a sounding board or getting feedback on something still half-jelled, is not only effective and enriches the end product, but it's also fun and builds good working relationships.

Dynamic Duos

It took P. J. Plauger, though, to really teach me about the benefits of visibility. Shortly after he started Whitesmiths, Ltd., I visited him at their New York "headquarters," a small apartment in Manhattan. Somewhere off in one of the rooms there lurked a minicomputer, stuffed in a closet in order to keep the clatter down was a printer, and around what should have been the living room were scattered several terminals. At each terminal were two programmers!

Of course, only one programmer was actually cutting code at each keyboard, but the others were peering over their shoulders, doing those annoying things that New Yorkers are especially schooled in, namely kibitzing. The room buzzed with a steady stream of questions about the algorithm or whether an initial value was correct, suggestions about how to break out of a loop, or drawing attention to a syntax error or a test done in the wrong order or a missing case. After awhile the two programmers would switch places, and the one at the keyboard would become the professional nudge.

I speculated about cash flow problems being at the root of their shortage of hardware, but Plauger assured me that this was their chosen mode for working. Pretty inefficient, huh? Nope. Having adopted this approach, they were delivering finished and tested code faster than ever. A closer look showed why. The code that came out the back of these two-programmer terminals was nearly 100% bug-free. Not only did it have fewer defects, but it was better code, tighter and more efficient, having benefited from the thinking of two bright minds and the steady dialogue between trusted terminal-mates. I came to think of this model for programming teamwork as the "Dynamic Duo." The principle operating here is very broad: Increasing work visibility leads to increased quality! Two programmers in tandem is not redundancy; it's a direct route to greater efficiency and better quality. (As the XP crowd knows. LLC)

The same principle applies to learning. Most people—not all, but most—learn more rapidly in small groups than they do alone. This is even true of many diehards who are convinced that they can't learn that way or who hate to work in groups. There are numerous contributing factors. Discussion brings up issues and ideas that might never have occurred to the isolated individual. Peers can often explain and interpret difficult concepts when an instructor cannot. New ideas and approaches emerge from the dialogue itself. Perhaps most basically, students in groups learn from each other, not just from an instructor or textbook. It's one of the reasons I nearly always use project and study teams in the workshops and seminars that I lead.

The rule seems to apply particularly to learning a programming language. Plauger has observed that, for language learning, there seems to be an optimum number of students per terminal. It's not one. It's probably two. Three also works, but one student working alone generally learns the language significantly more slowly than when paired up with a partner. At the other end of the scale, four or more working at one computer are always getting in each other's way—figuratively and physically. Groups this large often end up splitting into subgroups or will resort to "time sharing" and ultimately prove less effective. So if you really want to add C++ or Smalltalk to your repertoire, don't closet yourself with the manual and a tutorial program. Grab a programming buddy and sit down together at one keyboard. Knowing this principle may also offer new hope for budget-bound schools and for companies whose training departments have just been laid off.

Virtual Visibility

Interestingly, to get the benefit of work visibility, it may not always be necessary for anyone else even to say a word. Most of us have had some experience with one of those perversely elusive bugs. You study the test run and the listing, and you know that the problem is somewhere in one particular block of code, but no matter how many times you walk through that section, you can't find where it blows up. So you bang on the door of the next office and hang-doggedly ask for some help. Charlotte, after all, has a Ph.D. in Computer Science. You start to describe the background of the problem. As you explain the loop to her, something leaps out at you. Before she can say anything, you sigh a quiet "Oh!" then back sheepishly out the door as you mutter thanks. "Any time," she replies.

The very act of explaining or describing something to someone else seems to alter our thought patterns. I don't know if it is actually necessary to have someone else in the room. Perhaps it is sufficient to imagine you are explaining the problem to someone else, but I suspect it's never quite as good solo.

Like all guidelines to building better systems, the Principle of Work Visibility can be carried too far. One form of this particular reduction to an absurdity (or should it be expansion to an absurdity?) is the programming model that seems to be favored by certain major software vendors, what might be called the "mongrel horde" approach to program development. The formula is simple. Just get a lot of programmers and put them in a big room, a programming bull pit with acres of desks and terminals and everything in on-line databases and e-mail threads for all to read and remark upon. We all know what comes out of this approach.

The benefits of visibility in most situations leap by large quanta when a second person is put into the process, but the returns diminish with successive additions. There are exceptions, of course, for special kinds of activities, especially in the very early or late stages of system development. Brainstorming generally works better with more brains to whip up the storm; small groups may only manage to churn up a dust devil or two or may even sit around becalmed. Code or design walkthroughs also seem to benefit from the contributions of many reviewers walking through, the many eyes being all the better to spot the problems or weaknesses. On the other hand, for real problem solving, wrestling with intricately interwoven sets of constraints, and puzzling out a good software architecture, too many heads often end up butting up against each other. Generally speaking, this is probably yet another of those seven-plus-or-minus-twoish things, where maximum scale is modest.

Structured Views

The principle of work visibility reaches its zenith in some of the specialized teamwork and group models designed for software development. In Joint Application Design, or JAD (Wood and Silver 1989), a group of end users and developers work out requirements analysis and high-level design through a highly structured meeting process. The visibility of the process to the users and their chance to furnish input in an active way lead to better systems and improved rapport between communities of system users and system developers.

The so-called structured open team described in Chapter 16 (Constantine 1989; Thomsett 1990) is another model that exploits the principle of visibility to improve system quality and, ultimately, development efficiency. In such a development team, project members do a large portion of their work in each other's presence throughout the life cycle. Marc Rettig (1990) reports that one successful team spent half of each work day meeting as a group. Of course, these were not merely meetings as we usually think of them, but working sessions. The purpose was not to review minutes or keep each other apprised of progress, but actually to do work. In structured open teamwork, people analyze problems, design modules, and even work out coding details in groups. These working sessions are facilitated by a team member to make them more efficient and effective, but much of the real power comes from the visibility that the open process brings to software development.

Any software development group can improve software quality just by finding ways to increase visibility in the programming process. There will be detractors and resistors, of course. We all know programmers who come and go at odd hours when nobody is around, who encrypt their source files, and who hunch over their terminals to keep anyone who happens to walk by from peeking at their programs.

But remember, the Stealth Programmer is a disappearing breed.

From *Computer Language Magazine*, Volume 9, #2, 1992.

27

Rewards and Reuse

We recycle so many things, from grocery bags to toner cartridges, why not recycle code? Why not reuse our designs and models rather than always starting from scratch? The rewards of reuse seem to be enormous. What code is cheaper to write than the code you don't have to write at all? With higher levels of reuse supported by larger component libraries, we might double or triple effective productivity. All we have to do is change the whole culture of software development and maybe the personalities of programmers.

Old Problems

Reuse is hardly a new idea. The lowly subroutine was conceived so that the same instructions did not have to be written out each time a particular calculation was needed. Reusable component libraries have been around for almost as long as people have been programming. The first to yield to reuse were math routines, followed soon by input-output. Except for the sheer joy or perversity of doing it, no applications or tool developer writes their own sine-cosine routines anymore.

Then, what is the problem? Unfortunately, most programmers like to program. Some of them would rather program than eat or bathe. Most of them would much rather cut code than chase documentation or search catalogs or try to figure out some other stupid programmer's idiotic work. Software developers develop things; users use them. Other things being equal, programmers will design and build from scratch rather than recycle. All of them are convinced that they can write it tighter or faster or more elegantly than whoever came before. So, even though it might make them more productive, programmers are almost constitutionally biased against reuse. How do we encourage them to change their habits? Suddenly the chorus in the balcony starts singing contrapuntally: "Incentives. Market forces. Rewards schemes. Royalties. Reinforcement schedules. Culture change." Such lovely cacophony.

Lending Support

It really is not all that hard to understand the score. Reuse on any substantial scale begins with reusable component libraries. There are really only two basic problems involved in such libraries: getting things into them and getting things out again! For programmers to reuse components from a library, there must first be components in the library. Where do these come from?

Various models have been proposed and tried. One is simply to accept free donations from anyone willing to have their code published in the library. Some organizations have had trouble getting donations until they either offered to pay for them or at least promised that authors would not be hounded for maintenance or modification. This approach, a sort of "used-book store" model, appears to be inexpensive, building a large library with little or no direct investment in component development. In theory, components are generated as a side effect of regular development projects.

It does work, but the libraries typically resemble the familiar used-book store. I have spent many happy hours pawing through stacks and boxes of used books, but I think of this more as recreation than as a model for information retrieval or code recycling.

Typically there is little or no quality control and no accountability with this approach. To induce donations, contributing programmers are absolved of responsibility. What you need may be in there, but the odds are against finding it. If it takes the typical programmer more than 2 minutes and 27 seconds to find something, they will conclude it does not exist and therefore will reinvent it.

Components in libraries built with this open enrollment approach are like those thousands of old books of varied vintages and values heaped in disarray. Browsing through the dusty piles for an unexpected treasure can be great fun, but you would not want to do so on a tight deadline. If you know that you need a good current source on post-Soviet economics, you would go to a well-stocked and organized university bookstore, not the basement bookseller with the diverse exotica.

Meilir Page-Jones tells of a client whose "used-book" component library grew so unwieldy that they decided to appoint a reuse librarian whose job it was to keep things *out* of the component library, letting only the finest become part of the repository. Legend has it that this person became known as Conan the Librarian. For this approach to work, however, there must be substantial forces impelling developers to donate to the library.

Programming Royalty

Some companies, on the other hand, are biting the bullet of up-front costs and forming groups of full-time developers whose function it is to build components for reuse. These are not typical grunt coders, but highly skilled specialists with a knack for recognizing commonalities, defining abstractions, and building bullet-proof code covering just the right domain. They are rewarded for creating quality components with high potential for reuse. They may even get royalties for each use made of one of their contributions to the library.

If such developers are simply salaried, it could be in their interest to build fancier and more refined components than necessary, since one of the really hard parts of the job is finding what needs to be done. Initially, hundreds of nice little general-purpose components suggest themselves, but as the library grows, seeing what is needed next becomes increasingly difficult. One does not want to finish any one component development project too quickly, because then you either have to become really creative again, or sit on your hands and risk someone noticing you.

Again looking to the book trade for inspiration and understanding, this can be thought of as the "school textbook" model, in which teams of specialists try to figure out what should be taught and how, creating books by committee. Often the results are resplendent with splashy color graphics, tables, exercises, and catchy sidebars on every third page. And they're supported by workbooks, teacher's manuals, supplementary readings, and visual aids. They typically are also uninspired, inelegant, even boring, and all too frequently they are hopelessly out of touch with the real needs of schools and students.

Royalties to the author for reuse pose other problems. For one thing, the feedback provided by royalties, whether paid in cash or merely brownie points, generally comes too late. The money has already been spent, not only on components that see a lot of reuse, but also on ones that proved useless. For any selection process to work, there must be a large pool of parts with substantial variation in "fit" for the selective pressure of the marketplace or environment to work. This means that such libraries will, on the average, always be too big, with a large proportion of mediocre or inferior components from which a small number of "good" ones can be culled. It is hard to know even how the selection process should be driven. Is a widely used component really a desirable one? Perhaps it is so widely used because what is really needed is not in the library. Perhaps its use reflects its position in the index or how it appears in the browser. Perhaps it has simply been better advertised, even though a smaller and more powerful alternative exists.

And what constitutes a use? Each call or instantiation? Each inheritance from or reference to? One program might make 130 uses of a component that is never used in any other project, while another component might find a single use in all 27 systems developed over a year. Which component is more useful? Is a simple and obvious component that becomes widely used worth more royalties to the author than a subtle and ingenious class that saves days of effort on only one project?

Acquired Taste

Of course, other models are possible. Consider the acquisition specialist in a public library whose job it is to track community interests and needs along with industry trends and keep the collection growing appropriately. Like the used-book store, the public library is built from components (books) that are already extant, are acquired intact, and are entered into the library without further editing or refinement.

For a model better suited to building a reusable software component library we need to look further back into publishing, to the actual acquisition of works to be published. Series editors and acquisition specialists in the publishing industry play an active role in seeking out and developing new titles, working with authors not only in response to sensed needs or demands, but also to round out the "book list" for more complete coverage and to anticipate future needs. This model, or Page-Jones's idea of the "art patron" who not only acquires but commissions works, may be closer to what the software industry needs.

Merely assembling *reasonable* components does not make a library of reusable components. We have to get developers to reuse rather than reinvent. Many companies are trying to set up bonus and compensation schemes to reward reuse, but I am not convinced that these are necessary for high levels of productive reuse, and they may even be counterproductive in the long run. Sometimes information about performance may be all that is needed. In one organization it was enough to change how they reported programming productivity back to the group. Having invested in the development of a reusable component library, they were disappointed with its limited use. They had been posting monthly bar charts showing programmer productivity in lines-of-code written and delivered. They were persuaded to report instead the total number of lines incorporated into delivered code, which included lines linked from the reuse library. Reuse rose sharply. But is lines-of-library-code the right metric for reuse? Correct, reasonable, and appropriate reuse is probably a much more subtle factor, more difficult to define and measure.

Even if we get the right metric, linking the desired behavior of reuse too directly to tangible rewards may create problems. A close link between simple, quantifiable behavior and direct reinforcement, whether in brownie points or quarterly bonuses, can actually undermine the professional values on which effective reuse is based. As workers conform their actions to fit rational reinforcement schemes, underlying values and attitudes about quality work may actually diminish in salience, increasing the dependence on a finely tuned reward structure.

This is why at one of the three-initialed computer companies, their reusability group is focusing on the corporate climate and culture that shapes reuse and reusability, the common values about programs and programming that impede or advance the sharing of designs and implementations. Perhaps I was lucky to be brainwashed by early mentors who thought it was in their best interest and that of our employers not to keep reinventing the wheel. First in nuclear physics data reduction and later in routine business applications, we built and made extensive use of reusable component libraries. These experiences taught me that, with a rich component library supported by effective tools, the rewards are intrinsic. The payoff is finding the component you need in a reasonable time and then finding that it can be readily used or adapted for your use. Every time this happens, you are being reinforced for it. The habit of initially consulting the library or repository becomes ingrained without being tied to increasing the number of green stamps you get or your quarterly code bonus.

Elaborate gimmicks and extrinsic rewards are probably more important for anemic libraries and clumsy tools than for good ones. Perhaps they signal a need to reexamine the corporate culture itself and the professional values it reinforces or discourages.

From *Computer Language Magazine*, Volume 9, #7, 1992.

28

Superlearning

You've been meaning to learn Smalltalk or to become proficient in Java or to master the Unified Modeling Language, but there are only so many hours in the day, your client-server project is overdue, and your kids actually would like to see you sometime before they finish high school. Try superlearning! The promos say that you can learn object orientation in an hour. Or a foreign language in three seconds. Superlearning, accelerated learning, multi-sensory education. Powerful new techniques developed by the Russians or the Bulgarians or the Texans. Wouldn't it be great? Slip on some headphones, drift off, and wake up knowing COM and the complete Windows API. Or slip into a lecture, blow your whistle a few times, and walk out thinking objects. Don't you wish?

Today it's sleep-learning and subliminal reprogramming of the unconscious, but it all started with audio training programs, foreign language courses on cassette and, before that, on LPs and even 78s. Which brings me to Sputnik.

Launching Language

Sputnik changed my life. In 1957, the Russians surprised and inspired the world by orbiting the planet's first artificial satellite. This precipitated a change in how Americans viewed space, viewed Russians, and viewed brainy, science-minded young people. Until Sputnik, I was an unappreciated misfit. Almost overnight I became an appreciated misfit.

And I decided to learn Russian. There were no classes, so I ordered the newly published, but already obsolescent "Living Language" course on three LPs. The box copy promised quick, easy mastery of a difficult language. Over several months I reached a point where I knew the Cyrillic alphabet and could garble a handful of stock sentences, but I didn't learn Russian. That's hard and takes a lot of time. In fact, it took three consulting trips to Russia before I could get by on the streets of Moscow and Leningrad. Even then, they thought I spoke Russian with a Bulgarian accent.

Learning Smalltalk is certainly easier than learning Russian, but you can't learn either in your sleep. Despite the fact that an entire industry has grown up around it, there is absolutely no credible or consistent evidence that learning can be accelerated by certain forms of music or rhythms or subsonic pulses or that subaudible messages recorded over (or is it under?) New Age music can help you sell systems or lose weight or become more self-confident. None of this stuff is worth the charges on your credit card except to the purveyors of "super" learning.

So how do people learn complex things, like languages or programming languages, or how to program, or how to do therapy? How do they learn to think in terms of procedures or object classes or disabled communication patterns?

Economist Kenneth Boulding, one of the founders of modern systems theory, said that know-how—working knowledge—is not the same as knowledge. Knowledge, even fairly complicated knowledge, can be acquired in many ways, but know-how requires learning-by-doing. You can learn a lot about programming or psychotherapy by reading or watching other people or attending dazzling demos, but you only become a programmer by writing programs or a therapist by doing therapy.

Lectures are probably the least efficient and most ineffective method for teaching. And for obvious reasons they are almost totally useless for imparting know-how. Teachers and trainers should be accountable for how much they successfully communicate, not how much they superficially cover. Droning on over point after point from bullet-laden visuals doesn't communicate a heck of a lot to anyone.

What about multi-media presentations? I was there, on the faculty of IBM's Systems Research Institute when, circa 1970, James Martin first dazzled colleagues and students by using not one but two overhead projectors augmented by 35mm slides. We've come a long way. Now everyone uses two overheads! If you want to lead the pack today, you need a lot more. Color. Sound. Graphics. Animation. Games.

Quick Study

Does multimedia make a difference? Do people learn more or learn faster with color animations? Flashing lights and flashy shirts probably do serve a purpose. At least audiences are more likely to stay awake, which is important, since sleep learning doesn't work. Visible and audible punctuation can help people remember things, but it only works if it is closely, even intrinsically, tied to what it is people are supposed to remember. I remember vividly a spectacular video morph from a lecture over a year ago, but I have no idea what the presenter was talking about. I did like the way the car turned into a hundred-dollar bill, though.

It takes more than bells and whistles to facilitate learning. If there is anything real to be gained from multimedia, multisensory communication, it must come from the careful, calculated, and appropriate use of each medium. Back in the heyday of the structural revolution, I worked with a company making multimedia training packages for software development topics. Print, audio, and video media reinforced and complemented each other because each element in the training was presented in the particular form that conveyed the concepts or skills most effectively.

I spent more than a decade training people in some of the most difficult and complex interpersonal and cognitive skills known: understanding families as working systems and helping families that didn't work too well to work better (Constantine 1986). So I know that you can indeed help people to change how they look at and think about the world, to make what is called, in the current jargon, a paradigm shift. It just doesn't happen in an hour or even a day.

What is the real skinny on this multisensory and multimodality stuff? Learning styles vary. Some people learn better by listening, some by reading, some by seeing. For others, only doing it themselves will work. To some people a picture is worth a thousand words, to others it's only worth 17 or 18. To some very aurally orientated individuals, a graphic or visual may be worthless. Communicating through different sense modalities increases the odds that something you say, show, or do will get through. One sense modality can also reinforce learning in another modality.

Memories for some things are more readily formed or more persistent than others. Scents can lay down highly persistent memory traces after only a single exposure. Spatio-motor learning, the memory for practiced movements and actions, is not only highly persistent but can help in recalling associated thoughts and feelings. Handling things physically, manipulating materials that meaningfully represent ideas, helps to consolidate concepts for learners, but only if the physical manipulations are directly related to the concepts.

Multi-modal communication does not have to involve elaborate multi-media presentations. For example, on a panel at a conference in London I fielded a question from the audience about the relationship between reuse and object technology by holding up two pencils to form a large "L," describing them as orthogonal—independent concepts. Later, relenting under pointed questioning, I acknowledged that the two were somewhat related, that high levels of reuse might be somewhat easier with object technology; I held up the pencils in a broad V, illustrating that they were slightly correlated. Two days later, people were still talking about this mini-demo.

The relationship between reuse and objects is an easy one to demon-strate. The best that good presentation can do is to make easy things easy to learn. Harder things will always be harder. No matter how many senses are engaged, you cannot learn object orientation in an hour any more than you can learn programming in an hour. What you can learn is simplified—some would say watered-down—versions of basic concepts.

From *Software Development*, Volume 1, #11, November 1993.

29

Up the Waterfall

Do androids dream of electric sheep? Do managers on software projects have nightmares about plunging over waterfalls?

In the traditional view of the software development life cycle, a linear series of stages are completed in sequence, passing from requirements definition through analysis, design, construction, and testing. High-level design is completed before detailed design can be started. Problems are to be thoroughly analyzed and designed before questions about coding are considered. The development process proceeds smoothly from high levels of abstraction to low-level details, from the general and abstract to the specific and concrete.

Of course, it never really works this way. Still, the so-called "waterfall" model of software development continues to be hotly debated. It's a sometimes nightmarish part of our collective mythology. Once you go over a waterfall, your direction and progress are pretty much out of your control. You are going down, whether you like it or not. At best you can hope not to drown. I'll take some of the blame for long ago introducing such over-simplified notions, but, compared to the uncoordinated chaos reigning at the time, even these somewhat simplistic linear life cycle models were progress. Times have not changed all that much.

Getting Ahead

How software engineers and other programming types actually behave is that they are constantly getting ahead of themselves. No sooner do they see the title page on the requirements document and they are thinking code or screen layout. When they should be analyzing abstract usage scenarios, they're already thinking about icons for a tool bar. When they should be laying out communications paths through major modules, they start thinking about clever ways to utilize the applications programming interface.

This is normal. In fact, it's part of how normal people normally solve problems. In a sense, they work both ends against the middle, jumping forward and back between ends and means, bouncing up and down from high-level abstraction to low-level details.

But developers aren't supposed to work this way. Getting ahead of yourself in a long and complex project can create real problems. It makes it hard for you and your manager to know how far along the project is. Early commitments to details may later have to be changed, precipitating a cascade of other reworks and work-arounds. Getting into specific details too soon can also distract from the main work at hand.

Traditionally, developers and project leaders have had two basic options whenever this impulse to skip ahead arises. They could stick to the discipline and overcome the impulse, or they could give in to it and do the dirty deed before getting back on track. Either way has its risks. If you stay with the current task and ignore the distraction, important insights or ideas that could prove useful may be lost or forgotten. If you always go ahead and work on the details or the specifics whenever you think of them, you may never get back to the main thread. When you do, the thrust of your grand design may be lost.

Rationalized Reality

What we really need is a life cycle model that takes advantage of the ways most people actually tend to think and work, but which keeps developers from becoming their own worst enemies. The problem is how to capture just enough information that can be used later without disrupting the flow of the current problem-solving activity.

My boss and I were recently working on the user interface design for a desktop applet, trying hard to act like disciplined software engineers applying a systematic interface design strategy, but we repeatedly tripped over our own tendencies to get ahead of ourselves. We kept getting these great ideas about detailed interface layout and behavior when we were supposed to be identifying abstract scenarios describing user needs.

Determined to be organized and systematic, yet committed to making the most of how we spontaneously work best, we started using "bins" to hold all those great little flashes that kept coming up at the wrong time. First developed for managing meetings, bins are a brilliantly simple tool for group problem solving. A bin is just a place—a flipchart or file or notepad—in which to record things that are not for current discussion or debate but which ultimately need to be considered.

Out of this we ended up devising a new conceptualization of the development life cycle. We call it the "feed-forward/work-back" model. It's a rationalized successor to various sequential development models, including not only the waterfall model but also so-called whirlpool models that take developers through an iterative spiral of steps. Feed-forward/work-back is actually one of those very small ideas that could make a big difference in how you work. In principle it could be integrated into virtually any software development life cycle model.

Shuttle Bus

It's called "feed-forward/work-back" because of the kinds of loops it inserts into the development process. When you get ahead of yourself, you feed information forward but don't do the work. This is a feed-forward loop. When you discover an oversight or failure from an earlier phase or activity, you do the necessary work immediately. This is a "work-back" loop. Feed ideas forward, work your way back. That's it. Whenever you get ahead of yourself, you make a note to yourself and your teammates to reconsider something when you get to the appropriate point in the process, wherever that is.

Just think of each phase or activity in the software development life cycle as having its own in-box. It doesn't matter what particular life cycle model you are using, how many activities it has, or even whether it is strictly sequential or loops back on itself. For each designated phase or step or activity you create a conceptual container, an "in-bin," to hold things to be looked at and worked on at the appropriate time.

It is important to create an actual record or file of some sort to serve as the in-bin. If you're using informal group methods, put up a sheet of flipchart paper for each phase or activity. If you do something called "Physical Design Validation" in your software development life cycle, have a sheet labeled "Physical Design Validation—In-bin." If you are using document processing or computer-aided software engineering tools, create a file or folder or other document in the system for each of the in-bins.

When you get to a particular phase or activity, you start out by examining the in-bin, looking through it and sorting its contents for action. Some things may have become irrelevant or may have already been decided or dismissed. Ideas that once seemed spot on may now look way off target. Anything that is still valid or salient can now be worked on.

Sometimes distractions from the current thread of development go in the other direction; they concern matters that should have been taken care of earlier. In these cases, it is clearly best to attend immediately to the out-of-sequence issue in order to allow development to proceed safely and smoothly. You don't want a lot of lurking problems or loose threads bollixing up the system. When you find that some requirement is ambiguous, you go back and firm up the requirements. When you find that some architectural issues were left unresolved, you resolve them. When you find that a poor choice was made for file organization, you go back and rework the file design before moving on.

The aim, of course, is to use lots of feed-forward to reduce the amount of work-back.

From *Software Development*, Volume 2, #1, January 1994

30

In-Time Delivery

Our Alitalia flight from Boston to Rome departed late, just as we had been told to expect. Nevertheless, it landed in time for us to catch the direct train for Firenze, where we would have a few days to be pleasantly overwhelmed by the art, the food, and the wines of Tuscany before returning to Rome to teach a class on designing more usable software.

Note that I did not say that our plane landed "on time," but rather "in time." It's a subtle distinction in words, but a cultural matter of great import. Arriving at 6:30 for a 6:30 reception is being "on time." Arriving when the line at the bar has diminished and they bring out the hot *hors d'oeuvres* is being "in time." In time means functional timeliness. As for the Italians, it is not that they are incapable of acting with a sense of urgency, as when their pasta is in danger of cooking past the point of *al dente* perfection, it is just that in Italy, as in various other countries around the world, the cultural sense of time is not closely tied to clock time. A little early, a little late—what counts is the results, the outcome. Italy's neighbors to the north, the Swiss, are at the cultural antipode, operating their trains and their lives by schedules that you can set your Swatch by.

Software and applications development can also be understood on this cultural continuum from on-time development—schedule driven and calendar bound—to in-time development that emphasizes reasonable results within sufficient time to be of value to the users. In some settings, outside forces dictate how the clock runs. Some software for federal and state government applications must incorporate specific features by legally mandated dates, but even here, the twin clocks of on-time and in-time development both tick off the passing hours. The new edition of a tax preparation package faces an absolute 15 April deadline, but in the real world, it is not clear whether this means it must ship by early January or the middle of February to meet customer needs on a timely basis. Still, in most all cases today, management insists that software be delivered on time, and the drop-dead deadlines seem to be coming faster than ever under competitive pressures in a down-sized world of programming.

Rapid and Reasonable

As a result, rapid application development has become one of the methodological rages of our business. Development is "time-boxed" to an absolute schedule of progress and delivery. On-time delivery becomes the paramount if not the singular criterion of project success. High-performance "SWAT" teams of top-gun programmers are armed with the latest and best software tools to reduce the product development cycle time. Delivery within some imagined but absolutely determined market window takes precedence over other objectives. When the deadline is reached, whatever you have is what you deliver—bugs and flaws and all.

True, without deadlines and objectives of some kind, some project teams might never deliver, staying locked in analysis paralysis or designing to a fair-thee-well while the technology changes under them, leaving them stranded high and dry on an isle of obsolete systems. For some people, there is nothing like the terror of approaching deadlines to foster teamwork and productivity.

At one software conference I had a chance to witness this rapid development culture in the extreme. Imagine: your boss hands you the specs for a new app as you walk in the door and tells you that you have 40 minutes to demonstrate a working program. Forget models. Forget methods! This is crunch-mode coding, no more, no less.

This was the premise for the "Visual C++ Superbowl" at Software Development '94 (and a regular event at conferences since. LLC). A packed auditorium watched as teams of programmers from Microsoft and Borland cut code at warp speed (Symantec didn't show). Richard Hale Shaw of *PC Week* played Donahue while the judges and the audience alternately gasped, laughed, and applauded. It was, in a word, breathtaking, to plagiarize my friend and fellow judge, J. D. Hildebrand of *Windows Tech Journal*. I had forgotten how much fun programming could be. Of course, I was not demonstrating my chops on a 12-foot screen in front of 1,100 people, either. Although few programmers face situations as extreme as this, an increasing number of developers find themselves under the gun to produce software faster and faster. In classes and in my consulting, more and more programmers tell me of draconian deadlines and escalating pressure to deliver by schedules that are handed down as if from Olympus. Often they tell me, "We want to test more thoroughly, but we're told to just ship it as-is." Or, "We'd like to do a better user interface, but the boss won't let us." Or, "We have no time to do it right, we barely have time to do it at all."

In truth, rapid development of applications is real, but the deadlines under which it operates often are not. Targeted delivery dates are pulled from thin air by management and marketing people. I remember being told by one team that they had an absolute deadline for delivery within three months and therefore could not spend the time to model customer requirements or fully design the user interface to requirements. Of course, this absolute deadline had already been extended twice in increments of three months!

Just Do It

I started out programming in precisely this atmosphere, developing routine business applications on fixed-price contracts. We didn't need clairvoyance to see that much of the time we were solving the same problems over and over again. It did not take rocket science to conclude that a library of reusable components for basic business data processing operations would make it possible to build systems faster and more cheaply. But management wouldn't let us take the time to program the library. Billable time ruled all. We didn't have the time to build infrastructure, top management argued, we just had to cut code and ship software.

So we went ahead and built the library anyway, creating new components for it in the course of completing other projects. Sure, we sometimes slipped schedules, but then we almost always did. And eventually we had our library and began to demonstrate substantial gains in productivity. In reality, you don't need permission to do your job well. If you know that a project estimate is unrealistic, then cutting corners in analysis and design won't help. One way or another, now or later, you will take the hit. Since fuller understanding of the problem and better design are apt to cut development costs in the long haul, acting *as if* you had the time may often be the best strategy. The long-term cost to software vendors and in-house developers of delivering poor software, inevitably slipping the shipping date anyway, is certainly more than the cost of delivering good software even if it is late. As they say, if you don't have time to do it right, when are you going to get the time to do it over?

In-time delivery of decent software is what really matters for both business and professional success over the long haul. Developers should never simply accept unrealistic deadlines as given. To fulfill their true obligations to employers, they need to learn to negotiate deadlines based on trade-offs in scope and quality.

In some cases, even if the boss says just to ship crap, you may have to go ahead and do a good job anyway.

From *Software Development*, Volume 2, #7, July 1994.

Under Pressure

Lorne, Australia, is the gateway to The Great Ocean Road that winds along some of the most beautiful coastline in the world, past dramatic cliffs, thundering surf, and sugar-sand beaches where you can walk for miles and hardly see a soul. While I was living in Australia, the Victorian Branch of the Australian Computer Society invited me to Lorne for their annual conference. I was to help judge their first Software Challenge, a six-hour application development marathon using the latest in rapid visual development tools to build a truck weighing application for a recycling facility. This was the third such rapid development competition I had refereed, so I was becoming an old hand (see Chapter 30). I had, for example, learned not to groan every time a system GPFed and to keep from hyperventilating as the competitors came down to the wire, still debugging in high gear. I had also learned that I, too, would probably learn something from the competition, even though I wasn't a competitor.

About an hour into the ACS Challenge, I slowly toured the "war room" set aside for the programmers. Spaced around the room, teams of three were coding away in Visual Works and PowerBuilder and SQL for Windows, everybody, that is, save for one group: the cool young men from Ernst & Young. As I looked over their shoulders, I could hardly believe my eyes. The team, led by Craig Bright, was drawing diagrams! Instead of being hunched over keyboards like their competitors, they were gathered around sheets from a flipchart. They had refined the requirements definition and were busy mapping out the architecture of the proposed system. Noting my interest, one of them handed me a copy of their battle plan, a notebook with a scaled-down version of their regular methodology modified especially for this competition. There it was, all spelled out, with staged activities and specific intermediate deliverables—a complete, disciplined, rapid development process. Even in the heat of head-to-head competition, with less than a day to deliver on more than 200 function points, this group was demonstrating grace under pressure, calmly analyzing the problem and designing the solution. I was impressed.

Faith in Process

Many is the time I have told students that the less time you have to deliver a system, the more important it is to know what you are delivering. If you have only four days to code an application, your best chance of success is to take the first two days to design the thing well. Of course, I had never been called on to deliver on my own pontifications by programming a complex application in a single day. It is easy to be pious when your faith is unchallenged.

The Ernst & Young team was certainly one whose faith in process was being sorely tested, and their trials were far from over. Just after they arrived at the conference center, they had managed to bring forth sparks and smoke from their brand-new Pentium-based system. Some quick shuffling of software onto laptops had put them back in business, albeit lacking a bit in hardware power.

As they finally turned from their flipcharts and notes to their keyboards and monitors that morning, things were beginning to look tough again. On the surface of it, their competitors had gained a seemingly insurmountable lead; some of them could even already demonstrate a number of working features. Surface impressions are, of course, often misleading in programming. Indeed, at the midday checkpoint, when the judges reviewed the programming teams and audited the results to see how many function points had been delivered, the lads from Ernst & Young had turned their methodological cool into a commanding lead. Careful analysis and planning were paying off, even under these pressure-cooker conditions.

As they say, however, it's not over until it's over.

In last place at that initial evaluation was the team from Xpedite Professional Services Pty. Ltd., under team leader Sue Stevens. While others were busily cranking out functionality, they had been focusing on details, carefully crafting code complete with error and exception handling. Clearly, however, this approach was ill-suited to the highly compressed development cycle of the competition. In midstream the Xpedite team decided to revise their development strategy.

As the time for the final judging approached, the Ernst & Young team began consolidating the various pieces of their systematically constructed system. Working quickly to get all the files onto one machine, they inadvertently overwrote the working version of one set of files with the dummy versions used on the other machine. We've all done this sort of thing, accidentally reversing the direction of a transfer from what we intended. In fact, I had done it myself only a few months earlier with some PowerPoint files for another major conference. Fortunately, I had backups. Unfortunately, they did not. Having clobbered much of their programming, by the final judging they ended up delivering less functionality than they had demonstrated at the midpoint.

Delivering Value

In the meantime, the Xpedite team had turned their attention to detail onto the human factors of the user interface. While other teams were still building rather rough functionality, they were taking into account the real needs of the recycling-yard operator and delivering more useable value. Instead of standard tables and menus, they tailored their windows to the customer. The results took them from last place at the lunch break to winners before dinner.

What can we learn from the efforts of these valiant teams? More than ever it seems clear that rapid prototyping is not a substitute for a disciplined process. In fact, the combination of rapid visual development tools (see Chapter 23) with an appropriately scaled process of analysis and design is likely to be just the needed one-two punch for the challenge of too-tight deadlines. Taking the time to understand and plan saves time.

We must also keep sight of what it is we are producing. We are not delivering code, we are delivering value. More value with less code is worth a lot more than more code with less value. Raw functionality is worth less to our clients and users than easy-to-use systems that fit with their business needs.

It is also important to stay flexible, remaining ready to adapt our approaches and procedures to changing conditions and a changing understanding of what we are trying to accomplish. Textbook formulas are probably not going to meet the challenges of modern rapid development.

Finally, though it seems all too obvious, even with very short product development cycles, good version control is mandatory. Even under extreme time pressure—or maybe especially under such pressure—the time taken to make backups and track versions is time well spent. In fact, backups and version control should have been built into the Ernst & Young team's streamlined development method, which is what they promised to do when they returned for the next competition.

From *Software Development,* Volume 3, #10, October 1995.

32

Re: Architecture

What ever happened to software architecture? Looking at a typical sample of in-house enterprise applications and commercial off-the-shelf software packages, it's often hard to find much evidence of underlying organization. Architecture, whether in the organization of the internal functionality or in the structure of the user interface, is often among the first victims felled by today's time-boxed software projects, short release cycles, and rapid application development. There seems to be no time to think through the consequences of architectural decisions. Often there is barely time to think. Full stop. Systems are thrown together as fast as features can be thought up, with little attention to overall organization. Developers find themselves looking ahead only as far as the next line of code or the next feature.

New technology has not been of much help. Visual development tools (see Chapter 23) open up new routes to the rapid evolution of sophisticated systems, but the pace of visual development and the ease with which working applications can be constructed can also contribute to a paucity of planning. The tools may even encourage a style of development where small pieces of code that mix business logic with bits of interface programming and underlying functionality get hung onto the back of visual components, the whole interconnected by a spider web of message passing and event threads that nobody understands completely. The result is today's version of the classic "spaghetti code," in which everything is connected to everything else. When every change propagates unpredictably through the web of interconnected code, the potential for continuous software evolution shrivels.

Second Chance

Add iterative refinement to rapid prototyping and the last vestiges of architecture are likely to sink into the software swamp. That's unfortunate, because iterative prototyping is a powerful approach to delivering more usable software in less time. Prototyping allows you to deliver real capability early or to try varied approaches without a full commitment. A prototype puts something in front of users in order to get feedback based on real use. Even for relatively modest systems, it is all but impossible to get everything in the user interface right on the first try, no matter how much thought and effort you put into the design. Prototyping and iterative refinement offer a second chance—and a third and a fourth—to get user interfaces right. With each iteration the interface and internals are refined and enhanced, delivering more and delivering it more effectively.

Unfortunately, the structure of the first prototype, which may have been fine for proving the concept, stays around to shape the basic architecture of the evolving system. Round and round you go, and, with each iteration, the system grows. New layers of features are pasted on and functional enhancements are squeezed in until the basic organization that seemed so reasonable when the system was small begins to fall apart under the weight of revisions.

It would be tempting to suggest that we should simply return to some fabled days of functional decomposition when disciplined developers spent the time with a CASE tool to work out a sound and systematic architecture for the entire system before writing the first line of code. Unfortunately, by the time the traditional approaches deliver a system architecture, a RAD team equipped with rapid visual development tools will have already shipped a working system. What we need is a way to incorporate architectural considerations into a radically accelerated development life cycle. We'd like to gain something in sounder structure without slowing down the process much.

We may need to rethink the place of software architecture in the development process. Normally, we think of architecture as something that precedes construction, but just as code can be rewritten, it can also be "rearchitected." (The world of "Extreme Programming" calls this sort of thing "refactoring." LLC) One large Australian bank, for example, was forced to fall back on its legacy systems after an ambitious and overextended project to build a new enterprise-wide information system had to be abandoned. The old system, an accretion of generations of COBOL kludges, had a well-earned reputation as a brittle mess that broke whenever the smallest change or correction was introduced. The bank management despaired of being able to introduce the varied new financial products and services needed to compete in the dynamic banking industry of today. But all was not lost. While everyone else had been caught up in the frenzy of new system development, one dedicated maintenance programmer had been quietly rebuilding parts of the legacy system, cleaning up the code section by small section and restructuring the architecture in the process. Important subsystems had been reorganized sufficiently to support continued evolution.

Renewal

The experience of this bank points to the basis for a radical reorganization of rapid iterative development processes. To make iterative refinement from prototypes work over the longer term and for larger systems, you have to keep going back to the architecture to improve it. We might call this iterative architectural refinement, or "iterative rearchitecting" if you prefer to verbify your nouns. On each successive round of design and construction, the overall structure of the program is re-examined to identify how it could be improved to support newly incorporated features better. Refining the architecture might entail reorganizing data structures, partitioning the system into more or different subsystems, or replacing work-arounds or make-do algorithms with better code. More often than not, architectural refinement will mean redesigning and rewriting some code that already worked. Although this coding adds to the effort in the next development iteration, it makes the system more robust in terms of further refinement, reducing the cost of future iterations. Architectural reviews are particularly good for examining the object class structure, identifying potential or needed reusable components and looking for missed opportunities for reuse.

This process is a form of concentric development, a rationalized model for rapid prototyping with iterative refinement that starts with core functions to provide a basic set of capabilities to the user. These core capabilities are identified from a selected subset of the use cases or abstract scenarios the finished system must support (see Chapter 22). Starting with an essential core of complete use cases assures that the user has support for entire tasks, not just fragments of functionality. The system is then built in concentric layers of embellishments and enhancements. As each new layer is started, an architectural review identifies refinements or changes to the software architecture that will improve the robustness of the system in support of immediate and future enhancements. These architectural changes are added into the project workload for the current cycle of concentric development.

One company in Australia has been using a variant of this approach for four years with great success. They make three releases per year of major software. Some of the "slack time" that inevitably comes in the ups and downs of periodic releases is given over to architectural review and planning, so that the architecture is updated almost continuously.

Architectural planning can pay off big-time, even under the tightest deadlines. There is a footnote to the saga of the earnest team from Ernst & Young who took the time to architect their system in a one-day programming face-off (Chapter 30). An augmented team took on the next Software Challenge at ITWorld in Brisbane, Australia. They returned with a new tool (Borland's Delphi) and a revised process for what the competitors were calling "frantic application development." This time they had version control and backup as well as quick but careful analysis and architecture. They won.

From *Software Development,* Volume 4, #1, January 1996.

33

Quality by Increments

Whether it's "Total Quality Management," "Continuous Process Improvement," or ISO, most current notions of process and product quality emphasize enterprise-wide commitment to quality with heavy investment for long-term payoffs. Elaborate schemes for assessing and increasing "process maturity," such as the well-known Capability Maturity Model of the Software Engineering Institute, may have big payoffs, but they can also require a major commitment of resources just to get started (Humphrey, Snyder, Willis 1991) and may have unintended consequences (Bollinger and McGowan 1991). For the greatest, most enduring gains, substantial restructuring and comprehensive quality assurance programs may be necessary, but there are also small, practical steps that can be taken to yield immediate and substantial payoffs in terms of improved software quality and project performance.

Modest changes in how work is organized and carried out can dramatically affect quality in software development. These approaches are not based on technology; they do not involve computer-aided software engineering, object-oriented repositories, new life-cycle methodologies, expert systems for software metrics, statistical quality control, or any of a myriad of other allegedly advanced technical fixes. These steps all go back to basics, to the basic fact that even in high technology it is people who do the work. These approaches have in common that they look to how people and work are organized and managed. Most of these are things that can be put into practice almost immediately without large investments in training, tools, or inspirational posters.

Setting Priorities

First steps are often the most important, and the first step to improving quality is getting priorities straight. To improve quality in a product and the process by which it is created, quality has to be a priority. If quality is not important to you and to an organization, and it doesn't show in what management actually does and how they do it, quality won't be important to the software development staff. This does not mean posters that declare "Quality Is Job One!" or memos urging employees to strive for zero defects in software. In this area, what counts is how you walk the walk, not how you talk the talk.

- *Make quality important.*

Unfortunately, common assumptions and practices of modern managers often prevent them from making quality a real priority. One major hindrance is that many companies are dominated by the issue of time-to-market. Especially in high-technology fields like software development, management vision is limited, transfixed, unable to see beyond the so-called "market window." If you miss this window of opportunity, so the accepted line of thought goes, all is lost. The idea is to get into the market before anyone else, even if it means shipping a bug-ridden, inferior product. When concern for the market window takes precedence over quality, quality will suffer. It's as simple as that. Timeliness does matter, of course, but it's a matter of priorities. When the choice comes down to packaging and selling what is really a beta-test version now or holding on tight through another round of testing and refinement, which path is followed?

Many software developers continue to let the idea of market window drive their thinking and keep them from producing higher quality systems. Yet the history of our industry is littered with the ghosts of companies that were first in the market and are no more, as well as with innovative but immature products that lost out to later improvements.

- *Look beyond the market window.*

Another way that contemporary management thinking works against making quality a priority is that most companies, especially in the United States, seem more concerned with costs and cost-cutting than with return-on-investment. This is all too easy to do when the economy sours and profits are squeezed. Education, training, and staff development, all recognized as important contributors to quality, are considered to be costs, not analyzed as investments. Staff attendance at conferences and seminars may be an essential part of maintaining a competitive edge, but this is regarded as part of over-head expenses and is often among the first targets of cost cutting.

This is not a matter of soft-headed notions of "being nice" to staff, but a question of the financial basis of management thinking and decision making and how this affects the ability to improving quality. If the cost of a six-month delay in announcing and releasing a product will be paid off in another six months, then rushing to market is not a cost savings.

How money is spent ought to be justified, but the analysis should be based not on cost alone, which is only one side of the equation, but on return on investment. Australian consultant Rob Thomsett has shown, for example, that similar gains can be achieved through investing in CASE technology or in team building, but the return on investment with team building is an order of magnitude better. Still, CASE is flashy technology that can be shown to visitors, while effective teamwork is invisible, so many companies would rather spend on hardware and software than on peopleware.

- *Think return-on-investment, not cost containment.*

Rewards and Recognition

For quality to be a priority, people must be evaluated and rewarded for turning out quality work. But what do we reward? In software development, productivity, whether in function points or lines of code, is usually what gets the bonus or promotion or recognition, if anything. Or we reward herculean, last-ditch efforts to meet seemingly impossible deadlines. Ironically, in many companies it is in the best interests of project managers to ensure that all-out efforts are needed toward the end of a project. Such highly visible commitments are what is most likely to win approval whether the project succeeds or not. "Well, we lost the contract, but no one can fault Pete, who worked around the clock right up to the deadline."

The problem is not that people don't care about quality, as some managers complain. One study of 11,000 people in six industries (by Brooks International in 1991) found that more than nine out of ten employees felt a personal responsibility for doing quality work. But seven out of ten reported that quality was not an important factor in how their work was evaluated. And a bare one out of four said that their management really rewarded improvements in quality. What do we reward, then? The truth is, recognition and rewards of any kind are a lot less frequent than most managers think. Some 80% of managers claim they give their subordinates sincere and thorough praise, but only one out of seven of their subordinates see it that way (Lickert 1989).

If we want to improve quality, we ought to follow the Ferber Principle. Psychiatrist Andrew Ferber was once asked what was the most important thing for beginning therapists to know if they wanted to help client families improve. His answer:

- *Whenever you see something you like, applaud like crazy.*

Measurement and Control

Nearly everyone has heard the dictum that you can't control what you can't measure (DeMarco 1982). This is often a prelude to a hard sell on starting a software metrics or statistical quality control program. Formal measures have many advantages, but a moment's reflection will tell you that there are many important things in life that parents, teachers, managers, and others control but that they do not measure. Many of these probably cannot be measured. When it comes to people, the essential thing is attention, not measurement; what matters is what you monitor. Any effective parent knows that if you pay attention to tantrums you get more tantrums. Systems in general, and human systems in particular, have the peculiar property that the very act of observation changes what is being observed. This is the basis of the well-established Hawthorne effect: simply making a group the object of study, paying more attention to what they are doing, can lead to improved performance.

- *Pay attention.*

What, in particular, you monitor matters, of course, because whatever you monitor is affected. If programmers are evaluated on the tightness of their code, they produce smaller systems; if user friendliness is the criteria, you get friendlier programs (Weinberg and Schulman 1974).

In Australia, the new manager of a maintenance programming group wanted to improve not only the effectiveness of his team, but also its status and recognition in the company. Among other things, he started sending reports back to the original programmers about the bugs discovered and corrected in their systems after they were "in production." A programmer might get a note simply saying that over the weekend the system had crashed without closing the output file, but that Maintenance Programmer Quinnthorpe had tracked it to a loop in module Z091, which was corrected, recompiled, and tested in 1.6 hours.

An interesting thing happened as the result of this practice. The new systems being put into production got more reliable and started passing acceptance tests more quickly. The mere act of monitoring quality and reporting the results can bring it under control and improve it.

- *Give feedback.*

In another company, bar charts were posted every month showing programmer productivity in lines of code written and debugged. After the reports were changed to include all delivered code, not only that written by programmers but also all included modules from the reusable component library, reuse rose dramatically (see Chapter 27).

Feedback is the essential ingredient. When workers have access to information about their performance and its relationship to organizational objectives, quality goes up. This is the basis of the open-book model of management, in which workers are given not only reports about production and defects, but financial information about related costs, revenues, and profits (Case 1990; Finegan 1990). With this kind of information in hand, workers are in a better position to optimize how they spend their time and to improve their own work process. The key is feedback that ties individual and team performance to the larger financial picture, for example, reporting not only programming time and program defects, but the costs of these and the resulting profit (or loss) on a project. Many managers have learned that it's a two-way street. When more information is shared with staff, they share more with management, and a continuous flow of ideas for improvement results. In technical management, we tend to think of measurement mostly in terms of numbers with three-digit precision or better. But qualitative methods and measures or simple rankings may often be enough to evaluate and bring a process under control. The theory of measurement, a part of statistics, recognizes various levels of measurement. Numbers that you can multiply and divide are at one level, a so-called ratio scale, those you can add and subtract at another, lower level, called interval scaling. But even where results can only be quantified enough to say that one thing is better than another by some unknown amount, statistical analyses are possible.

You do not need to measure altitude to the nearest meter to find the lookout tower at the top of the mountain. All you need to know is whether each step is taking you down or up. For many processes, effective strategies for improvement can be based on measurement as crude as just knowing whether you are getting better or worse.

Data and Information

Most managers would probably claim to value information and would like to think that they base their decisions on data. Unfortunately, these same managers often keep themselves from getting the information they need and may be oblivious to some of the information they do have.

The true scientist knows that there is no such thing as an experiment that fails. Whatever happens yields information that can lead to revising the hypothesis or refining the technique. In family therapy training I learned that whatever happens in a session is informative, or, as we used to tell our trainees:

- *Remember, it's all data.*

The true manager knows that all news is good news. Information about a process has intrinsic value and should be valued. How you react to information affects how accessible it will be in the future. Where one side is rewarded, the truth will not be known. The problem with punishing the bearer of bad news is not only that it's hell on messengers but eventually it assures that only good news will reach you. The "bad" news, which is often the most critical to know about, isn't delivered.

I once had a boss who told me that he would never hold it against me for keeping him informed of problems, that he particularly wanted to be kept apprised of difficulties that might jeopardize the agency we both worked for. He not only kept his word, but also left the resolution of such problems to me and my staff. This helped keep the lines of communication open and insured that he had access to information critical to his decision making.

In improving any process, the most important information to know, of course, is about problems and failures, yet this is precisely the information that managers may be warding off. Finding a bug in a program ought to be the occasion for a celebration. In fact, all program faults should be not only recorded, but also studied.

- *Record and study defects.*

Keeping detailed logs of all problems—defects and mistakes, customer complaints, design changes, analysis errors, "improvements" in beta testing—is one essential step. The other is to study these systematically and periodically. This means setting aside as part of every project the time for systematic reflection. If we don't study and learn from our mistakes, how can we avoid them in the future?

To improve quality, it is especially important that we never confuse opposition or criticism with disloyalty.

- *Encourage criticism.*

It is often the contrary view or the critical perspective that offers the most information about potential improvements to the process. In fact, the quality of problem solving is critically dependent on critical input. Groups that include a "resident critic" or "devil's advocate," or that exploit dialectical processes of opposing ideas and active critique, perform better (Constantine 1989; Priem and Price 1991).

Of course, it is not simply enough to know that something is wrong or even how it is going wrong; we have to do something about it. Program bugs are not just information about something wrong in specific programs; they are also information about problems in the process that generated the programs. The first question is how did it get there? The goal is not to fix blame, but to learn how to change the process so that it is less likely to happen in the future. Organizations that continually improve their processes take each failure as an occasion to retrain or to refine the process and improve it.

- *Correct the process, not just the program.*

Work Visibility

A powerful principle of quality improvement is found in the title of a hit song from the 1960s:

- *Let the sun shine in.*

Invisibility is the enemy of quality. We can't improve what we don't see. One of the best ways to assure that somebody sees a problem is to make what software developers are doing more visible.

Experience has shown that the quality of software can be markedly improved simply by increasing the amount of work that is done face-to-face (Chapter 26). When two or more people work together on the same problem, quality goes up. On the average, increasing the visibility of work increases quality. Why? Basically, in order for two programmers cutting code together to introduce a bug or a departure from standards and practices, they have to collude; to find the bug or spot the departure, only one has to see it. Forget about what you've heard about "groupthink" or collective mediocrity. It turns out that such effects exist but depend on special conditions. Group leaders can do simple things that go a long way toward improving the quality of problem solving and avoiding groupthink. Simply by delaying or withholding their own opinions, group leaders can significantly improve the problem solving of any group (Anderson and Balzer 1991).

The "two-to-a-terminal" model of programming, which I have called the "Dynamic Duo," dates from the era that introduced "ego-less programming." Ego-less programming was based on the notion that programmers had too much ego invested in their code. If only they could work in an ego-less style, becoming less defensive and more open to the review, suggestions, and criticisms of others, they would produce better code. There were a number of problems with this way of thinking, not the least of which is that people have egos. Modern management thinking, rather than trying to stamp out or overcome egos, seeks to take this reality of human nature into account and turn it to the collective good.

The watchword today is "ownership" or "buy-in." Progressive organizations seek to increase the sense of personal ownership—ego investment, if you will—that employees have in the products of their efforts. For example, the structured open model for teamwork (see Chapter 16) is an approach to organizing project teams that uses consensus-based problem solving to increase work visibility and individual ownership.

An essential variant on the theme of work visibility is the idea of separation of powers. It's implicit in the Dynamic Duo approach to programming. While one programmer is at the keyboard, the other is looking over his shoulder. The programmer at the keyboard has one set of responsibilities associated with defining the algorithm and mapping out the flow in code. The other is looking for the holes in the logic, trying to spot weaknesses or errors.

- *Separate powers.*

This principle is an essential component of "cleanroom" programming, an approach that has produced some moderate to large-scale systems demonstrated to be virtually bug-free (Cobb and Mills 1990). In this model, one person or group writes the code, trying to "get it right." But someone else compiles and tests it, trying to find what is wrong with it. There is more to the model, but simply this kind of separation of responsibilities in itself seems to improve quality. Knowing that someone else on the team is not only going to see the code, but take over compiling and testing, seems to lead to greater care and more effort to get it right the first time.

Skills and Stars

Decades of research and practical experience has taught us that often more than an order of magnitude in productivity separates the best programmers from the worst, and the best are typically twice as productive as the average ones (DeMarco and Lister 1987). Some groups have dramatically improved quality and productivity by the simple expedient of cutting their programming staff, keeping only the best half. One approach to quality is to take only the very best players, give them all the resources and motivation they need to do the best job, and let them do it. This may be especially appealing in an era of "downsizing."

- *Use only the finest ingredients.*

Of course, every manager knows that there are "stars" in any organization, but not everyone wants to get rid of all the supporting players. What we'd really like to do is find a way to help the others "get better." Which brings us to the principle of cross-training. The idea is to create more opportunities for software development people to learn from each other.

- *Let each one teach one.*

One of the most effective and efficient ways to accomplish this cross-training is to build it into the way projects are organized. This goes back to work visibility. By doing more of their work in face-to-face groups, team members automatically learn more from each other. In addition, rotating responsibilities as a normal part of software development gives opportunities to practice, helping to gradually disperse skills and knowledge through the group.

Differences in natural talent and achievable levels of skill will always persist. Some programmers will always be better at cutting clever code, some better at modeling essential abstractions; one team member might always be a better group facilitator than the others. But in an organization that encourages and makes room for cross-training and skill dispersion, the average level of skill in any of these areas is always increasing. Over time, people will pick up more and more of each other's specialties. They will never reach the point where everyone can do all the jobs with equal skill, but the differences will diminish. Most importantly, team members become increasingly able to fill in for each other. The organization as a whole becomes less critically dependent on the skills and presence of any one member. An entire project need not then become stalled simply because one person becomes ill or takes a job in another city.

Degrees of Freedom

Ironically, in many organizations that sincerely want to improve quality, common practices create conditions preventing improvement. Things as simple as how deadlines and budgets are established can make or break a project in terms of quality. In the typical situation, all factors—budget, allocation of resources, staffing, methodology, and deadline—are fixed when the project is given to software developers. Where can we get improved quality? We need at least one degree of freedom. If all the variables are constrained, the system is over-determined and there is no way to win. So what is sacrificed when there are problems? Quality! Under tight deadlines, such as those driven by some imagined market window, it often comes down to, "We don't have time to do it right." This points to one of the simplest changes that has been found to help improve the quality of software.

- *Negotiate deadlines.*

    Software developers need to be directly involved in establishing delivery dates and project deadlines. Setting a completion target should be approached as a negotiation in which there are recognized trade-offs. "Yes, the project can be delivered by the end of the year if you don't mind having a defect rate around 15 per KLOC. Or we can promise a lower defect rate if you don't mind cutting out half the screens."

Summary

Approaches to raising software quality do not have to be complicated or involve large budgets. Some simple things can make a big difference. First, get your priorities straight, make quality a priority. Don't let the market window run your business. Think in terms of return-on-investment, not cost containment.

Then, pay attention, recognize and reward quality. Give feedback, and be generous with information. Keep listening: remember that all news is good news, especially bad news. Encourage critical feedback. Record and study defects, and correct the process, not just the program. Let the sun shine in; make work more visible. Promote cross-training: let each one teach one. When quality is especially essential, use only the finest ingredients. And always negotiate your deadlines!

Revised from *American Programmer*, February 1992.

VI

Software Usability

Introduction

The user interface is the point of contact between programs and people, the river that marks the boundary between the user and the used. Software developers stand on both sides of this river. As programmers they are, in a sense, inside the computer, where they see the usual mess or the exceptional elegance of the actual code that makes things happen. At the same time they are users of computer software, outsiders looking in, seeing not the code but the arrangement of features and fields that make their development tools and support systems either more or less usable. They have, therefore, a double interest in the user interface: as designers and as users.

Usability is arguably the quintessential measure of software quality. It does not matter much whether a program has spectacular graphics or speedy algorithms or even bug-free performance if it is all but impossible to use. If a system does not do something that is useful, if it does not provide services or capabilities that meet user needs, can it be said to be a good system?

As computers themselves have become more accessible and more people directly and regularly interact with them, matters of usability and user interface design have received growing attention in the software world. The purview of software designers has gradually expanded outward from the internal structures of program and data to the user interface. At first, much of the concern centered on the technology, on the software side of the design. Software developers gradually learned to deal more directly with detailed choices of the devices and mechanisms used to interact with users, along with their arrangement within the user interface. From this concern with the technical details of the user interface the focus then shifted further outward, toward the users themselves. Software and applications developers were admonished to deal with real users, to converse with them more often and in more depth in order to understand their preferences and incorporate their ideas and suggestions, even to bring representative users into the design and development process itself. Programmers who once kept their distance from users except when forced to get their approval on requirements specifications now find themselves dealing with end users in meetings and planning sessions or even as continuing members of the development team.

From this user-centered view we are now seeing some movement toward more focus on uses than users, more emphasis on the intent of users than their preferences. This "teleocentric" or purpose-centered view of systems considers real needs to be more important than wants. The hope is to build software that better supports the work of real people, that serves useful purposes and makes tasks easier or simpler.

Whether this trend will continue and how far it will go is unclear, but here are some of the important issues regarding the user interface, the users, and the uses of software as we now understand them.

Consistency and Conventions

We are surrounded by user interfaces. The term may have gained currency through computer software, but every system and every piece of equipment that has users by definition has a user interface. As psychologist and former Apple Fellow Donald Norman has shown us (Norman 1988), we can learn a great deal about how to design and build better user interfaces for software simply by looking around us, by thinking about how the controls of common appliances, utensils, and tools make it easier or more difficult for us to use them.

Think about the last time you rented a car or borrowed one from somebody. Probably it was a different make or model from the one you usually drive. You slipped into the driver's seat, buckled up, and checked the mirrors. Then you drove off. The question is, how many seconds did it take for you to learn the user interface of this system? Did you attend a training workshop or view a video on how to use this particular car? Or were you able to figure it out on your own without having to read the manual?

The user interface of most of today's automobiles, with a few annoying exceptions, conform to the Great Law of Usability (Constantine 1991b). This law states that the user interface should enable a user who has expertise in the application domain to use the system without training and without reference to a manual or other instructions outside of the system. In other words, a good user interface allows users who already know what they are doing to just go ahead and do it without having to learn something new.

Know-How

Of course, you already knew how to drive. You probably qualify as an expert automobile user—not necessarily a professional, but fully qualified and trained. For the expert, driving becomes what psychologists call an over-learned skill. You can do it without giving it much conscious attention. Consider this remarkable little experiment the next time you are driving and talking with a passenger. As you are talking, let yourself become aware of the fact that you are also driving. How is this happening? Driving is a very complex information processing task, as a team of Army scientists and engineers learned when they tried to program a computer to drive a van. And even an ordinary casual conversation is far more complex than driving a car. Yet experienced drivers can attend to the thread of the conversation and relegate most of the problems of driving to background processing using stable subroutines.

When you slipped behind the wheel of that unfamiliar rental car, you were aided in adjusting to the new user interface by two things. It probably fit quite closely with the way in which you "naturally" carry on your over-trained dialogue with a car, and it was probably not dramatically different from the one in your own car. The instrument panel and controls of most cars follow a few basic conventions. Gear shifts are either on the steering column or on the floor between driver and passenger, the speedometer is typically dead ahead on the dashboard, the steering wheel is round, and the turn signal, to the left on the steering column except in countries where you drive on the left side of the road, is tilted clockwise for a right turn, counter-clockwise for left, just like the steering wheel. The interface is both consistent with established conventions and internally consistent. Now and then you encounter something odd and have to play around a bit to figure out how to get the headlights on, but even this is likely to take only a few moments.

It surprises many people to learn that almost none of the standard user interface features of an ordinary passenger car are regulated by state or federally mandated standards. The law does not even require a steering wheel or even that it be round. Some special cars are indeed built with alternative steering devices for special classes of users. Some years ago, a German automotive company got cute with an oval steering wheel on one of its sporty models, but drivers hated it. The steering wheel is the way it is because long experience has shown that rotation of a round wheel is both a good metaphor and an efficient mechanism for controlling direction of travel.

Rising Standards

It was not always thus. In the early days of the evolution of the automobile, numerous other controls for steering were tried. Tiller bars were common in early models, in part because the actual mechanics were simpler. But steering wheels eventually won through a process of natural selection among engineers and the driving public. This evolution was possible precisely because automotive designers were not constrained by premature standards nor were they compelled to be different for the sake of being different simply because someone or some company claimed intellectual property rights on the "look-and-feel" of circular steering controls.

For most of the really important aspects of user interfaces, standards are unnecessary. Superior arrangements and mechanisms will gradually win out in the marketplace of products and of ideas. Tiller bars, like steering wheels, establish a fairly simple translation between control movement and directional change, but they have critical limitations. If a group of well-intentioned industry leaders or a government standards body had mandated a standard "look-and-feel" for steering controls when tiller bars had the lead, automobiles would have been kept limited to local travel at modest speeds.

The First Law of Conventions was aptly stated by K. D. Mackenzie a quarter century ago (Mackenzie 1966). When there is more than one way to do something and the choice among alternatives is essentially arbitrary, pick some one way and *always* do it that way. When the choice among alternatives is not arbitrary, it is important to pick a good one.

P. J. Plauger, who is both sufficiently principled and sufficiently masochistic to devote substantial time to international standards efforts, talks of the Principle of Good Enough (Plauger 1993). A standard for information interchange or for a programming language or for telephone interfaces does not have to be ideal or perfect, it does not even have to be "right." In practice, ideal standards are politically and technically impossible, anyway. All that is needed is that a standard be "good enough." As a rule, human cleverness and evolving technology will overcome most limitations or shortcomings anyway.

The question is, just what is "good enough" when it comes to such widely used facilities as graphical user interfaces? The most important kind of consistency is consistency with the way people think and work when they are not forced to do things the way some software system does. The human cerebral cortex has remarkable plasticity. People learn. They can adjust to amazingly difficult interfaces, but there is always a cost.

Most of what people know and do has nothing to do with computers. (Sorry programmers, but that's the harsh reality!) Although some things are hard-wired into the human brain, most things people claim as intuitive are really conditioned. In fact, psychologists now define intuition in terms of complex associations and processing that have been learned so well they are no longer fully conscious activities.

Counterintelligence

When you force users to interact with a system in a way that counters those conventions that have already been programmed in through experience or wired in through evolution, you increase frustration and fatigue, and you build in an added, permanent increase in errors. Even small increases in the probability of error due to the user interface can be significant. Consider even a tiny increase in errors in the data entry processes for today's gigabyte databases. Or consider the consequences of such effects due to problems in the interfaces of the software development tools by which computer software is itself designed and created.

Unfortunately, most current graphical user interfaces are just not good enough. They are inconsistent, unnecessarily complex, and full of conventions that are seriously and demonstrably wrong. Microsoft's public admission that Windows might not be a perfectly suitable basis for control of household appliances and other consumer products is monumental understatement. The problems are not in details of style that might be tweaked into suitability, but are fundamental flaws in the most basic mechanisms.

To pick but one example, consider scroll bars as the mechanism and metaphor for controlling movement of a drawing or writing surface in relation to a smaller "window" through which only a portion can be viewed. Scroll bars are to on-screen navigation what tiller bars are to automotive navigation (Constantine 1994d)! They slow and limit the user, giving feedback that can be misleading and confusing, leading to wasted moves, increased errors, and disruption of thought processes. They require the user to move in a way that runs absolutely counter to how the brain works. To move left or right, you have to first move down, to move up or down, you start by moving to the right.

To understand how problematic a simple but counter-intuitive interface can be, do this little experiment. Turn your mouse one quarter turn counter-clockwise and then try positioning the on-screen cursor. This spatial transformation seems simple, but is almost impossible to get the hang of.

Outside of the world of computers are systems and applications that must solve similar problems of navigation through panning, scrolling, and zooming. Two that are worth thinking about as a source of ideas for graphical user interfaces are microfiche readers and video cameras. Among the dozens of mechanisms for controlling on-screen navigation that have been designed, including by the author, are any number that are demonstrably and dramatically better than scroll bars (Constantine 1994d). If you don't think this could make a difference in real work, considers how many times a day you or your customers pan and scroll your way around documents, diagrams, and displays. Calls for standardization in graphical user interfaces may be a bad idea that seems good at the time. The question is whether you want to be stuck forever driving your computer with a tiller bar.

From *Computer Language Magazine*, Volume 9, #11, November 1992.

35

Complexity and Creeping Featurism

I hate moving. I hate upgrading software. I hate the transition to a new machine. In principle, migrating to the next platform or version is simple and efficient; in practice, it throws my normally somewhat disheveled everyday existence into extended and unfathomable chaos. Most of all, however, I hate learning a new word processor.

As a purveyor of ideas, the two pieces of software closest to me are my graphics package and my word processor. These tools are my constant companions. I want them to be nice to me and to get along with each other. They define the limits of what I can do in expressing myself in words and pictures, and they put ceilings on my productivity. They enable me to leap tall in-boxes in a single bound, or they trip me up on trivial tasks. As with underwear or deodorant, my preferences for certain of these tools over others is deeply personal, fierce, and irrational.

I originally migrated to Windows because the graphics package that I needed (or was it wanted?) ran under Windows. Migration connotes some sort of steady progress, but this felt more like defenestration. Having taken the plunge, I was faced with the annoyance of switch hitting between my word processor and a suite of tools under DOS and my drawing tool under Windows. Like palindromic arthritis, this is not crippling, but it is a constant pain. In the interest of smoother collaboration with a growing cadre of colleagues who all used the same Windows/Macintosh word processor, I accepted one of

those come-on offers to upgrade. To appreciate the aptness of the term
"upgrade," picture a grade that goes up—steeply!
I am not saying this word processor was not user friendly. It has more
cute buttons than a professional seamstress and more files of context-sensitive
help than your high school guidance counselor. Using the handful of simple
everyday operations is no big deal. In fact, it probably does almost anything I
would ever want it to do, but finding where all those handy things were hiding,
especially those treasures that spell the difference between meeting and missing a deadline, took many months.

Progress

Despite the fact that most major word processors have been through a dozen
versions, they have not become easier to learn. The ads make that claim, but
what they really mean is that it takes less time to get started. Almost anyone
can begin doing useful work within minutes of completing the installation. After that you hit the wall. The best of today's word processors is significantly
harder to really learn—to master—than the early systems on CP/M or Apples.
Here we are, several generations down the pike from such forgotten gems as
Electric Pencil and Spellbinder, and the tools, though much more powerful, are
in many ways also more unwieldy.

Part of the problem is that simple, early text processors evolved into
word processors, primarily by doing more; then word processors were trans-
muted into "word publishers" with still more capability. Then high-end systems, such as WordPerfect and Word for Windows, became almost
indistinguishable from full-blown desktop publishing software in terms of
what you can do with them, even if they operate in somewhat different ways.
They are crammed chock-a-block with bells and whistles, and it takes a slew
of hooks and handles to get them to ring and toot in the right places and at the
right times.

Word processors, and a growing legion of our most important software
tools, have become victims of creeping featurism, a serious malady of user
interfaces that strikes software in its prime and can, if left unchecked, cripple
the user. Untreated, creeping featurism can leave users with an agoraphobic
response to large, open dialogue boxes, or even with a lingering fear of
unknown menus. Sometimes the clearest sign is a vaguely anxious feeling that
somewhere, lurking in some unexpected cascade of pull-down menus, is that
wonderful shortcut that resided on Ctrl-Alt-F5 within your last system.

Selling Points

Features sell. Software reviewers stress features and highlight them in neat comparison tables packed with check marks and dashes or circles of various shades. Vendor advertisements vie for the most bullets on the function list. Consumers learn to discriminate at a glance between a "full-featured" personal information manager and one with only limited functionality. Most buyers will never use more than a small fraction of all those options and operations, but it's a comfort just knowing that they are there against some unlikely and unanticipated need. After all, more is better, right?

Creeping featurism is a chronic degenerative disease. The syndrome is defined not by the number of features but by how they are acquired and by how they are embodied in the software and presented to the user. Creeping featurism results from the slow accretion of capabilities and is reflected in a bumpy and irregular user interface marred by idiosyncrasies and special functions that seem to grow like warts or carbuncles in the oddest places.

Creeping featurism is debilitating because when you add a new feature you have to put it someplace. In an extant system it is quite possible that none of the available places to put things make much sense. If nonprinting comments were not in the early versions of the word processor and were not planned for in the original interface layout, the function for creating and editing them may just have to be stuck somewhere stupid, like on the function key for importing and exporting DOS text files, to pick one unlikely but real example.

Creeping featurism often results in scattering related operations or options in different parts of the user interface. After four or five rounds of revision, the dozens of "tack ons" and "work arounds" lead to a user interface covered with little appendages, oddments of switches, and addenda to menus. With time, the shape of the interface more and more reflects the internal dictates of program constraints and organization: how the programmers had to think of the functions in order to find places to hang them. Old timers, with calloused thumbs and bent fingers from years of wrapping their hands around these features, get so used to them that they hardly think twice when they key in Ctrl-F5-C-C. Continuing to support these reprobates commits vendors to still more interface barbarism, since new features must not interfere with the controls for these old ones.

What the user really wants (or is it needs?) is a simple interface to control these complex systems. Unfortunately, today's software is too often only simple on the surface and gets messy as soon as you try to do any real work with it. Of course, by then, you are out of the software store and bound by the shrink-wrap agreement.

Humans deal with complexity by chunking, by lumping together similar or related things into chunks that can be tossed around mentally as a single unit. Really good user interfaces do the same thing, by reducing to a minimum the total number of distinct ideas or techniques the user must learn. This takes careful thought in the first place and regular reworkings to overcome the messiness introduced by creeping featurism.

For example, from the standpoint of a person using a word processor, straight lines are lines are lines. The user wants to draw a line and put it somewhere. Whether it runs down the margin to "redline" text, or separates text body from footnotes, or boxes in a table, or frames a sidebar comment, or is a 3-point rule in a snazzy letterhead, it's just a line. It looks like a line when we print it out, and we call it a line when we tell a co-worker to "get rid of that line down the side." Yet most word processors treat each variant as a separate and unrelated phenomenon.

My old word processor had two basic ways to draw lines, or rules, as typesetters say. This split interface was based not on any external user considerations but really on internal implementation details. The older, more primitive feature used line drawing text characters. The newer, more versatile way used graphics. In an ironic twist, the old way was semi-WYSIWYG—you drew under control of the cursor keys and could see what the results would be as you created them. The new way required entering choices and values for the type of line, position, and weight. Even after you finished, you couldn't see what you did without going into a print preview mode, a legacy of the old DOS text-based restrictions.

But now consider my next word processor! It has five completely different ways to create lines. These are indexed separately in the manual and accessed through different menus or buttons in the software. Some lines you can get rid of by pointing at and pressing delete, some you can't. Obviously, creeping featurism has struck again. The end result is more complexity than is necessary and the appearance of more complexity than there is.

Darwinian Design

I am certainly a firm believer in evolution, in malleable software designs that are steadily reworked to conform to the user in response to an ever deepening understanding of what it is we are trying to do with our tools and how the tools can best help us. On the down side, the evolutionary process in software engineering can result in a patchwork of parts and pieces that may work but that punishes the user. After two or three integer version releases, the entire user interface should probably be redesigned from scratch to cover the same functionality with a fraction of the controls.

In the meantime, I had to paw through the thicket of creeping features to figure out how to make a simple 3-point rule from margin to margin with my wonderful(?) new Windows word processor. I was sure it was in there, somewhere, but it took awhile to track it down amidst the zits and pimples on the user interface.

From *Computer Language Magazine*, Volume 9, #10, October 1992.

36

Going to the Source

What do users want, anyway? And how do you find out? Software developers are being told to produce the systems their clients and customers want, to become more user-oriented. Companies in every field are trying to be more competitive by listening to "the voice of the customer" and becoming "customer-driven." It is not enough anymore to have software with the right features. The software needs to have a good user interface: to be easy to learn and easy to use. But how do you know what users want in a user interface, anyway? Many companies turn to market research, to telephone and written surveys that ask users or potential users what they want.

Sometimes it appears they don't even know themselves, and often it seems that what they want may not be at all what they need. A major developer of accounting software accumulated over 15,000 requests and suggestions for changes from its customers between one integer release and the next. Many of these were patently ridiculous, and careful study showed that others would have been mistakes to incorporate into the software.

Wishing Well

In folk tales, peasants who are granted three wishes invariably seem to call disaster down on their village. If you ask users directly what they want, they will typically ask for more features. If you simply respond like some obedient software genie, you will unleash another epidemic of creeping featurism (Chapter 35). Worse, the surveyed users may not have a clue what to ask for, but, flattered by the attention and taken by the sense of responsibility, they will just make something up. Then the real trouble starts.

To the user, the user interface *is* the system. To find out what is needed or what is right and wrong with a given system, you do need to go to the source. If you don't ask, you probably aren't going to find out. Developers who rely on their own expertise or judgment alone, or who trust spontaneous feedback and complaints from customers, put themselves at a competitive disadvantage.

User surveys are an obvious tool, but the truth is that most users just won't take the time to respond to questionnaires, and those who do often do so casually, with little attention to needed detail. Telephone surveys or in-person interviews are likely to get a little more information from users than if you make them do the work of writing things down, but all surveys suffer from problems of recall. I remember there were confusing things with the 3-D features of my new graphics package, but now that I've learned how to use them, I can't recall just what confused me at first. The essential information for the developers is already lost, namely, the exact point when I hit the wrong button or got results that didn't look like what I expected.

For most software developers, beta test sites are a major source of feedback. Especially if a company establishes a close working relationship with a number of good sites, valuable information can be obtained this way. However, there are also serious limitations to beta testing for interface design and refinement.

In particular, if a product is fairly flaky or is still quite rough around the edges, a customer may run into literally hundreds of small glitches or minor difficulties in a single day of typical use. Trying to make note of all these as they arise interrupts the flow of work so badly that all but the most dedicated and compulsive beta testers end up recording only a fraction of the problems they actually encounter. Equipping users with a voice-operated tape recorder increases the capture rate, but this, too, tends to interfere with normal patterns of work.

To get around these limitations, it is becoming fashionable for major software companies to build usability labs or usability research centers. These facilities use both audio and video recording and are usually fitted with one-way mirrors for observing systems in use. The centers are typically equipped with a range of computers and workstations.

Aside from the cost of setting up and operating such a research facility, a major shortcoming is that people do not behave in the laboratory like they do when they are on their own turf. If you want to know how people work with a particular piece of software, you need to study them *in context,* using some form of contextual inquiry, such as the approach pioneered by Karen Holtzblatt and her colleagues at Digital Equipment Corporation (Holtzblatt and Beyer 1993). The essence of a contextual approach is to investigate what users do when they are doing their usual job in the usual setting. It's like the field research that a cultural anthropologist or ethnographer would undertake. People are observed in their work and informants are interviewed about how work is carried out. A skilled interviewer can elicit remarkably detailed information about actual usage with minimal interference in the work process.

Of course, to actually watch a person using a system, there must be a system to be used. Prototypes are often employed in early phases of development, alpha and beta versions later. A really good field researcher can sometimes get useful data from nothing more than paper prototypes, simple static drawings of proposed screen layouts.

You can also get ideas for new tools and features by seeing what people do with the tools they already have, where giving them something just a little different could significantly simplify work flow, for example. You might also give them your competitor's software and learn what is wrong with it. Or you can even study how they do their jobs in the absence of a software tool. The idea isn't simply to automate the manual process, but to learn how and where software support can actually help.

Office Visits

The central idea of contextual methods is to get out of *your* office and interact with users in *their* offices. Not only does this give you better data on which to base your design decisions, it costs less. Building a half-million-dollar usability research facility may get you written up in the trade rags and may signal the marketplace that, by golly, your company is truly committed to better user interfaces and to client-centered design, but hopping into your car with a notebook and a tape recorder may lead to better software.

On the down side, most people do not particularly cotton to having someone looking over their shoulders as they try to do their jobs. And, being watched changes how they do it. When an interface designer or usability investigator sits at the user's elbow taking notes, an interaction is set up that changes what the user does. The designer gives the user unconscious cues: a sudden intake of breath, a quick scribble on the pad, a quiet "ah" or "hmmm," leaning back or leaning forward, shifting in the chair restlessly. In myriad ways subtle messages are communicated about what the user is doing or ought to be doing instead of the incredibly stupid moves being made. The temptations to "help" are great, and typical developers just love to step in and take over when someone else is making less than optimal use of "their" software. Untrained or inexperienced investigators often make even more blatant interventions. ("Here, let me show you an easier way." "Ah, just click there." "No, not quite.")

It works the other way, too. The user knows you are there watching. They know you understand the system, perhaps better than they do, so they look to you for guidance, whether with outright questions or glimpses over the shoulder.

All in all, it is probably better not to be there. So does this mean just go back to the office and start building that usability lab so you can stay behind the one-way mirror? Not necessarily.

A simple technology works amazingly well. A video camcorder is aimed over the user's shoulder, focused on the keyboard and screen. Beside the screen is an adjustable mirror oriented so the user's face is visible to the camera. That's it.

In a typical investigation, a user is video taped making use of some piece of software. This tape is first reviewed by the investigators to study what the user is doing. Being able to see the user's face gives the investigators additional clues about what is happening. When the user is surprised, annoyed, confused, or impatient, it says volumes about details of the interface.

The investigator then sits down with the user to watch selections from the tape. The idea is to tap into intentions and reactions, what the user was thinking about and actually trying to do while using the software. Here's where the mirror comes into play again. When people see themselves, especially their own faces, on a recording, they can often recall with amazing accuracy and detail their own "inner dialogue" and feelings from the time of the recording session. If you take the trouble to obtain it and understand it, this information can tell you what your users *need*.

In the short run, giving customers what they want—or said they wanted on some market survey—can be a winning strategy, but in the long run it probably pays off more to give them what they really need, especially if you can package it so it looks like what they wanted or thought they needed. After all, deception in service to the user is not a vice!

37

Colorful Language

As the modern Zen master put it, what is the color of one hand clapping? Something to ponder as we take a look at color in user interfaces.

Color has become an important aspect of graphical user interfaces, at least in the selling of software. For years I resisted getting a color monitor because most of my work was straight text processing. My venerable Hercules-compatible video card gave me everything I needed, and I could work for hours in front of that flat-screen amber monochrome monitor without headaches or blurred vision. Why should I switch to anemic color, lower resolution, and the flickering jaggies? I did own a color monitor, an overgrown CGA turkey that came bundled with my first laptop, but it mostly functioned as an end table. I didn't see the software world in full color until I finally moved up to my current workhorse system, which came with 1024 by 768 video in 256 colors on a 72-hertz noninterlaced display. My eyes were opened.

Until then, I saw color as a sales gimmick for video games and executive decision support software, which are often indistinguishable. Although I never went through the usual crazies with the Windows desktop color scheme ("Look, Maude, it's psychedelic!"), I did start reassessing the role of color in communication. Color can be more than just more fun. It can be an important part of the communication between software and user. The trick, of course, is in knowing when and how to use it.

Colors carry certain connotations, mostly culturally shaped, but some of which may be wired in. Children, even infants, seem to show more interest in bright colors and vivid contrasts. Red, orange, and yellow, especially in an otherwise black-and-white context, draw our attention. But people do not always behave in ways consistent with conventional assumptions about color. Popular wisdom has it that blue and green are cool colors that calm the viewer, but research doesn't support this. Some studies have suggested that surroundings painted in a kind of hot pink may actually be the most psychologically and physiologically calming, even though most people hate such a decor.

Some corporate GUI standards specify that potentially risky or irreversible actions be flagged in red. Unfortunately, typical users behave in a way that defeats the intent. Rubrication actually increases the likelihood of casually selecting an item or icon. For many people, a red item in a menu is like a red flag to a bull; once they spot it, they simply have to click on it.

Color Communication

Color can be used as an added dimension of communication that can aid in interpreting complex information. Both my daughters went through an experimental public school that used an innovative approach to reading. If English were a phonetically regular language with uniform spelling, there would be little need for spell-checkers and hardly a word of debate about teaching phonics versus reading by rote. But the same sound in English can be spelled dozens of ways. In fact, many of the greatest irregularities in spelling and grammar tend to fall in the core vocabulary that has come down most directly from Proto-indo-european, which makes it harder on the young protoreader.

The Gatagno "words-in-color" system cleverly used color as an auxiliary clue to "decoding" the sounds of words. All the different forms of the "ay" sound—"eigh," "ei," "ai," "ey," "a," etc.—were printed in the same color, a sort of visual training wheels that the kids were intended to outgrow.

This clever scheme seemed to work, but it is also possible to be monumentally stupid about educational uses of color. One object-oriented methodology maven has been preaching multi-sensory educational techniques to reach the whole brain through sound and color and action. Of course, his visuals at one major conference, though projected on a magnificent high-resolution true-color display system, were just heaps of straight text in mind-numbing monochrome. The only appeal to the right brain or to that artistic seven-year-old lurking within every systems analyst was some black-and-white clip art in the lower right corner of each slide. Alas, it was the same art on each slide and had nothing to do with illustrating or reinforcing the point.

Children and other human-type creatures do learn concepts more easily and more thoroughly when communication is reinforced through representations in various media and modalities, especially when abstractions can be given colorful tangible forms that can be manipulated. Kids are helped in learning the alphabet by colored letters they can pick up and play with. Smart trainers have been using this for years. Part of the success of so-called CRC cards in object-oriented design (Wirfs-Brock et al. 1990) is that these little 3-by-5 or 4-by-6 stand-ins for object classes are concrete things that can be played with by developers as they think through various architectures and scenarios.

Our earnest methodologist, on the other hand, used colored game pieces to involve the audience in learning his pet methodology. Unfortunately, the colors, muted pastels of almost uniform saturation, were neither easily distinguishable nor very informative. The one possible pedagogical justification for the colors was overlooked altogether because tokens representing closely related concepts were given distinct rather than similar or related colors, while tokens for very different concepts were given shades of light blue-green and green-blue so similar that in the slightly dimmed light of the auditorium they were virtually indistinguishable to most people and blurred into grayish uniformity to an important minority. About one in every 12 males is color blind, along with about one out of 20 females.

Which leads to an important rule of color in user interface design: never rely on color alone to make any potentially important distinction among visual elements. If it is important to tell a static class relationship from a dynamic instance relationship, for example, then displaying one in red and the other in blue is not enough. The lines should differ in weight (thickness) or style (solid, dashed, etc.) as well.

If color is employed as an essential part of the user interface, the humble designer ought to leave open the possibility of the end user knowing best—or at least having the final say. Under Windows you can change the color of most anything, but I have never been able to figure out how to change the color of the text cursor in Windows apps. The anorexic little cursor that inhabits most text applications is almost invisible when it's the same color as the text. I ended up making the text color dark blue, which is nearly as good against a paper-white background, but makes it much easier to find that blinking cursor.

Color Scheming

As hi-res color displays begin to dominate not only the office but the lecture and conference circuit, graphics have gained new prominence, with misguided attempts by corporate sponsors of conferences to impose a standard "look-and-feel" for entire conferences through distributing "templates" for presentation packages like Persuasion or PowerPoint.

Part of the problem is that the templates are either developed by software types who have no sense of aesthetics and understand little or nothing about communicating information, or else by graphics arts types who may have a sense of aesthetics, but still know little or nothing about communicating information. The former produce the same garish garbage as can be found in many personalized desktop color schemes; the latter produce those lovely templates with lushly shaded backgrounds that have become the hallmark of the audio-visual upper class. The typical color scheme shades from rich purple through bright blue, with royal-blue headlines and mint-green "bullets." Beautiful look and feel! Only trouble is, half the audience can't read half the slides. At one recent conference nearly everyone over forty admitted to me that they couldn't read the gorgeous rear-projection displays, but instead relied on the printed handouts, which were done in black-and-white, of course.

Your corporate look-and-feelers, worried about looking and feeling good, are on the wrong track. The perception of shape depends on contrast. As a rule, greater contrast enhances readability. It has long been known that, under normal lighting conditions, text is most readable when it is presented as black text on white background. Light on dark is substantially harder to read, and color on color can be eyestrain city.

Which raises another issue: fonts. You can sometimes tell the age of the software development staff by the fonts appearing in the user interface. All too often, software uses or defaults to what I term "under-40" fonts: small print in typefaces with low line weight. Only those under 40 can read them! The problems are worsened by high-resolution displays because system fonts are usually bit-mapped. More than once I have seen a great software demo ruined because nobody gathered around the exhibit booth could actually read the menus or diagrams; they just nodded politely as if they knew what was happening.

The rising hegemony of "presentation packages" creates other problems as well. They promote what I call "six-shooter slides"—you know, bullet, bullet, bullet, bullet, bullet, bullet. Visual aids should be just that, aids to understanding and recall, visually illustrating, expanding, or reinforcing a presenter's commentary. Six-shooter visuals are the weakest and least effective way to use a potentially powerful tool. The fact that they are in pretty colors adds nothing. Color and graphics capabilities ought to be employed to some practical end in communication, not merely used willy-nilly following the Sir Edmond Hillary Principle of Design—because they are there.

Like Siskel and Ebert, I am convinced that some features are best appreciated in the original, uncolorized form. Colorful language may be best rendered in stark black-and-white. As to the color of one hand clapping, I think it may be the same color as a window.

From *Software Development*, Volume 1, #1, January 1993.

38

Improving Intermediates

Ski trails come in three varieties—green, blue, and black—because skiers, too, are of three kinds: novices, intermediates, and experts. I happen to be an intermediate skier, have been for years, and expect to be all my life. I'm what ski instructors refer to euphemistically as a classic "improving intermediate," meaning I'm middle-aged, keep getting better, but not by much and not very quickly. I'm happy. I love skiing and have even survived a few of those dreaded (or lauded) double black diamond trails, usually because I miss the last turnoff onto the kinder, gentler slopes. Mostly, though, I keep my eyes out for those user-friendly blue squares and reassuring green circles.

Skiing has a lot to teach us about the relationship between users and systems and how software developers can improve that relationship. It would be a punishing experience to learn to ski on one of those steep expert slopes strewn with bone-jarring bumps. A few tyros, mostly youngsters under twelve, seem to go directly to the mogul fields following their first try on the bunny slope, but I've always suspected that they were really bionic mutants. For most of us, those wide gentle slopes marked with friendly green circles are essential for early learning.

On the other hand, you can only learn so much if you stay all day on the bunny slopes. Sooner or later you have to move on to the bigger challenges of the blue and the black (or, occasionally, the black and blue).

The power users of skiing, experts who twist their way down the slalom course and fly over the mogul fields, would have us believe that theirs is the only way. But improving intermediates can enjoy transcendent moments, too,

203

as when you come off the top at Heavenly Valley, with the turquoise jewel of Lake Tahoe shining below and the desert to the east, a brown and ocher sea stretching to the horizon, and the crisp morning air stings your face as you whisper through a dusting of fresh powder.

Three-Phase Design

Okay, so what has this got to do with software development? Aside from daydreaming about skiing Tahoe again, I wanted to introduce the triphasic model of human interfaces (Constantine 1994a, 1994c). The triphasic model says that system users have different needs at different stages in their development as users, and that the user interface should be designed to accommodate these changing needs. To do this, software must present different faces to users of different levels of ability, each designed with its own distinct features and particular technical goals. Like the network of trails at a good ski resort, these interface components are not really separate but are intricately interconnected.

The three interfaces in the triphasic model are the acquisition interface, the transition interface, and the production interface. The acquisition interface is the system the naïve user sees on first encounter with the software. A good acquisition interface enables the beginner to do work right from the get-go. The production interface makes it possible for an experienced, fully trained user to produce sophisticated results with high efficiency. In between is the transition interface, for the improving intermediates among software users—those who are beyond the slow and sloppy point-and-click of the beginner, but are not and may never be real power users who can slalom their way with shortcut keys through multiple applications in cascaded windows. Just as the novice, intermediate, and expert trails at the ski resort are distinct but interconnected, so a well-designed system presents a threefold interface with smooth transitions among its parts.

Disenfranchised Majority

I think one of the most serious problems in user interface design today is that most of the attention is given to laying out the bunny slopes of software. Expert users are grudgingly accommodated by leaving open access to rather rough and ugly "advanced" features or by cobbling together a random set of keystroke shortcuts and an awkward macro facility. But the "improving intermediates," who may well be the most numerous and most important category, are virtually ignored.

If a system is useful and reasonably well designed, users will not remain novices forever. A minority of them may eventually become experts or power users, but the majority will probably spend their days as improving intermediates. Their needs are neither those of experts nor novices; they need a user interface that allows them to steadily and incrementally add knowledge of the software and increase their skill in using it. It should not punish them for what they don't know or need, and it should not send them unexpectedly hurtling down the double-black-diamond slopes of dialogues only a C++ programmer could love.

At best, commercial software and software development tools seem to have green trails and double black diamonds, but almost nothing in between. The transition interface, which helps the former novice continue to improve in efficiency and versatility, needs to be designed as a distinct collection of interface features that are systematically tied to what the beginner already knows and what the expert will need to know. User-configurable button bars and tool palettes are probably a good idea but not the answer, since they either saddle users with the standard set—invariably either too complex or too limited—or make them figure out for themselves which features are which.

The entire interface could be modal, offering a novice mode and a series of intermediate modes with expanding interface richness and versatility. Novices should probably not see or be offered access to the black diamond features, except through clearly marked "lifts" or "trails." A check on a preference list tells the system what general level the user has reached or wants to use. Custom interface layouts could start from this range of standard ones. Oddly, many freeware computer games are readily configurable by player ability, but expensive productivity packages and software development tools come in one-size-fits-all configurations.

Maps

Ski resorts typically provide other user-friendly features that ought to be part of every software interface. Trail maps show how to get from where you are to where you want to be and guide the skier who is seeking out or trying to avoid certain kinds of trails. Software systems should incorporate or provide their own trail maps, visual guides to the layout of features in the maze of buttons and dialogues, pull-down and pop-up menus. On-line help, at least as typically done with the help engines of popular GUIs, is of only limited value. Such on-line un-help is every bit as difficult or clumsy to navigate as the menus and dialogues themselves and, worse, is invariably organized differently than the interface itself.

On the ski slopes, the trails themselves are clearly marked, the same way as on the map. In software, menu titles frequently give little or no clue to what lies below, and the "help" system, separated from the interface features it is supposed to help with, often employs a different vocabulary. If I am trying to figure out how to make a footnote go away in my word processor, the darned help system should just show me, opening the right menus in sequence and pointing to what I need to use.

Different tools and approaches, even different rules and principles, may apply to the transition interface than to the acquisition or production interfaces. Usability testing (see Chapter 36), which studies users actually interacting with a system, may help fine-tune the acquisition interface, but it is likely to help little with the transition or production interfaces. Why? Because the camcorder runs out of tape or the psychologist runs out of attention span long before users progress to intermediate or expert levels of ability.

With the help of good engineering and extensive usability testing, some GUIs have succeeded in furnishing a reasonable acquisition interface. The original Apple Macintosh interface was designed to a target of twenty minutes from sealed box to productive work, for example.

The problem is that, as the user progresses, the typical interface remains the same. Beginning users of a system really need what amounts to software training wheels. Training wheels have helped many a kid learn to ride a bicycle, but training wheels were not meant to be permanent. Training wheels, in fact, do not actually help kids learn to ride a bicycle; they help kids learn to ride a bicycle-with-training-wheels! In order to develop the balance and motor skills to ride a bicycle, the training wheels have to come off.

There you have it. Just when you were reluctantly ready to accept the need to design and test the user interface for your next product, you find out one interface is not enough. You need green, blue, and black versions, with trail maps and markings, and maybe even detachable training wheels. Okay, so the analogy isn't perfect.

I think I'll go and hit the slopes!

From *Software Development*, Volume 1, #2, February 1993.

39

Unusable You

2.70! The number may not be familiar, but the M.I.T. mechanical engineering course it designates is famous. Students get a kit of miscellaneous parts, then compete to design and build the best robot ping-pong ball sweeper or computerized mobile bridge or some other challenge dreamed up by faculty. Professor Woody Flowers, PBS science maven and originator of course 2.70, wants to help tomorrow's designers and engineers make more usable products that really work for humans. His undergraduate design courses have spawned competitions for high school students, and he even arms middle-school students with cameras to search out and document unfriendly or unusable designs around them.

If dumb design is so obvious, why is it that millions of VCRs and microwave ovens around the world flash 12:00 or 88:88? Why doesn't GUI-based software speed up our work? Despite human factors departments and usability testing labs, leading vendors keep on releasing stupid software with major usability problems that a 12-year-old can spot from across the room.

Consider this: My computer tells me I have 8,283 files filling nearly 550 megabytes of disk space (Ah, those were obviously the good old days . . . before Win95 and 98. LLC). Making sense of and finding things in such a digital jungle is a big part of staying ahead in consulting. File size and creation date are often clues to getting the right version or variation, so we like to see these when we go to open a file from an application. A good time for basic housekeeping—rearranging files and directories, renaming or deleting material—is while we're looking at and thinking about files as we open or save them. Everybody knows this, but only a minority of software is built this way. We need an add-on/add-in that standardizes and extends the garden variety Open, Save, and SaveAs dialogues under Windows so that every app displays file stats and descriptions and allows routine file maintenance from within the dialogue.

Good idea. Some major products supply this capability. With one such marvel installed, you hit Ctrl-O and, in the upper left of the file open dialogue, where it always was, appears the familiar combo box for file name with scrollable file list below showing, as always, too few of the files and no file stats. Highlight a file name, and a gray box in the lower right(!) reveals date, time, and size for that one file. Only one set of stats is visible at a time, visual attention must shift repeatedly between upper left and lower right, two distinct and widely separated visual elements must be mentally connected into one conceptual entity, file descriptions cannot be compared without memorizing, and instead of a quick and easy visual scan through a list, a clumsy sequential, mechanical operation is required. This brain-dead design violates basic interface design principles and fails to support the work the user is trying to accomplish.

We are not talking about rocket science; these problems are obvious to untrained teenagers. All the leading development companies have trained user interface specialists and elaborate usability testing facilities. I know from talking with these companies that they are concerned about usability issues and seem knowledgeable about user interface design principles. But something goes wrong between the intentions and the software that ships. I've been looking into some of the reasons that good companies keep shipping crummy software. A systematic investigation is in the works, but here are some of the things that stand out at this stage.

Job Description

In order to have usable software, the user interface has to be somebody's job. Without responsibility and accountability, better user interfaces don't happen. I've been saying this for years. Now I'm beginning to think that usability has to be *everyone's* job, that everyone on the development team has to be focused on end-product usability and take it seriously from first brainstorm to final box.

One way to develop this focus is through systematic usability inspections (Constantine 1994b). These resemble traditional design and code walkthroughs, but focus on the user interface and usability issues to identify usability defects. This gets developers thinking about users and issues of software usability. A single inspection just before freezing a final release is not enough. Developers and interface specialists should inspect work flow models, early paper prototypes, initial designs, and working prototypes, as well as alpha and beta versions of the software. With each successive inspection, usability improves, as Jacob Nielsen has shown (Nielsen 1993). With each inspection, developers also learn a little more about good user interface design and the defects to avoid.

Too Little, Too Late

Software developers often throw away useful findings on product usability because they get them too late. Leading vendors of development tools and other shrink-wrapped software like to prove their commitment to usability by pointing to shiny new testing labs where representative end users can be observed and evaluated with elaborate video and computer equipment as they try out software. Empirical usability testing is more glamorous than usability inspection, but lab testing has some major disadvantages. For one thing, usability testing comes too late. Realistic evaluation of end-user interaction with software requires a working system, usually a beta test version. By this time the user interface mistakes have all been made. Finding them all will be difficult to impossible. Since the basic structure and functionality of the software is cast in concrete code, it's typically too late to do more than tweak and fine-tune superficial aspects of the user interface. The result is a user interface that may be polished but is still misshapen. The real problems are often in the architecture of the software and user interface, in how the features fit together as a whole or fall apart, in the basic model on which the software is built.

Even when there are fundamental flaws in the architecture or the need for major rethinking of how the software and the user interact, usability testing often does not reveal them. It is better at identifying smaller problems within a given overall approach. Just as you can't test your way to bug-free code, you can't test your way to defect-free user interfaces.

Even expert evaluations, which are typically cheaper and more efficient than usability testing, are often conducted too late to be very useful. In one application, a thorough user interface inspection identified a little over a hundred usability defects, which were prioritized by the severity of their impact on product usability. The client fixed a handful of surface defects among the lower third of problems but only one of the dozen defects categorized as serious. The rest were all judged to be too hard to change because of the underlying program architecture.

Surface Features

Much software development is feature-driven. In the marketplace, the one who finishes with the most or the fanciest features wins. Yet feature-laden software with attractive 3-D graphics can still be seriously deficient in user interface design. Software usability resides in the total organization of the user interface, not in how features look so much as in how features work and how they work together to make the user's job easier. Getting this right takes attention to interface architecture and attention to interface detail by everyone throughout product development.

Perhaps this is why software vendors attend so much to layout, look, and feel, not because these are so important for usability, but because these are the only things they know how to fix.

From *Software Development*, Volume 2, #4, April 1994.

40

Editing Interfaces

My company just finished editing a user interface. Officially, the contract was for an "expert usability evaluation," but what we were doing was editing. Good user interfaces start with good architecture, but achieving real software usability requires recognizing where a user interface has gotten it wrong, then making it right. Often, successive rounds of critical appraisal, revision, and refinement are needed to remove the defects. This is editing, and editing is one of the core skills for software and applications developers. It's pretty much the same story whether you are editing a program, a book, or a user interface.

I have long been envious of writers whose fingers fly over the keyboard, producing first drafts that are already final copy. For myself, writing is a slow, sometimes frustrating, and often fitful process, the first fruits of which tend toward the indigestible. Fortunately, I am a pretty good editor. Over the years I have learned how to step back from my writing, peruse it with jaundiced eyes, and identify the problems in need of rework. An article may go through four or five rounds of heavy-handed rewrites before I am satisfied that the results are ready for prime time.

In truth, much of what I know as a writer I learned from years as an editor of books, journals, and newsletters. Do enough of this, and editing gets into the bloodstream. The editorial frame of mind becomes a way of approaching the world. For me, some habits of editing have become so ingrained as to be almost automatic and unconscious. I can be scanning a book in a store and will spot a typo as I flip the pages. It is as if misspelled words were in boldface, leaping out of the page to grab my attention.

Chalk Talk

This ability can be a somewhat embarrassing talent, especially when coupled with poor impulse control. On one occasion, I was waiting for a table in one of those trendy little French cafes with a chalkboard menu. Without hesitance or thought, I crossed over to the chalkboard and casually corrected a misspelled word. My daughters were mortified.

Some people are born with a flair for orthography. Not I. Programmer-author P. J. Plauger once remarked that he is almost constitutionally incapable of misspelling a word. This he told me in preface to a suggestion that I get someone who could spell to go over my manuscripts. Instead of taking his advice, I learned to spell.

Two things taught me. Years spent as a journal editor, trying to rescue the obscure, mangled, or awkward prose of pedants and researchers, started the process. Spell checkers finished it. I finally got spelling down pat after years of using a word processor with built-in spell checking. Spell checkers are marvelous teachers because they do not actually check or correct spelling, they just tell you if they don't recognize a word. The early checkers didn't even offer guesses. So you ended up having to grab a dictionary either to reassure yourself or to get the spelling right. In any case, you got immediate feedback and played an active role in your own learning. Now, it has become hard for me not to see spelling errors.

The story is much the same in editing user interfaces. Once you begin thinking in terms of usability, you may find it difficult not to see usability problems wherever they lurk. You start noticing the way signs in a hospital confuse or mislead visitors, how hard it is to remember which button to press on a VCR remote, or the way a neighbor's driving directions can be interpreted in multiple ways.

Of course, finding the flaws in other systems is not the hard part; the big challenge is seeing the shortcomings in our own work. For instance, that expert usability evaluation I mentioned was sandwiched into a busy travel schedule. Our report, identifying some one hundred usability defects in the client's user interface design, had been carefully proofed before being dropped off for printing and binding at one of those 24-hour copy services. On the morning of the consultation, with our client and his staff and his boss gathered around a conference table, I opened the report and instantly spotted a glaring typo on the very first page. Isn't it always the case?

Editors and writers know this effect and exploit it. If you want to proof your own writing, shove it in a drawer for a few days before rereading it. If you want to identify usability defects in your user interface, set aside the designs, sketches, and screen shots for a day or two while you work on something else. When you come back, it will be easier to look at your work from a fresh point of view and to see the problems.

Champions Made

Magazine editors often approach their work from the point of view of an archetypal ignorant reader. Pete Bickford, erstwhile User Interface Champion at Apple, has a similar take on assessing user interfaces. He used to say that his job involved playing the part of the dumbest user on the planet. It's a mindset in which you tune out all the things you know about computers or the application or the programming. If you can look in the upper right corner of a Windows application window and see a button to multiply something, you are on your way to becoming a more effective editor of interfaces.

Studied imperviousness and practiced innocence are not enough, however. Editing is creative as well as critical. You can't just cross things out, you have to also write things in. What you write involves judgment informed by knowledge of good form. Just as you can't be a newspaper editor without knowing the basics of journalism and the rules of grammar, you must understand the rules of usability if you are going to edit user interfaces. You need to recognize unnecessary complexity or awkward workflow, then know how to simplify messy organization or smooth out jerky operation. You even have to learn to see the things that aren't there, such as the missing feedback to the user or the functionality that isn't visible where and when it should be.

Defect Defense

In editing interfaces, it helps to be negative, to be able to take on the attitude of the stereotypical New York theater critic or book reviewer, focusing on weaknesses and mistakes, on problems and shortcomings. This may be the easiest part for programmers and engineers, who seem almost by nature to be a critical lot. Put any two of them in front of a whiteboard and you get three strong opinions—followed by an exchange of verbal artillery. They are quick to point out the flaws in each other's designs or the limits of proposed solutions. On the other hand, their typical response to criticism, implied or proclaimed, is to explain.

A key rule for editing interfaces, then, is never to defend or explain anything. There is almost always a reason why you put that button over there or refreshed the thumbnail image when an item was clicked, but the real issues in usability are not the internal reasons but the external consequences. To stay in tune with your capacity as creative critic, you have to stop yourself from justifying or explaining your own design and programming decisions.

Just as editing can teach a lot about writing, the more you practice critical editing of user interfaces, the more you learn about good user interface architecture. If you find yourself reaching for a blue pencil when someone hands you a screen shot, go ahead. You may be on the way to a new career as an interface editor.

From *Software Development,* Volume 3, #11, November 1995.

41

In Service

It may be called client focus or "the voice of the customer," but it's about service. I had a chance to learn more about this when I first opened a bank account in Australia. I dutifully filled out the forms, proved my identity, and plunked down my first deposit. Did I want checks? Yes, of course. Did I want a keycard? A what? A card for EFTPOS. EFTPOS (pronounced "eftposs") is an everyday word in Australian English. "Is this the EFTPOS line?" the person behind you at the supermarket asks. "I want to EFTPOS this order," another customer says. Those in financial services will understand that EFTPOS stands for "Electronic Funds Transfer, Point Of Sale." In Australia, you buy groceries, pay bills, and get cash, all with EFTPOS.

So, of course, I wanted the bank to give me the card, even though the bank policy required me to call for it in person. After picking it up and carrying it unused for a week, I went to get some cash.

Out of Service

The screen on the first ATM displayed an "out-of-service" message, so I moved to the next one, an ancient looking beast with a one-line, gas-plasma display telling me to insert my card. I searched for the slot. With no indication of the correct way to insert the card, it took me three tries before the hidden rollers sucked my card into the machine. I entered my PIN on request, asked for cash, keyed the account type, entered the amount, and verified by hitting the "OK" key. Nothing. After a considerable delay, I read a message saying that the action was not activated for this account; I was directed to consult my bank service representative.

I had no idea what the message meant. Maybe I had entered the wrong PIN or made some other silly mistake. I tried again as the queue behind me grew. No luck. Same thing at another machine. Finally I went into a branch office of my bank where the service representative at the enquiries counter greeted me with a terse, "Yes?"

I explained that I had an EFTPOS card that didn't seem to work. "Well now, what did you do?" she asked in a tone that brought back memories of the principal's office in elementary school. I explained that I had tried to take out cash. "No, what did you do?" she inquired again, with an imperious emphasis on the final word. So, I recounted, to the best of my ability, precisely what I had done: select withdraw cash from the green keys, select primary check account from the blue keys. "Ah, there you have it." What? "There it is, isn't it? You do not have a check account." I explained that I had opened a checking account, pulling a book of checks from my coat pocket as proof. "No. Those are not checks. We do not offer check accounts to individuals. You have a savings account. If you would enter your selections properly you wouldn't have this problem." I was about to ask to see her supervisor when I noticed her badge; she was a supervisor. I mumbled something and slipped away.

It is easy to see this incident in terms of a bad attitude or even poor training, but customer-orientation or its lack can also be shaped by software. The kind of systems we design and deliver to our customers can make a big difference in the kind of service they can deliver to their customers. Good software would have saved me from ever having to enter the bank for a lecture from Helga the Horrible. The software supporting the ATM knew I did not have any checking account; it knew that I had one and only one account, a "savings" account. The message could have said something to that effect.

Small details can make or break service. Like many consultants, I find it convenient to order software and equipment by phone. On one such occasion, I was still idly fingering my credit card as I read through the last of the items I was ordering. Suddenly I realized I had given the sales operator the details for my personal credit card instead of the company account. I asked her to change the card number. There was a long silence and a sigh. "I'll have to redo the order," she said. Couldn't she just go back to that field and change it? No, that field was locked once she left the screen; she would have to start over again. Click, click, clickety. "Could you spell your last name for me again, please?" I protest that I had already given it to her. "But it's on the record that had to be deleted."

Apparently the brain-dead programmers of this application never really thought through how such a system would be used. There was no provision for backing up or undoing parts of a transaction. The result? A frequently flustered salesperson and at least one irritated customer considering placing his next order with another company.

It can also work the other way. Good software can facilitate good service by empowering people. Consider my experience with Cellar Door Direct, a wine club based in South Australia. Months after getting a circular I called them up to order some wine. All I had at hand was a Post-it note with my scribbles on it. Unfortunately, the code for the wine I wanted was not on the telephone operator's current screen. I heard her page through some data until it came up. "That's the Jarrondale '92 Shiraz, right?" She quoted a price that sounded too high to me; I remembered it being on sale. "What price do you have?" she asked. I told her what I thought was the right amount. "Well, I don't show that sale price anymore, but let me enter an override." Click, click, clickety, and a few days later a case arrives at my door. The combination of flexible software with flexible staff has cemented the customer relationship.

Messenger Service

For another example, Sydney pioneered a marvelous service called Cuisine Courier. You choose from the menus of local restaurants and for a paltry $2 fee they courier your order right to your door. When you ring them up, you just give them your telephone number and the system supplies the rest. "Mr. Constantine, is it? Are you still at this address? Well, then, what menu would you like to order from?" You give the shorthand code and the operator confirms with the full name of the restaurant, likewise for each of the menu items. "That should arrive within 45 minutes." Three quarters of an hour later there's a knock at the door and it's time for a feast.

How do they do it? Good systems design! As soon as your order details are confirmed, the system faxes it directly from the computer to the restaurant. By the time the courier arrives at the restaurant, the order is ready and documented with directions for delivery. No worries, as the Aussies would say, because everyone is working from the same data.

As software developers we need to keep in mind how such small details, as well as the overall architecture of our systems, can work in service to the ultimate customer. Our decisions may determine whether "the voice of the customer" is heard as a complaint or a compliment.

From *Software Development,* Volume 4, #3, March 1996.

Usable Objects

Introduction

When I began my return to the world of computer software in 1986, objects were clearly heating up as a topic, although many developers and their managers then looked askance at what might have seemed like just another trend de jour whose 15 minutes of fame would soon fade. However, it seemed to me that there was more to the story, that objects represented another cornerstone in the foundations of software engineering practice (see Chapter 24). Encouraged by George Schussel of Digital Consulting, Inc., I organized and chaired the Object-Oriented Systems Symposium, a traveling forum that, over several successful years, provided a platform for such leaders and thinkers as Grady Booch, Dave Thomas, and Rebecca Wirfs-Brock.

Skeptics and holdouts remain, as they always will, but the revolution is largely over; object-orientation has become the dominant approach to software design and development. Every revolution seems to generate its own orthodoxy, however, and object-orientation is no exception. The revolutionary guards of the new paradigm became quick to condemn anything tainted with traces of the discarded and discredited paradigm of procedural programming, and that included use cases. Now that they are ubiquitous, it seems hard to believe that use cases were ever considered heretical (Lockwood and Constantine 1993), but many among the old and new converts to the object paradigm condemned them as counterrevolutionary. Both revolution and counterrevolution eventually succumbed to pragmatics, however, and most object-oriented methods, including the much touted Unified Process (Jacobson et al. 2000; Kruchten 2000), eventually embraced some form of use case modeling.

These two central themes of modern software engineering practice, use cases and objects, are closely linked to the theme introduced in the previous section—usability. Both objects and use cases have been applied—sometimes with elegance, sometimes with ineptitude—to the design of user interfaces. Both have, at one time or another, been trumpeted as the answer to the usability question. Both have been misunderstood and misapplied almost as often as they have been used with success. In a series of closely related articles originally written for *Object Magazine,* this section examines that complex intersection of software objects and use cases with user interface design and software usability. The reader whose interest is piqued by this outline will find the ideas developed more fully in *Software for Use* (Constantine and Lockwood 1999).

42

Objects in Your Face

Graphical user interfaces have nothing to do with usability, they have to do with graphics. After all, what's the point of having a fancy GUI if you don't use it to draw pretty pictures? And, with display performance a vanishing issue, why not animate your pretty pictures? The aim is marketing and the target is reviewers and software purchasers who look, but not too carefully, then write a rave review or order a site license. Users who care more about getting real work done are another group altogether, which is one reason you hear a lot more about user interfaces than usability, more about "user-centric" design philosophy than about supporting work, more about listening to the voice of the customer than about listening to the problems of workers.

Enter object technology. Where once everything had to be "structured" to be worthy of attention, now it must be "object-oriented." If it ain't object-oriented, it ain't up to date. If software is not built out of "objects" and "classes," then it can't possibly be any good. Objects, so the simplistic claims go, are natural and intuitive. What's more, they're politically correct—they're reusable!

Now user interfaces have become object-oriented. Or so it says on the outside of the box.

On the Face of It

Just when you thought you could rest in the knowledge that objects were securely ensconced where they belong: in class libraries of immense reusability and deep within the coded heart of robust software everywhere, just when you thought you finally understood polymorphism and genericity and persistent objects, just when object technology starts to make sense, suddenly, objects start appearing on your monitor screen. If objects are good inside the software, they must be good outside as well. If objects are good for developers, they must be good for users. Or so the advertising says.

So what does the object revolution look like when it escapes the programming language and reaches the user interface? Picture this: On the screen is a simulation of a pocket organizer, a "day-timer." Click on the "index tabs" to go to any section, click on the corner of a "page" and the page flips. My, how clever! Of course, most of the time half the screen is wasteland and you have to twist your neck to read the index tabs, first clockwise, then the other way, as text flips from side to side with the turning pages. Ah, but it looks familiar, and everyone knows that familiar metaphors make software easier to use, right? It is especially important not to notice that there is less information on the super-VGA screen than on an old 80-column DOS display, even though it is displayed now in a much smaller font. After all, it's in color, which is great if you are not among the one in twelve males who are color blind. This "personal information manager" must be good, because it is surrounded by and covered up by and interlaced with all those pretty pictures. But wait, they're not just pictures, they're objects! You can manipulate them and communicate with them and make your life wonderful with them.

Yet another personal information manager shows a picture of a rotary index file (such as a Rolodex™) on the screen. Click on the lid and it opens up to reveal little index cards with names, addresses, and phone numbers on them. Click and drag on the "knobs" on either side and the index cards flip past on the screen.

Some call this object-oriented, but other, more impolite names and descriptions can be heard among people who actually use this stuff. Not that we don't need extra flourishes of the mouse to add to the risk of repetitive motion injuries, not that we don't need that extra bit of a break from work while we ooh and ah over the cartoon cards flipping over in the middle of the screen. After all, this is an object-oriented user interface!

What is an object-oriented interface? Is it just icons, button bars, and pull-down menus, your garden variety icky-sticky GUI? Or is it point-and-click and drag-and-drop, the dogma of direct manipulation? (To be acronymically correct, we are now talking about OOI GUI WIMPs.) Maybe it's any user interface implemented in an object-oriented programming language, or perhaps just the user interface of any system written using OOP techniques, independent of the language. Perhaps it means the interface is peppered with pictures of "real-world" objects. Maybe users interact with the system by sending messages to objects. ("Document, print thyself.")

In truth, "object-oriented interface" simply means the object-oriented revolution is over. The new paradigm for thinking has succeeded so well that even marketing executives and ad copywriters have discovered objects. Objects sell!

Of course, we all know objects are better. They're better because objects are intuitive, and pictures are intuitive, and pictures are objects—or some such reasoning. But a quick look at the unlabeled icons on some popular new e-mail packages or word processors or presentation software will show just how intuitive these interfaces are. How many of those icons can be interpreted correctly at first glance? How many can be remembered from session to session? How many can be learned in less than a year of daily use? Whatever it says on the outside of the box the software came in, if it takes more than a second to figure out an icon, it ain't intuitive! If you forget which blob to click on to set columns, it ain't intuitive. If you keep selecting the wrong menu to make page headers, it ain't intuitive.

Does any of this matter? What difference can the shape of an icon make or the details of copy-by-click-and-drag? A lot. Small errors and small irritations add up, slowing down rather than speeding up work. Work is what some of us try to accomplish in our hours at the desk. Software that runs counter to the way people think about or carry out tasks means a permanent increase in errors. If the program makes the user do an extra step or think twice or reinterpret things, no matter how familiar it becomes, the user will continue to make more mistakes than the necessary minimum. These extra errors are, in truth, not human error at all, but defects in the interface, in the software.

The user interface *is* the system to the user; it is what end users see and interact with in trying to get work done. They do not see the clever use of multiple inheritance or the inspired construction of some method or the meticulous reuse of library classes. They do not see most of the stuff that software developers futz over so much. They see the user interface. Period. The user interface is more than just look-and-feel; it is how the system works, how it behaves. For users, the really important question about the interface of any piece of software is whether and how it lets them use the system to support their work.

Do clever icons and cute animations, dialogues in pictures, and buttons that talk make software any easier to use to accomplish real work? Work is behavior. It is made up of actions, steps and activities interconnected by other activities. It does not consist of objects but of operations. When it comes to accomplishing work, far more important than the objects are the objectives: what work is done, how work is done, and why work is done. When this is kept in mind by developers, better systems are possible, systems that help users work better.

Physical Fallacy

Back in the dark ages of the industry, when software engineering was still data processing, analysts and programmers learned the hard way that simply automating the old manual procedures led to bad systems, clumsy emulations instead of clever enhancements. Today we have "object-oriented" interfaces, and what has happened to the old Rolodex™? It has moved from the top of your desk to your so-called desktop! The implementers of these mindless models of manual systems miss the fact that the original Rolodex™ was itself a technological breakthrough, substantially departing from the clumsier technology of loose index cards, which, in turn, were a significant advancement over bound ledger books. A Rolodex™ or DayTimer™ or DayRunner™ that can be empowering when you can hold it in your hand becomes merely awkward and annoying when it is simulated on the screen.

The problem is that object technology is handicapped by some naïve mythology. Object technology guru Ivar Jacobson has noted that naïve object models lead to software that is not robust in the face of changing requirements and varied uses. Naïve object models are based on simplistically searching the application environment for "real-world" entities, then loading all behavior onto object classes based on these entities. The practice of attaching all behavior to buttons and icons based on real-world entities is equally naïve and leads to less robust interfaces.

Sound software architectures include many components, whether object classes or functional modules, that arise from the needs of the software, that are part of the solution more than part of the problem. These essential components must be created, not just discovered lying about the room in some silly "object game." Developing good internal architecture—or good interface architecture—requires the software engineer as a thinking problem solver, not as a playful painter of representational reality. Instead of naïvely allocating actions to simple stand-ins for physical pieces, good design distributes behavior and responsibilities in software components based on sound software engineering principles that keep related behavior together and leave objects uncoupled from each other.

Everyone who understands object technology knows that software objects are not real-world objects and do not behave the same. The **Patient** object in a hospital information system may legitimately be expected to know its diagnosis and the status of payment from its **Insurer**, but we do not expect it to respond to a "kneetap" message by jerking some software "leg." Objects, despite what the gaily clad gurus of object naïveté might tell you, are not "real," they are abstractions—abstractions in the minds of analysts, designers, and programmers—no more a part of the "natural" world than any of the other abstractions we humans invent to make it through the workday.

There is a real connection between object technology and good user interface design, but it is subtle and somewhat indirect. In better supporting encapsulation and information hiding, objects enable more rational and effective partitionings of the total problem into subproblems. Sound object-oriented software architecture makes it easier to keep the implementation of the user interface and the implementation of the underlying functionality of an application distinct but interrelated. Sound object-oriented software engineering subdivides object classes representing and supporting different facets of the problem (Jacobson et al. 1992). Interface objects, which encapsulate interactive behaviors with the characteristics and features of external interfaces, can be kept distinct from domain objects that encapsulate data and behavior associated with the concepts and constructs of the application domain, and from control objects that encompass coordination and communication spanning multiple objects.

To the extent that objects are an enabling technology for more effective and extensive reuse, object orientation can contribute to better user interfaces because consistent reuse builds consistent user interfaces. Consistent user interfaces are more usable because there are fewer distinct things users have to learn and remember to make effective use of them. Consistency allows users to reuse skills and procedures learned for one purpose on other parts of an interface or on other systems. Setting local text attributes from a tool bar, for example, should not be significantly different from setting text attributes as the global defaults for an entire document. However desirable it may be, consistency can be hard to achieve when every feature and facet of a user interface is separately conceived and constructed. It is substantially easier to build consistent user interfaces from standardized class libraries and project repositories of reusable object classes.

Today's short-lived "wisdom" in human–computer interaction is that good user interfaces consist of explorable collections of familiar objects. Far more important than free-form explorability is that the user interface be well organized in ways that support real work. It has to reflect the conceptual and intrinsic organization of the work, not the physical artifacts of its current incarnation. This means thinking about what users are really trying to do and what will make it easier. It means keeping simple things simple. Locating the telephone number of a colleague should not involve repeated rotations of a simulated on-screen knob. Correcting a mistake should not trigger an on-screen conflagration as a simulated wastebasket bursts into flame.

Good object interfaces are simply good user interfaces, interfaces that support work and leave people in charge. They take over things that computers do better and let humans continue to do what humans are good at. Software engineers can do better than copy the simple-minded simulacrums of today's crummy software. A typewriter is not merely a mechanical pencil. An honest-to-goodness personal information manager is not a pocket appointment book displayed on a monitor screen.

The question now for software developers and user interface designers is whether object-oriented software will be more a matter of object interfaces or objects in your face!

Revised from *Object Magazine*, July 1993.

43

Getting the Message

What does an object look like? Who uses it, and how do they use it? What makes it useful?

In one sense, users and the user interfaces they face have been the raison d'être of object technology. It was to solve problems in graphical presentation and in user interaction with what were then called cathode ray displays that Ivan Sutherland first devised many of the core concepts in object-oriented programming. Indeed, an academic colleague of mine once remarked that nearly everything in modern object technology can be found in Sutherland's 1963 thesis on Sketchpad (See Sutherland 1963).

Since those primeval days, the literature of object orientation has grown to elephantine proportions, yet what is said of users and user interfaces remains hardly more than a hair on the hide of the object-oriented corpus. We flaunt our fabled seamless development and weave its fabric from the vocabulary of applications and usage, yet our methods make little more than mention of how to understand users and their language or how to teach our systems to speak it.

Where's the User?

While teaching at the University of Technology in Sydney, Australia, I analyzed some of the most popular and successful texts on object-oriented analysis and design. It was a very scientific sample: I checked every book on the subject in my office, then walked down the hall and went through Professor Brian Henderson-Sellers's bookshelves. Not surprisingly, we owned a lot of the same books, but between us we had 15 different recent texts on object-oriented development, including nearly all of the most widely used and referenced. Out of nearly 6,000 pages in total, a mere 161 pages discussed any aspect of users, user requirements, usability, or user interfaces, and nearly three-quarters of these were in just three books. More than half of the books devoted three or fewer pages to any subject connected with users and use. A full third did not even have any relevant index citations, and one book, while devoting a whole page to the topic of software usefulness, did not bother to index it. Perhaps the situation is changing, as several books attest, including *Designing Object-Oriented User Interfaces* (Collins 1995) and *Object Modeling and User Interface Design* (van Harmelen 2000). Not a moment too soon or a page too many, we might conclude.

To many who use objects in their development work, it is still unclear just what it is that object technology might bring to the user interface and offer to users. After all, object technology is really the technology under the hood, the technology of implementation, not the technology of interaction. Like the rest of software engineering, the evolution of object orientation has been largely directed toward improving this machinery under the hood, with barely a nod to the niceties of whether the hood release might be located somewhere that the driver can reach.

In this oversight, we need not feel too much shame. We have mirrored the histories of many new technologies, which are often dominated in the beginning by daunting challenges of implementation and performance, only later affording the luxury of close attention to external detail. Such was the case in early automobile design, where building reliable engines and solving the problems of power transmission took legitimate precedence over comfortable seats or easy controls. That changed, of course, and perhaps it is time that object technology consider the comfort and convenience of users.

For the most part, users don't care what is under the hood of the systems they use. Don Norman, usability guru and champion for a human perspective on the use of technology, says simply that, to the user, the user interface is the system (Norman 1988). There are exceptions. The technology under the hood becomes important to the user under special circumstances. It becomes important if the car can't accelerate enough to pass a truck safely or the compiler can't churn out efficient code. It matters if the engine has to be repaired or retuned every 5,000 kilometers or if Windows has to be rebooted every few hours because of memory leaks in the office presentation package.

User interfaces are about behavior as well as about appearance. If a particular object-oriented visual development tool imposes a big enough performance hit, then the technology under the hood can protrude through the dashboard. Slow responses to queries and snail-paced scrolling through data can become as much features of the user interface as are the icons on the tool bar.

As the literature and rhetoric of object technology has grown, many have spoken or written in passing about object-oriented user interfaces. Few have tackled the more tantalizing task of saying just what such interfaces might be and how they might be useful.

From GUI to OOUI

What is an OOUI besides another double-oh acronym? Is there such a thing as a truly object-oriented user interface and would any self-respecting person want to use one? If it is nothing more than a GUI with direct manipulation of visual objects, OO adds nothing to the UI mix.

One of the persistent problems in the OO world becomes particularly vexing when it comes to talking about user interfaces. This problem is the distinction, or more often the lack thereof, between objects in software or in software models and objects in the quotidian sense, that is, in the external physical world, the world so often cavalierly called "the real world." Many an object-technology novice has been seduced into thinking that all you have to do for object success is find the objects in the real world, stitch up some code for the classes to which they belong, and ship your software. What could be more seamless? As Ivar Jacobson and other methodologists have persuasively pointed out, many of the most important objects in well-designed software systems do not correspond in any simple fashion to real-world or domain objects.

The quotidian and technical meanings of "object" continue to be casually conflated and confused. In everyday terms, all user interfaces incorporate objects for users to manipulate. That some objects are monochrome characters manipulated through keyboard commands does not make them less worthy of the name.

In his book on the subject, Dave Collins (1995) offered a "definition" of OOUI based on three characteristics: (1) users perceive and act on objects, (2) users classify objects based on how they behave, and (3) all the interface objects fit together into a coherent overall conceptual model. Sounds good, but the first part is about users, not user interfaces. It can be argued that object perception is hard-coded in the human brain if we are speaking of ordinary objects and is a phenomenon true only of software developers if we are speak-

ing of software objects. The second part, concerning classification, is also
about users and not interfaces. It is almost certainly not true of everybody or
even of any one person in all circumstances. People classify ordinary objects
in terms of many features and factors other than behavior. You might note that
all politicians act pretty much alike but that a friend of yours looks like Bill
Clinton, for example. As to the third putative property of an OOUI, a coherent
model is merely a characteristic of well-organized user interfaces of any
stripe: good interfaces hang together and make sense as a whole.

Another view of OOUIs might be that they are interfaces that surface the
constructs and structure of the object-oriented paradigm, presenting users with
objects and class hierarchies, methods and messages as a medium of exchange
for interaction with systems. This view holds some potential but also hides some
pitfalls. In the most rigorous and naïvely reactionary interpretation, users would
interact with an object-oriented interface by moving messages from object to
object, but this is not likely to be particularly natural or highly usable.

No user whose sanity has not been eroded through years of small-talk
with object-oriented compilers would ever describe what they do with a
graphical user interface as "sending messages to objects." Users do not send
messages to objects. They do things with and to those objects. Even the idiom
of so-called direct manipulation is a kind of digital misdirection. Users do not
directly manipulate anything when they move a mouse on the desk to cause a
pointer to move and a picture to change on the display. That we can learn to do
such things and accept them as reasonable is even more a tribute to the human
brain than that we can program a computer to play some part in this panto-
mime of pointers and pixels.

Surface Features

Does it ever make sense to expose any of the machinery of object technology
at the interface with end users? For the most part, when the logic and structure
of the program show at the screen, something is wrong. It reflects inside-out
design, where the interface ends up as little more than a thin and blotchy skin
over a lumpy interior. Outside-in design, by contrast, means that internal components and their external manifestations reflect user needs rather than partisan
programming.

So-called "factory objects" placed on the interface might be an example
of a useful exception. Visual components that when clicked or swiped create
new instances of a class are an interesting and under-utilized form of object-
oriented user interface technology. A "pad" of "fax cover sheets" could be
used to open a blank form ready for completion and eventual transmission.

Not everyone would find such a "document-centric" scheme the most felicitous, so it is probably worthwhile thinking through how best to provide appropriate alternatives.

Collins contrasts OOUIs with other UIs that are not object-oriented, but the straw screen he erects is the ancient command line interface. Command line interfaces put the verb (command) before the object (parameters). Sometimes it has been argued that the object-verb grammar of OOUIs is more natural and more flexible: select the picture and click the recolor tool or drag the document to the printer.

If what you want are usable user interfaces, forcing this syntax on the user in the name of object-oriented purity is not necessarily a good idea. The carpenter may start with a nail but then brings the hammer to the nail, not vice versa. In real-world tasks, objects as objects and objects as operators are not typically interchangeable. Hitting the nail with the hammer makes sense, while the reverse is absurd.

If one of the claimed strengths of object-orientation is that it maintains consistency with the language of an application domain, then surely this should apply to OOUI design. Indeed, good UI design is always consistent not only with the language of users and the domain of their work, but also consistent with the tasks within that domain that are of interest to users. This consistency is only possible if we take the time to understand what users are trying to do and how they are trying to do it.

Coming down from the abstract heights, consider a particular but representative problem: the design of interaction with a "stapling" feature in a document management system. Just as physical sheets of paper or documents can be stapled together to be handled as a unit, a stapling feature on the UI allows collections of documents to be grouped on a semipermanent basis so that they can be manipulated as a unit by the user.

In the real world, the office worker may take a stack of documents to the stapler to staple them. This corresponds to the "object-oriented" drag-and-drop idiom: click the document stack icon, drag to the stapler icon, and then release. Note that this is operationally almost identical to selecting the object by clicking, then moving the pointer to the stapler and clicking on it, with one important difference. For many users, drag-and-drop is one of the more difficult idioms to master, and they will prefer clicking on two targets in series, which is generally easier, slightly faster, and more reliable. Yet other users, contaminated by experience with command line interfaces or corrupted by years of doing real work instead of working with computers, may prefer to select or pick up the stapling tool, then click on the document stack to be stapled.

Any claim that the drag-and-drop idiom is the most natural and lifelike is further weakened by the fact that a reasonable implementation does not leave the document stack in the jaws of the stapler object any more than the printed document remains on top of the printer icon. Even MacMetaphor purists recognize opportunities for the computer to do some of the manipulation, and will happily allow dragged objects to unrealistically spring back to their original locations.

In the real world, workers have no problem mixing object-primacy and function-primacy metaphors. They take the paper to the stapler or pick up the stapler and apply it to the paper without confusion. A good user interface affords similar flexibility or goes it one better. Without ambiguity, the interface could allow all the major variants in interaction: (1) drag stack to stapler; (2) click stack, then click stapler; (3) click stapler, then click stack; or even (4) drag the stapler to the stack. A good implementation communicates these possibilities to the user. The stapler should have the right affordance, by its appearance suggesting that it can have things dropped or dragged onto it and that it will respond like a push-button to clicking. When clicked, it should appear to push in. When approached by a dragged stack, it should highlight to indicate its readiness. If you drag a printer to it, it should burp. An appropriate animation, with or without an audible crunch through the speaker, tells the user when the stapler does its job. Pick up the stapler as a tool with nothing selected and the pointer turns into an iconic "hand-held" stapler.

Is this UI approach object-oriented? The object purists would probably say no, the object evangelists would probably claim it along with anything else they think is cool and might work. You could certainly implement it in an object-oriented language or go retro and piece it together from procedures. What will matter most to your users is whether it fits with the work they are trying to do.

The choice of implementation technology may become of interest to users when it comes time to incorporate new features or to accommodate changing requirements. A robust technology that permits rapid and reliable integration of new capabilities yields more utility in the long run than one that resists changes. If by object-oriented user interfaces we simply mean ones built from communicating software objects, here may be the big payoff. Of course, to deliver on this promise, we will need to get the message, too, living up to our street rep of constructing flexible and reusable components.

Revised from *Object Magazine*, September 1996.

44

Abstract Objects

In the underground-classic science-fiction film *Dark Star*, undaunted Lt. Doolittle tries to teach phenomenology to an intelligent bomb bent on blowing itself and the ship to smithereens. The universe is an abstraction, he hastily explains, and all we can ever know of it are the abstract constructs of our own minds filtered through our limited and unreliable senses. Translation: don't jump to potentially fatal conclusions from possibly faulty constructs.

Getting down to concrete cases, object technology is built on abstractions. Classes abstract the properties of numerous instances, and abstract classes act as conceptual place holders for the organization of constructive ideas. Even instantiated software objects are insubstantial abstractions, mere ghosts in the machine, at best the body-doubles for absent actors and entities in the external world.

Sometimes, teaching those benighted procedural peasants who wander into classrooms to escape their structured strictures, we start by indicating the real instances of chairs or employees or video tapes around them. Sooner or later, though, to become oriented in the object world, they will need to learn to think in software objects and to build sound abstractions. This is not an unprecedented challenge to human learning. Before there were objects, there were abstract data types. When the modules in the machines were still just simple subroutines, decomposing concrete problems into abstract functions was at the heart of good program design. Truth be told, all of software engineering is based on abstraction and abstract models. Abstraction gives us the power to think large, to construe the unconstructed and the unconstructible, and to explore the avenues of possible programs without having to walk them all first. Abstract thinking is, developmentally speaking, a more advanced and sophisticated mode of thought that takes years for children to acquire. Some few adults perhaps never learn to cut free of concrete literalism, but it would be unseemly to name names.

Paper Abstract

Relative to the rest of our discipline, usability engineering and user interface design are the specialties that might be considered to be developmentally delayed. Or maybe these days we would have to say "abstractively challenged." Interaction designers and user interface engineers do their thinking on paper or on-screen with representations that almost invariably look pretty much like the things they are designing. They do sketches or careful drawings, mockups or prototypes. The pictures may sometimes be crude, monochromatic, and unaesthetic, but they still look like screens and forms and dialog boxes populated with menus and toolbars, pick lists and radio buttons. The truest of usability specialists and graphics designers will even draw faces on their stick figures and people their Post-it notes with penciled munchkins. They draft elaborate concrete scenarios and paper their offices with storyboards that would delight Disney Studios.

There is, it would seem, something deceptively concrete about those phosphorescent images flitting over a glass screen. Even disciplined designers who structure their code through color-coded diagrams or specify search algorithms with mathematical models will suddenly wax literal when it comes to laying out user interfaces.

The advent of elegant and powerful visual development tools, such as Borland's Delphi or IBM's Visual Age, seems to have further promoted a primitive mode of engineering and even elevated it to the level of standard practice. With these modern tools, people design user interfaces not by design but by construction. They paste together objects, manipulating real list boxes and data grids and others of the growing panoply of modern GUI widgets. Of course, real sticklers for accuracy and object-oriented purity might be quick to point out that some putatively object-oriented visual development environments are more accurately labeled instanced-based rather than object-oriented, but the best and the worst of the tools all support much the same degree of concrete reasoning with apparently real widgets. Within these tools, things stand for themselves, and that's that. A form is a form is a form.

About as abstract as most user interface designers might get is to draw up a quick sketch on paper, replete with sloppy icons and skewed scroll bars. When the users complain about readability or crack wise about the dearth of artistry among the designers, developers quickly abandon sketches for software. After all, it is faster and easier just to throw some real widgets on a form with Visual Objects or Visual Basic or Visual Age or Visual Goober. In mere minutes, a user interface can be created that actually runs. It looks and feels like the real thing because it is. And, like many a real thing in real software, it went directly from impulse to fingertips and onto the screen without passing through deliberate design.

The responsibility for this sorry state of affairs rests not entirely with the tools or their makers any more than with the practitioners who use them. Object-oriented methodologies and tools do not offer effective models to represent user interface designs in the abstract.

In order to represent the architecture of user interfaces in the abstract, we need three things. First, we need a way to represent the various contexts within which users will interact with the system without committing to whether the final realization will be a window or a screen, a form or the panel of a tabbed dialogue. Second, we need ways to represent the contents of these various interaction contexts without having to decide whether a feature is to be selected by a command button, a radio button, or a check box. Finally, we need a way to show how all the interaction contexts fit together, where you start and how you get from one to another. This rather wide territory is covered by two simple conceptual tools: the content model and the context navigation map.

The Context Concept

Work is contextual. Whether working in a warehouse or an office, in the garage or on the screen, people carry out tasks in well-defined contexts with predictable collections of tools and materials. To perform a particular task, people turn to a particular place with the appropriate tools. To paint a picture, you stand before the easel with palette and brush in hand. To whip up a late night Italian meal, you go to the kitchen, gather some tomatoes and basil and garlic, a pot for the pasta and a skillet for the sauce, a spoon to stir and a grater for the pecorino. To repair a broken chair you go elsewhere and gather different supplies and equipment. Even when the site remains the same, the context is changed to conform to the requirements of the task at hand. The dental assistant arrays a different set of tools and materials on the tray for a root canal than for a routine cleaning.

How do we represent such varied contexts for use without getting concrete? Without drawing floor plans or screen layouts, how do we show what should be gathered together and what should be separated? The interface content model is one approach. Variations on the theme may have been worked out by various people, but the immediate inspiration was a technique for capturing requirements with Post-it notes on flipchart paper (Holtzblatt and Beyer 1998).

In the content model, a sheet of paper represents a single interaction context within which one task meaningful to some user will be completed. Each thing needed from the system for the user to complete the task is represented by a Post-it slapped onto the paper. For active tools and controls, "hot" colors—pink, yellow, or orange, for example—are used, while "cool" colors, like green or blue, represent data and information or other material to be manipulated. Each Post-it is labeled with the purpose or function it serves from the perspective of the users, not with the particular widget that might eventually implement the feature. We might put a tool labeled "color changer" and material labeled "clip art image" onto a sheet representing the interaction context for "preparing slide graphics." Post-it notes are easily moved from one sheet to another or crumpled and tossed into the trash. The content model becomes a flexible medium for playing around with the content and organization of a user interface without having to draw pictures or select specific widgets. The focus is on the problem, on users and what they need to do their jobs, more than on the details of real user interface design. Even the fact that content models do not look like screen designs helps users and designers alike to keep thinking in problem-oriented terms.

Pitiful Prototype

Some people refer to such sheets of papers with colored slips on them as "low-fidelity prototypes," but thinking of them as prototypes misses the point. They are not poor prototypes or inexact interfaces; they are good abstract models of user interfaces. They make it easy to try out alternative ways to break down tasks or group features, to experiment with different architectures for the user interface.

To complete a picture of the user interface architecture, we also need an overview that represents all the interaction contexts and how the work of users might take them from context to context, something analogous to a state-transition diagram or an object communication diagram. A context navigation map is a model that represents each interaction context by a named symbol and shows the possible transitions among them with connecting arrows. The navigation map is another level of abstraction removed from the content model because it hides information, ignoring the contents of interaction contexts, that is, the tools and materials they contain.

Where is all this abstraction taking us? Just as object-oriented programmers turn shapes into classes and annotations into code, eventually we will want to see interaction contexts transformed into real screens with scroll bars and shape tools, text editors with menus, and toolbars populated with lots of "intuitive icons." Why, then, go through the intermediate steps of abstract layouts and symbolic transitions when we could just as well just drag widgets onto a Delphi form?

The advantage of using abstract models is that they are often simpler than the real thing. They make it easier to grasp the whole and see the forest for the trees. By avoiding messy and distracting detail, they allow designers to concentrate on the essentials, on the bare bones of the real problem.

User interface design is often easy; good user interface design can be devilishly difficult. It can involve complicated interactions among dozens of screens with dozens of dialogs and a gazillion details. The whole thing has to be consistent and work together and make sense to the user. It needs to be simple for the inexperienced and efficient for the expert. It needs to work the way users think.

Just as in photography, as long as you are zoomed in on a close-up, it is hard to see the landscape. Abstract models allow us to defer some of those multitudinous decisions and details while we plan the scene with an eye to the big picture: the work and the users trying to accomplish it.

Abstract models also encourage innovation. By leaving open more options, they invite us to fill in the blanks in imaginative ways. As soon as we drop a pair of scroll bars on a window, we have locked ourselves into one way of moving around on a drawing. If, instead, we label a pink Post-it with "drawing navigator," we start thinking in terms of other possibilities, perhaps a navigation window with a bird's-eye view or a cameralike pan-and-zoom mode. When the time is right, we can consider the alternatives and fill in the blanks. The longer we resist committing to an easy or a standard solution, the more likely we are to find a better way.

As the French pointillist Georges Seurat was fond of pointing out, it is the blank canvas that invites invention, not the completed portrait. Perhaps it is time that object-orientation brought the power of abstraction to the problem of interaction.

Revised from *Object Magazine*, December 1996.

45

New Media

End-users, seated before their 19-inch monitors, may have no inkling of whether or not the software in use is object-oriented. We might even argue that, unless they read the details on the box in which the software was shipped or find some buried reference in the documentation, this matter of implementation technology is hardly of interest. So long as the system runs with reasonable efficiency and supports most of what users are trying to accomplish, their basic needs are being met. If it is relatively easy to learn and to remember how to use, users are well served.

On the other hand, if the technology of objects is to make good on its promises to streamline and simplify the process of design and development, if it truly enables us to supply systems more closely suited to the needs of our users, then software that is merely "good enough" is less than what our customers can rightfully expect from us. Object-oriented software ought to become recognizable to users, not by the awkward familiarity of its interface classes or because it mentions Smalltalk or C++ implementation on the box, but by the superior capabilities it offers to users and the more effective and elegant manner of its presentation. There are no excuses for failing to bring to the user interface the power of our new-found economy of expression and our expanded abilities to reuse and refine components through object technology.

How specifically, then, should we use our fine-honed skills and our high-powered tools? What form would apt and appropriate new interfaces take? How might we go about introducing innovations in the interactions between users and our object-oriented systems?

Consistent Inconsistency

Consistency, we are told, is the touchstone of good user interfaces (see Chapter 34). Users prefer and are more comfortable with interfaces that look and act like the ones they already know. Every intended innovation, every new device or arrangement, faces an uphill climb against some sort of natural resistance. Even demonstrably better interfaces may be rejected outright by users who do not want to or are unable to learn new ways to interact with their computers. Apple Macintosh users are duly famed for their insistence on consistency and their rejection of software that exhibits "un-Mac-like" behaviors or features. Few remember that among early testers of the Macintosh OS were some who found it utterly unusable, decrying the lack of standard commands and the absence of any form of the accepted "C:>" prompt.

Innovators have an array of clever concepts on which they can draw to design user interfaces that are simultaneously original and completely familiar. Many of the constructs for composing the internal structure of object-oriented programs also have application when the attention turns to the user interface. Generalization and specialization, composition and recomposition, extension and overloading—all these can help us develop effective new interface facilities and new ways of communicating with them. Often the most successful innovations in user interfaces are not dramatic breaks from the past, but variations on established themes that combine familiar elements in inventive ways, "radical evolution" as artist-inventor Bill Buxton terms it.

The worst form of inconsistency is the familiar object that behaves bizarrely. A door knob that looks as if it would twist but which must be pushed to release a catch will bedevil anyone trying to open the door. A GUI widget that appears to be a drop-down list but which calls up a dialog box when clicked will annoy and confuse users. A display that looks to be a passive presentation of data, but which must be double-clicked as if it were a program icon to refresh the contents, might never be correctly deciphered by the casual user.

Innovations or inconsistencies can show up in various facets of the user interface: in the appearance of objects, in their behavior, or in the idioms through which we interact with them. Alan Cooper, an outspoken critic of many contemporary user interface practices, introduced the term *interaction idioms* for the idiomatic gestures and sequences by which users communicate with graphical user interfaces. Some of the commonly accepted idioms for conversing with GUI-based software are single-click to select or activate, double-click to open or launch, lasso to select a group of objects, and drag-and-drop to move objects.

The cleverest innovations are those that present new possibilities in appearance, behavior, or interaction idiom, but which require no new training to use them effectively. An "intuitable" interface is one within which users can readily guess the correct meaning and use of its elements, even those elements that they have never seen before. How readily users can make the right guesses depends on many things. Good guesses depend on familiarity, but also on clarity. They depend on how well the interface expresses itself, communicating to the user—through words and shapes and symbols and position—what the designer is trying to say about how the system can be used and how it will behave.

"Explorable" interfaces allow users to investigate what can be accomplished with a system and to try features without incurring serious consequences. Robust internal objects designed to supply reversible methods can contribute to usability because the ability to cancel or undo any action is a prime contributor to explorability. Easy navigation through nested menus or dialogs is another familiar way to support exploration.

At the heart of the object-oriented paradigm is communication through messages. Good communication with users is also the key to innovative interfaces that teach users how to use them. Psychologist and usability guru Donald Norman (1988) introduced two concepts that can help designers devise components and idioms that are new yet are still readily understandable and usable. *Constraints* are elements of the user interface that communicate limitations on actions, that prevent the user from doing things that will not work or will waste time. Dialog boxes and work areas, for instance, have boundaries. Modal dialog boxes stop the interaction until the user takes some action within the dialog. Slider controls move only in one dimension. An open window that cannot accept a dragged item will change the cursor to the slashed circle recognizable as meaning "no way." As these examples suggest, the clever use of constraints can gently steer users and channel their actions in the direction of successful operation.

Affordances are the other side of instructive interfaces. Affordances are aspects of user interfaces that invite, encourage, or reinforce certain kinds of interactions. A rectangular control shaded to look like it sticks out from the screen invites the user to click on it with the pointing device, to treat it as a push button. When it then appears to depress into the screen as a result, the affordance of pushing is reinforced. Triangles or arrows pointing upward suggest that something will move up or increase as a result of using the control, ones pointing downward suggest the opposite.

Mix-in Media

In much the same way that common internal capabilities can be combined through multiple inheritance and mix-in programming, visual components and interaction idioms can be combined to create new capabilities that are immediately recognizable and usable to users even without prompting or instruction. For example, in many applications dependent on databases or persistent objects, usage can be simplified through use of arrays of displayed items that allow editing in place, with data cells serving both for display of values and input of new values. If the editable cells in the display resemble entry fields, their potential behavior is suggested to the user. New users are likely to guess the behavior correctly and will try editing such fields in the course of exploring the interface.

Some systems go another step in combining features within such display grids, embedding a selection list within the individual cells of some columns. If only a fixed set of values are acceptable, as in a field for company department codes, direct selection by the user can lead to less typing and fewer errors. When cells that function as drop-down selection lists look no different from any other, clicking on or tabbing to them may result in seemingly bizarre and unexpected behavior from the software or can leave the user unaware of all the possibilities. The simple expedient of making such cells resemble drop-down lists or "combo boxes" makes their meaning clear and their usage apparent. A small button-like rectangle at the right end of each such cell, with a downward-pointing triangle and "push affordance," invites the user to click on the button and to expect to see a selection list drop down.

Another simple generalization and recombination involves spin boxes, common GUI widgets that allow a user to "spin" a numeric value up or down by clicking on a small up-triangle or down-triangle within the right end of an entry-and-display field. Resetting the time with strictly standard widgets would require two spin boxes, one for hours and one for minutes, which breaks up the time display into a visually awkward and unfamiliar arrangement. Alternatively, the time could be displayed in the usual HH:MM format within a conventional text box to which have been added a set of spin buttons at each end. Users immediately recognize the spin buttons to the left of the hours as controlling hours, even though this is a nonstandard arrangement within a nonstandard component.

Overloading Without Overload

Operator overloading, so dear to programmers and computational linguists, can be either useful or abusive when carried to the user interface. Some overloadings are quite reasonable and delight users, others drive them to distraction. Giving the label at the top of a display column the appearance of a control button invites the user to click on it. Popular software often interprets this action as a request to sort the data in sequence by the column whose label is clicked. The control is overloaded, in this case serving as both a passive label and as an active command button. In some contexts, such as the Windows Explorer, the overloading is taken a step further, making the label button a toggle that reverses the sort sequence when clicked a second time. Such overloading can be made more usable through further overloading that provides active feedback, although care must be taken to avoid sending conflicting messages to the user. The column sort controls should not look like drop-down selections or spin buttons, which would convey the wrong affordance. A small triangle in the label can unambiguously inform the user of both the direction of the current sort and the column on which the data is sorted. After an initial exploration, the first-time user has no difficulty understanding and using such a feature.

For another example of effective overloading, many applications include visual interface components to which data items can be dragged and dropped to initiate some particular processing. Common examples of such "drop zones" include printers and trash-can icons on the screen. In some cases, there may be sound reasons to have both a drop zone to which documents might be dragged and a related control button to trigger an operation on already selected data. Some users prefer the drag-and-drop idiom, but others find drag-and-drop tedious and difficult, preferring to select data, then click on a control. Though not universal, a convention employed in some applications is to communicate "drop affordance" by making the "drop zone" look like a shallow depression or well. "Push affordance" is, by standard practice, communicated by a protruding, convex appearance. A single "drop kick" control, consisting of a button-like protrusion in the center of a shallow well, tells the user, "Drag something here or press—your choice."

Miscuing the user can lead to errors, confusion, or unused features. At the bottom of most standard application windows is a status line with various settings displayed in what appear to be shallow wells. In some applications, certain of these wells also function as active controls, although it is never clear which because no affordance suggests their behavior. While a single click might be ignored by the control, a double-click might in some cases toggle a setting from one value to another or in other cases bring up an auxiliary dialog.

Just as there are sensible rules and patterns for effective specialization and subclassing of object classes, there are reasonable ways to extend the components and idioms of interfaces to create effective new capabilities.

Reuse of internal program components and interface classes usually promotes consistency, but familiar behavior must accompany familiar appearance if the result is not to be bewildered and irritated users. Incremental improvements that introduce modest extensions to existing components and arrangements are more likely to serve users well than radical departures from standards and conventions. Through consistent extensions, generalizations, and combinations, creative new components can be designed. Through appropriate use of affordances, constraints, and overloading, they can be made more understandable and more usable.

Revised from *Object Magazine*, March 1997.

46

Useful Cases

As if a nascent Hollywood script writer were hidden within every systems analyst and software designer, almost everyone nowadays seems to be turning into a scenarist. Variants on scenario-based design are springing up as fast as academics with time on their hands and consultants with flagging practices can crank out another article or compile and peddle another anthology. Every major object-oriented methodology, right down to the latest and most unified, has embraced scenarios or use cases or some other aptly or ineptly named sequential task model. Articles have been written, books have been printed, columns have been penned, classes have been taught, and discussions have been led until most professionals in the field can speak comfortably and knowledgeably about use cases without stammering or pausing to wonder whether or not the term is really English.

A number of pioneering practitioners have also reached the conclusion that use cases ought to be good for user interfaces (see Chapter 22). If use cases can be used to guide the design of object communication and the partitioning of methods across classes, they should be useful for designing human-computer communication and the partitioning of features among user interface contexts. The logic may be less than compelling, but there is, nonetheless, an intrinsic appeal to the idea, a sort of technological equivalent of sympathetic magic. After all, both terms have a common root word and they even rhyme. "Going places with use cases for user interfaces," could well be the slogan of the hour.

Story Bored

Of course, interaction designers and other user interface specialists have for years been using various forms of scenarios, including storyboards, the cinematically inspired visual equivalents. Look where it has gotten them. Office software suites are looking more and more like wide-screen Hollywood epics, complete with a cast of characters and their irritating comic sidekicks. (Frankly, though, I would take a road runner to an animated paper clip any day.)

Scenarios, despite the we-do-them-too claims of me-too hustlers and the creative redefinitions of battalions of boundary blurrers, are not the same as use cases, as Ivar Jacobson has always been quick to explain. Both are task models and both employ a narrative form to describe the sequence of events, but a use case is an abstraction: a single case (kind) of use. A scenario documents a concrete instance of interaction. It tells a literal if not always literary story (Constantine and Lockwood 2000). To write a scenario about a user interacting with a user interface, you must have a user and an interface in mind, and you need to be able to refer to that interface and its features in your narrative. This means that scenarios aren't much help when it comes to designing user interfaces, because the user interface is one of the characters in the story. You have necessarily conceived at least a partial design for the user interface before you even started writing the scenario. Scenarios are not useless—they can be helpful in building understanding of a problem or for refining interaction with an existing user interface—but scenarios are usually too concrete to offer much intellectual leverage for designing the structure and contents of brand new user interfaces (Constantine and Lockwood 1999).

Use cases have become coin of the object-oriented realm because they are useful. Having proved their worth in requirements engineering and object-oriented software engineering, they would seem to offer some potential advantages for user interface design. Use cases doggedly stick to an external, or "black-box" view of the capability supplied by a system, while scenarios, like short stories, can be written from almost any point of view. Indeed, erstwhile programmers have a tendency to view the system as the center of the universe and to write their scenarios from an inside-out perspective.

Use cases not only take an outside-in view but also step back from the literal language of scenarios to the more abstract language of variables and classes. A scenario might read, "Paula Programmer clicks on the icon on her desktop to launch the Tech-Support Wizard, is offered the option of connecting by dial-up or through the network, chooses dial-up and is connected, gets prompted for customer number and types '4477-610,' clicks on 'Problems with printing' in the displayed list of problem areas, et cetera." A use case, in contrast, might specify more generically, "User clicks on tech-support icon launching application, connects to system, types in customer number when prompted, picks from displayed problem list." We have taken a step back that takes us a step closer to the real problem faced by the user.

Unfortunately, most use cases still incorporate many implicit, unstated assumptions about the user interface of the system. In this example, the tech-support system is identified by an icon, the user has a customer number and the number must be typed in, and the problem is selected from a displayed list. Such assumptions might not seem too presumptuous, but experience teaches us that it is our unspoken and, therefore, unquestioned assumptions that are apt to hurt us most in the long run. They commit us to particular design solutions without ever having specified the problem and considered the alternatives.

Use cases of the conventional, concrete variety are a stew of implicit design solutions mixed up with statements about the problem being solved. It is often difficult to distinguish and separate the ingredients. Is the use of a customer number really part of the problem or is it merely one already assumed solution to the unspecified problem of identifying the user? To support good user interface design we really need a more abstract and purified model, somewhat like use cases but uncontaminated by presumptions about the design of the interface that is yet to be designed.

Good Goals

For these reasons, Lucy Lockwood and I developed essential use cases as a simplified, generalized, and more abstract model compared to their concrete cousins (see Chapter 22). Abstraction (as argued in Chapter 44) encourages innovation and robust design. The rationale behind essential use case modeling is to describe user tasks in and of themselves, stripped of any technological assumptions or constraints. An essential use case represents the abstract essence of something that a user may be trying to accomplish; it is cast in terms of user intentions rather than user actions. The users of the programmed tech support system, for example, intend to get help, to say who they are, and to make clear what problem or problems have been encountered.

Essential use cases not only separate the user problem from the designed solution, they separate user intentions from the system responses that support the realization of those intentions. Instead of one, free-form narration of the interaction—the story-telling approach taken in scenarios and most concrete use cases—essential use cases take the form of a structured narrative that divides the dialog into two columns: what the user wants to do and what the system should do in supporting response. These two columns are termed the *user intention model* and the *system responsibility model*, mimicking the format Rebecca Wirfs-Brock introduced for concrete use cases. For the task of using a programmed tech support system, one essential use case might be called <u>getting technical help</u> and could take this form:

```
getting technical help

  User Intention            System Responsibility

  request help              acknowledge

  identify myself           offer help

  specify problem           give answer
```

The essential version of the use case omits extraneous details of the interaction and leaves open the visual or physical form that the interface might take. Its high degree of abstraction and focus on goals invites the designer to consider alternative ways to accomplish the same ends. For example, the same essential use case just given could describe using a network-based technical support system or a voice-processing application over a telephone. Because essential use cases are generally shorter and simpler than concrete ones, they often lead to smaller systems with simpler interfaces that are easier and more efficient to use. Because they are a goal-oriented task model, they help keep the design focused on the goals and real needs of users.

The essential use cases for a given application are, as would be expected, almost invariably interrelated. We could, of course, write every essential use case narrative as a complete, self-sufficient, and independent document, but we would end up with a bigger stack of documents than necessary. We can save paper if we organize and simplify the collection of essential use cases by extracting common elements and allowing use cases to refer to each other.

Much as we use inheritance to define classes and subclasses within object-oriented programs, we can organize essential use cases into a classification hierarchy in which abstract cases serve to hold descriptions of common or shared portions of narratives and subcases carry the specialization. Similarly, we can construct complex use cases out of simpler ones through composition. One extremely powerful means for organizing and simplifying essential use cases is extension, an innovation first introduced by Jacobson (Jacobson et al. 1992). We can extract and define as separate extension cases those parts of a narrative that are optional or exceptional alternatives, thus allowing each extension case to extend any number of other use cases. For example, in our programmed tech support problem, a user in the course of enacting a use case might sometimes give up and request live support. This use case, `request-ing live help`, extends other use cases, since it represents inserted optional or exceptional interaction based on an alternative or subordinate goal of the user.

The primary purpose of essential use case modeling is to guide the developer toward a simple and robust user interface design, but essential use cases can serve other purposes over the course of the product development process. Essential use case models are an ideal medium for capturing and verifying system requirements. The short and sweet narratives of essential use cases, combined with the map defining all the interrelationships among narratives, constitute a remarkably compact and readily interpreted description of all the external capability to be supplied by a system.

Because an essential use case narrative is basically just a dialog written in two columns, both users and customers find them easy to understand without much explanation or any special training. Essential use cases become a simple and natural medium for communication between developers and their customers or users concerning the scope and requirements for a system. Later, as the system is being programmed, external test cases can be derived from essential use cases, as can acceptance test cases when it comes time for acceptance testing.

Helping Hand

Though often slighted, documentation and Help are important contributors to the usability of systems, so important that the longest chapter in *Software for Use* (Constantine and Lockwood 1999) is devoted to Help design. In fact, good documentation and well-organized, responsive Help can make a difficult system significantly easier to use, and, conversely, inadequate or badly organized Help can ruin an otherwise reasonably designed system.

Organizing documentation and on-line help by essential use cases is an innovative and effective route to improved software usability. The essential use cases for a system represent all the things that users might want to and can accomplish with the software. Each well-written essential use case is a single task that is complete and well-defined from the external user's point of view and narrated in the language of users and the application domain. Essential use cases are ideal, then, for organizing task-oriented or "how-to" help, with each case being given a separate entry and documented by a set of instructions for enacting the use case. Even the relationships within the use case map—extension, specialization, and composition—are appropriately and naturally reflected in the documentation or Help files as links or cross-references.

Essential use cases can thus support consistent requirements tracing, not only from initial analysis through user interface and internal design and testing, but right through to documentation and creation of on-line help. Sticking to the essentials—in the form of essential use cases—can help us as designers and developers give users just what they need: smaller systems with simpler user interfaces that are better documented and easier to use.

Revised from *Object Magazine,* June 1997.

47

Efficient Objects

Engineering is based on measurement. A bridge has to be long enough to span the river and strong enough to support a specified static load. It must have the structural stability to cope with maximum expected wind velocities and to remain standing after tremors of a certain magnitude. Measurement is no less important in software engineering, yet software metrics are still often regarded as an advanced or esoteric subject of interest primarily to academics seeking research grants or defense contractors meeting government paperwork quotas.

Software metrics are a matter of putting things into numbers, hence they can be based on almost anything that can be counted, rated, or ranked. The best known metrics are measures of program size or complexity. On the simple and straightforward end of the spectrum is the venerable count of code length, which has, over time, become inflated into KLOC, thousands of lines of code. On the other end of the spectrum are function points and feature points and their other elaborately institutionalized kin. The more sophisticated metrics each have their advantages and their adherents, but when all the rhetoric and research is said and done, for many purposes, just counting classes or methods can be worth almost as much as the most elaborate and theoretically informed measurement scheme.

For numerous reasons, size and complexity metrics are often the first to be considered by software project managers. What is being measured is obvious and easy to interpret. Using size and complexity metrics enables monitoring the progress of development and measuring the productivity of developers quantitatively. Supported by a good base of historical data, such metrics can make it possible to estimate development time and costs with far greater accuracy and reliability than the more popular subjective approaches, which frequently amount to little more than fabrication *ex nihilo* and multiplication by a fudge-factor.

Designer Fit

For designers, quantitative measures of design quality are potentially far more important than simple measures of code quantity. Design metrics are based on countable or measurable aspects of a design that predict significant facets of the finished product, anything of interest to developers in terms of the anticipated implementation, operation, or maintenance of the software. For example, component cohesion and intercomponent coupling, two well-known design metrics, predict how easy it will be to modify or extend a program based on a particular decomposition into interconnected pieces. First introduced in the early days of structured design (Yourdon and Constantine 1979), cohesion and coupling have since been extended into object-oriented design in the form of measures of class cohesion and interclass coupling and have been extensively researched in both their classic and object-oriented forms (Henderson-Sellers, Constantine, and Graham 1996).

By answering the basic question, "Is this design better than that?" design metrics confer a number of tangible benefits on designers and developers. They allow us to compare alternative approaches and settle conflicting claims without resorting to management fiat or Frisbees at 30 paces. They can tell us early in the development process whether or not we are on the right design track and where serious problems might lurk around the bend. They allow us to judge, as we continue to work on and refine a design through successive iterations, whether the design is changing for the better or merely changing. The right metrics in the right circumstances can tell us how good our design is in some absolute sense. Is this version comfortably close to optimal or do we still have a long way to go? Are additional trials or refinements likely to pay off significantly?

Metrics also have a strategic role to play in the business of software development. Numbers carry clout that mere words may lack, especially when the value of verbiage has been eroded by too many years of inflated claims and empty promises. Under the threat of competition, downsizing, or elimination, software and applications developers are increasingly being called on to justify their existence and to do so with hard evidence. Metrics can benchmark performance against industry standards or best practices. Metrics can document improvement over time in productivity or delivered quality. Metrics can demonstrate the competitive advantage of inside knowledge—or of outside independence. Few things speak more eloquently to the business executive than numbers. Ease of use or enhanced usability are easy to claim, but quantitative comparisons can make the claims more convincing. A 37 percent reduction in data redundancy or a 28 percent improvement in transaction throughput can be a most persuasive punch line to a pitch for a new product.

Usability is one of the most basic dimensions of software quality, yet for software usability the field of metrics has been opened only fairly recently and remains only sparsely planted. Most usability metrics have been after-the-fact measures that assess the ease or efficiency of use of completed software systems. The mainstays of usability engineering have long been laboratory and field testing, both of which require working systems or good simulations for users to use. While usability testing in the lab or in the workplace can furnish invaluable feedback to developers, the information often comes too late in the process and at too high a price. In today's world of accelerated development and time-boxed delivery, designers need quicker and easier ways to assess the quality of their user interface designs while those designs are still on paper and can be quickly and easily changed.

Numbers Game

Use cases (see also Chapters 22 and 46), which serve many purposes in object-oriented software engineering, can also be used as the basis for some powerful and practical user interface design metrics. Three such metrics—Essential Efficiency, Task Consolidation, and Task Concordance—have been devised over several years as part of a larger suite to help designers in evaluating and improving their designs. These metrics have been crafted to have a sound and straightforward basis in established principles of software usability, such as simplicity, efficient operation, visibility of features, and meaningful organization.

Use cases define the external functionality a system must supply, and an essential use case embodies the bare-bones, idealized essentials of some well-defined task that a user would want to accomplish (see Chapter 46). The narrative body for an essential use case thus describes user-system interaction reduced to its simplest, most abstract and generalized form, devoid of assumptions about or references to specific user interface components or technology. It describes an ideal in terms of the minimal interaction necessary to accomplish a given task. Any actual user interface design can be expected to take more discrete steps to complete than in the ideal interaction. The essential use case narrative thus represents a target against which to gauge the quality of any practical design.

We can turn this concept into a practical metric just by comparing the number of steps it would take a user enacting a use case through a particular user interface design to the number of user steps in the essential use case narrative. Converting the ratio of these numbers to a percentage gives us the Essential Efficiency of a design. Higher Essential Efficiency means a cleaner, simpler design through which a user can expect to carry out a task more quickly and efficiently. The metric gives us, in a sense, an absolute measure of quality: if our first design delivers an Essential Efficiency of 98 percent, for example, we know that further refinements are not going to yield much improvement.

User interface designs must organize the various visual objects into screens and dialogs; good designs organize them to suit the tasks carried out by users. As UI guru Alan Cooper puts it, screens, windows, and dialog boxes are like separate rooms (Cooper 1995). Most people would prefer to finish a task in one room, without having to go from room to room looking for needed tools or materials and doing small pieces of the work here and there along the way. Every time users are forced by software to change interaction contexts, switching screens or dealing with another dialog box, their thoughts and work-flow are interrupted. With each interruption, they are not only slowed down but also make more mistakes. Good user interface design allows each use case to be completed with few changes in the interaction context relative to the overall complexity of the use case. Because the needed data and functions are consolidated, such designs tend to be not only easier to use but also easier to learn to use in the first place.

We can devise a simple measure of efficient organization based on the number of times the user must switch contexts in the normal course of enacting a use case. Task Consolidation is basically the percent of the required (nonoptional) steps that can be completed without switching contexts. A high Task Consolidation means that all the data and functions necessary for a use case have been brought together in one place, within one interaction context within the user interface. A lower value of this metric means that users will have to switch frequently and unnecessarily from window to window or screen to screen, reducing efficiency and increasing mistakes. This metric takes into account that context changes are more acceptable for optional or exceptional subtasks and that long or complicated use cases may have to be spread over more than one screen or dialog.

Both Essential Efficiency and Task Consolidation apply to only a single use case but obviously can be extended to weighted averages for collections of use cases. Task Concordance, in contrast, directly measures the fit between an entire set of use cases and the overall organization of a complete user interface. In terms of efficient use, a good user interface architecture is one that, on average, tends to make the more common use cases easier to accomplish. Rare or exceptional use cases can justifiably be more complicated to enact without dramatically affecting the overall efficiency of using a system. In other words, were we to rank all the use cases in order of their anticipated frequency, we would want to find them similarly ordered in terms of the number of user steps to enact them. The concordance (correlation) between the ranking by expected frequency and by enacted length is, thus, another measure of the quality of the design in terms of efficient organization. It is highest when the most frequent tasks are the shortest and when the longest tasks are the rarest. The usability metric Task Concordance is expressed as a percent of agreement between the ranked frequencies and ranked lengths.

What Counts

One of the appeals of mathematics is that everyone who correctly calculates the square root of 9 gets the same answer. Unfortunately, not all software metrics behave this way. Different people doing function point analysis can end up with significantly different numbers. To get repeatable results, elaborate counting rules are needed, and analysts must be properly trained and, preferably, certified.

Counting rules are also required for usability metrics such as Essential Efficiency, Task Consolidation, and Task Concordance, but the problems are relatively simple by comparison. Uniform results require agreement on such things as what constitutes a single user step or what is an unnecessary change of context, but these are relatively modest clerical matters that can be detailed in a few pages.

In the process of calculation, these simple design metrics based on use cases provide guidance to the designer in terms of where problems in the user interface are to be found and what might be done to improve the design. These are not passive and uninformative numbers but examples of "instructive metrics," measurements that become active guides to better designs. Using such metrics, inefficient use cases are highlighted, unnecessary context changes become painfully obvious, and parts of the design that are far from optimal are easily distinguished from those that are already more than "good enough."

The three metrics described assess only selected aspects of user interface design quality, primarily those dealing with efficient use. For more comprehensive evaluation, these metrics would need to be combined with other appropriate measures into a broadly based metric suite. Although metrics are not the answer to every design problem, with the aid of well-conceived design metrics user interface design "by the numbers" can lead to orders of magnitude improvements in the usability object-oriented software.

Revised from *Object Magazine,* September 1997.

48

Coherent Objects

What makes a thing easy to understand? What makes a thing easy to use? What is it about a collection of objects, not in isolation but arrayed in some context, that makes them into a practical set of tools? Consider the interconnected objects in a piece of software or the visual objects displayed on a graphical user interface. What makes them understandable? What makes them usable?

Anyone who has ever tried to cook in someone else's kitchen is familiar with the basic issues. It takes a few minutes to figure out where things are, and still you may have to inquire after the whereabouts of the vegetable peeler or the colander. Gradually, though, as you begin to locate the various collections, a certain logic is manifest, and soon you are managing quite well.

Unless your host is particularly perverse or the kitchen has already been reduced to hopeless disarray, you can expect to open some one of the drawers and find the cutlery together. A jar on the counter may hold a collection of wooden spoons. Pots and pans are perhaps stacked together in a cupboard, with their lids arrayed on a pegboard. Or the pots are stored in a pantry with lids in place.

Having the right utensils and appliances for cooking is important, but equally important in determining the difference between the joy of cooking and the frustration is how a kitchen is laid out and how its contents are stored and arrayed.

Imagine shuffling the utensils so that measuring spoons are with saucers, paring knives with matches, and pot covers are atop cereal bowls. Store the microwave in a closet and put the refrigerator in another room. Load the sink with cans, put dishes in the refrigerator, and line up all the knives and forks along the countertop. Suddenly the best-equipped kitchen becomes all but impossible to use.

Some modern user interface designs are not far from this degree of chaos. They put paragraph and line formatting under the `Format` menu, but headers and footers are formatted through the `View` menu while page formats are found under the `File` menu. Such is the adaptability of the human brain that, with time, almost any arrangement, however chaotic, can be learned, but arrangements that make more sense will make the learning go faster and the cooking—or word processing—much easier.

Of course, like software user interfaces, kitchens can be organized in more than one way and still make sense. Most kitchen schemes mix more than one kind of logic. Some things are organized by category, some by application, and some by a other expediencies or constraints, such as the presence of a toddler. Nevertheless, although there may be great variability in personal preferences, some categories are more logical than others. Some forms of organization are conceptually elegant but maddening when it comes to real use. Most people would find a kitchen quite hard to use were it to be organized by shape—square things in drawers, round flat things in lower cabinets, round hollow things overhead, and so forth—however simple and evident its logic might be in principle.

On the other hand, some categorizations, such as objects collected based on construction material, are more reasonable and workable than one might think on first reflection. Assembling the glassware, the silver, or the china makes sense and works, in part because these are often functional as well as material collections. Another effective way to group things is to collect objects that are typically used together, such as placing in one cabinet tools for mixing and baking: mixing bowls, mixer, measuring cups, and the like. There are subtle choices. Forks are typically found with other forks, in the vicinity of other tableware, but each place setting of knife, fork, and spoon is not usually stored as a separate unit—except, perhaps, in the galley of an airliner.

The quality of a kitchen organization or the layout of a user interface depends, then, on how the collected objects relate to each other and to the tasks to be performed. Task Consolidation (see Chapter 47) is a measure of interface quality that assesses the extent to which a given design consolidates in one place those features that are used together in a common task—a single use case. Visual Coherence, which is introduced in this chapter, is a metric to evaluate how well-organized a user interface is in terms of collecting related objects and separating unrelated ones.

Sticking Together

Object orientation has long recognized the importance of good software organization. Classes, we are taught, must be well-chosen and well-defined. They must communicate among themselves in reasonable and rational ways. A robust object architecture will continue to be defensible in the face of the inevitable and inexorable onslaught of changing requirements, added refinements, and repeated repairs. It will make sense not only to its designers, but to that legion of other professionals who must someday decipher and redefine its meanings.

The everyday language we use to talk about these issues, whether in kitchens or in software, reveals in its etymological roots what the basis of sound organization is. We speak, for example, of a good design, a persuasive argument, or a usable interface as being coherent or comprehensible. Coherent groups comprise things that cohere, that "stick together." Because they stick together, they are more easily comprehended, that is, grasped, whether by the mind or by the hand.

Sound object-oriented architecture begins with sound object classes built on a strong conceptual basis, classes that assemble those methods and attributes that make sense together as a coherent whole. This principle of coherence is embodied in one of the basic measures of the quality of software designs: cohesion. Cohesion has been around for a long time. First introduced as one of the core concepts in structured design (Yourdon and Constantine 1979), cohesion has become one of the foundations of modern software engineering practice. Wrapped in various guises, including the well-known and widely debated Lack of Cohesion of Methods (LCOM) (Chidamber and Kemerer 1994; Henderson-Sellers, Constantine, and Graham 1996), it has been successfully refined and extended to apply to evaluating the quality of object-oriented designs.

What does cohesion mean and why does it matter for OO design? Cohesion is a measure of the degree of semantic or conceptual interrelatedness of the parts any programming whole comprises. It is based on the principle that putting closely related things together in one place and separating less related things makes everything easier to understand. The parts will come together into wholes that are more easily recognized and comprehended as gestalts—as integral and integrated units. The tableware is in one drawer, while serving utensils are in another, and neither is mixed with the teacups. Cohesive software object classes and the systems built from them will be simpler for software engineers to understand, whether for purposes of construction or use, reuse, or modification.

When objects are brought out to the user interface, when they present themselves to end users and respond to users' actions, the objective is similar. People will more quickly make sense of a better organized user interface that brings together related things and separates unrelated ones. They will make fewer mistakes in interpretation and commit fewer errors in the course of interaction.

Cohesion itself, at least as traditionally defined in software engineering, is not quite what is needed to evaluate the organization of visual objects on the user interface. We need to measure coherence and comprehensibility in terms of how objects appear on the user interface: their visual organization. Visual Coherence is such a design metric to measure the quality of the organization of visual objects on the user interface.

Fitting Ideas

Visual Coherence is a measure of the fit between the visual organization of objects as they appear on the user interface and the conceptual organization of the ideas those objects represent. A more coherent and comprehensible user interface results when things that are thought of together appear together and things that are not thought of together are separated.

To measure Visual Coherence in practice you need to know two things. You need to know what the semantic groupings are for the concepts represented by visual objects appearing on the user interface, and you need to identify the visual groupings on the user interface itself.

Fortunately, modern graphical user interface design practices make it fairly easy to identify the visual groupings. User interface designers put lines or rules between sections of a dialog. They draw a border around a set of option buttons or make a frame around a toolbar. They may shade the background differently in one part, or make it appear to be raised from the screen or depressed into it. Or they may do no more than leave a little extra space between one group of command buttons and another. In any case, it is usually quite easy to eyeball the user interface and draw lines around the various visual groupings.

Semantic grouping, being invisible and intangible, is a little trickier. Fortunately, a good domain object model helps. Domain classes, their methods, and their attributes define one view of the semantic organization associated with a given application. Through a simple exercise of sorting through the basic concepts embodied in an application, we can define clusters of related concepts based primarily but not exclusively on the domain class model.

Computing Visual Coherence then becomes easy. It is only necessary to look at every pair of visual components in each visual group and count the number of pairs where both visual components are associated with the same semantic cluster. Visual Coherence is just the number of pairs in which both objects are associated with the same cluster expressed as a percentage of all possible pairs. We can continue the computation recursively to take into account groups of groups and thus assess the Visual Coherence of as much of the user interface as we wish (Constantine 1996a, 1996b).

Coherent Application

Visual Coherence may seem like a grand concept in theory, but it can hardly be said to be self-evident in practice. Fortunately, it has been researched. In one series of studies (Constantine 1996a) three different versions of a quasi-standard print dialog box were painstakingly constructed. All three were superficially plausible designs using the same number of visual components and the same number of visual groups, and all were laid out to similar aesthetic standards. The differences were in the degree of Visual Coherence. One design, the "structured" version, was highly organized, with a Visual Coherence of 62 percent; another, resembling the Windows common print dialog, had an intermediate Visual Coherence of 42 percent. The biggest challenge was to come up with a plausible but conceptually chaotic design. This "disordered" version had a Visual Coherence of only 29 percent, despite its reasonable appearance on the surface of things.

Professional software developers and user interface designers in the United States and Australia were recruited to evaluate the designs. They looked at each design in terms of how easy it was to understand, to use, and to learn to use based on various task scenarios. Aside from the one or two small blips of the sort that show up in all real-world data, the results came out much as would be predicted. Designs with greater Visual Coherence were considered to be easier to understand, easier to learn to use, and easier to use in practice, as indeed they are.

Good visual organization just makes sense.

Revised from *Object Magazine*, March 1997.

Brave New Software

Introduction

You cannot not communicate. This is sometimes known as the First Law of Human Communication (Watzlawick et al. 1967). All action or inaction is a form of communication — it makes a statement — and all communication is, in some sense, in some sphere, political. From pointless prattle to significant silence, communication has an impact. Language and communication are matters of syntax, semantics, and pragmatics. It's the pragmatics of human communication that makes it unavoidably political.

Software is a form of communication. As Ed Yourdon and I said way back in the turbulent 1970s, good software is written to be read; it's a message from one programmer to another programmer — or to a future self. It is also a message from the programmer to the user, filtered through the slow and somewhat inept interpreter known as the user interface, saying something to the user about how the developer viewed and made sense of the world. The system and its user interface are the media through which the programmer's mental model is communicated to the end user. Whether the message gets through and in what form depends on many things, among which both the intent and the ability of the developer are paramount.

As communication, then, software makes a political statement and plays a political role. How software portrays people, what it permits or prohibits, where it directs or misdirects the attention — these are political messages. Because it is so ubiquitous, software may well be among the most pervasive of modern day political forces. Video games that glorify violence and bloodshed, for example, are not neutral technology, but powerful messages about what the world is about. Whether you like them or abhor them, build them or would ban them, video games that make males the heroes and females the victims are playing sexual politics.

Software developers are paid to build better systems, not build a better world, or so some would claim. Science and technology seem to offer safe haven for professionals who just want to get on with the work or have fun playing with the technology. But we are not just professionals; we are also people sharing a shrinking planet. There are no balconies for a disinterested audience, only this one vast stage, the world.

What are programs for, anyway? Who do they serve? I will try not to get too preachy on you, but there are things we ought to think about as we plan and program our brave new software. What does a product say to the public, to its users? What does it communicate to those who enter into its dialogs? Does it empower people or delimit them, ennoble or demean them? Does it enlighten or does it confuse? Does it challenge and elevate or only reflect indifference? Does it make a difference?

So many questions. Your answers will determine your final grade.

49

Arrogant Programming

Were Dante a scion of the digital age, surely he would reserve a circle of hell for the perpetrators of dastardly code. I am not referring to the virus makers and system crackers of the world, for whom hell may be far too good. No, I am thinking of the purveyors of commercial code of such self-centered demeanor that it disregards the operating system, other applications, and often the users and customers as well. These apps with attitude are written as if they were the sole resident software on a stand-alone system, operating with a sense of executive entitlement and reckless disregard for others, be they of human or program form.

I have come to think of this as arrogant programming. Arrogant programming is a species of programming practice quite apart from the many varieties of stupid or sloppy code we all so often meet. Arrogant programming is self-absorbed programming, programming with an exaggerated sense of its own importance.

I think there are at least three subspecies of arrogant programming: egocentric, lazy, and grandiose. The classic variety is ego-centric. This form of arrogant programming is mildly autistic in its relations with the world, reflecting, perhaps, the social disconnectedness of its developers. Programmers can become so absorbed, so focused on their little corner of the software universe, they forget that other programs and programmers are out there.

The lazy form of arrogant programming reflects the avoidance of hard work. It is easier to be arrogantly lazy than to address the hard problems of writing code that lives comfortably with networks or tolerates erratic input or treats users with respect. It is easier to pretend that your program stands alone and owns the machine.

Finally, there is the arrogance of grandiosity, of overly clever code written on the premise that the authors know better than users. Such programs take over control from users and usurp their options. Arrogantly clever code is actually harder to write than merely ego-centric code and much more difficult than arrogantly lazy code, but the end result is much the same. In all three variations, the product is programs that talk too loudly, that spread themselves all over disk drives, that careen all over the screen and walk all over the operating system.

Discourteous Drivers

Consider one of the industry's leading manufacturers of printers. Their hardware is among the most dependable available, powered by robust embedded programming. Alas, their print drivers are another breed. These drivers come with a warning not to install them through Windows as you would any other printer, as if to say "We're special." Special, indeed! One release of this company's setup facility replaced the Windows Print Manager with its own version without so much as a by-your-leave.

Later releases continued to insist on their own setup procedures, some of which did not even bear the standard name of Setup or Install. Once installed, the conceited code threw a quarter-screen self-portrait of the printer onto the screen every time a print job started, even though you already knew what was happening and even when you didn't want to know, such as when another computer on a peer-to-peer network started a print job on your shared printer. The flamboyantly uninformative display with its oversized bitmap interrupted your train of thought and blocked your view until you made it go away. Then you tried to pick up where you left off. So, where was I before I was so rudely interrupted? Oh, yes, writing about arrogant programming.

This sort of message box is in your face, as if the print driver were the only thing running on your system or the only thing of interest, as if what you most wanted to see was that overgrown icon reminding you what printer you bought. A dog you can train, a friend you can take aside for a quiet chat, but there is no way you could ever teach such software any manners. You could not turn it off, even if the printer sat right on your desk and you could see the data light blinking and hear the laser whining.

If this printer was connected through a switch box and it ran out of paper, the driver gave you a "printer not responding" message that could not be made to go away because the programmers never thought that you might want anything other than their printer as the one and only center of your hard-copy universe. The print driver was so self-centered that it stayed in a tight loop waiting for the printer to respond, while Windows was slowed to a crawl.

Such programming declares, "My printer, my driver, my running out of paper is so crucial and time-critical, that I have to lock up your system until this crisis is fixed." If the status from the printer could not be read, the self-absorbed little piece of software would sit there until hell froze over or you crawled your way to the Print Manager or succumbed to the primal urge to give the system the three-fingered salute. This was the scenario every time you ran out of paper—every time!

Backwards

Print drivers aren't the only offenders. With multiple gigabytes of programs and data on every laptop, my office once decided to move up to portable high-capacity tape backup. The tape drive was fine if noisy, but the driver programming was arrogant. The backup software started off by querying the tape drive through the parallel port SCSI adapter, but the program was written on the assumption that the tape drive was already connected, turned on, ready, and with a cartridge inserted. Anything else and the backup software went off into la-la land, taking the operating system with it.

Or consider one version of an application designed to couple with an external multifunction fax machine through a parallel port. The drivers would complain and give error messages if you started Windows without the fax being plugged in and turned on. If you wanted to switch to a printer, you had to delete the fax driver and exit and restart Windows before switching to the printer or else the driver would keep throwing unstoppable error messages up on the screen.

Some of my favorite candidates for that special circle in hell are those companies who are too cheap to invest in proven installation technology and who roll-their-own install programs. Systems that cavalierly alter the operating system files without permission and without creating backup copies are still all too common. One creative lab producing sound cards not only required installing its Windows drivers under MS-DOS but hogged so much memory in the process that you had to uninstall everything else from CONFIG.SYS and AUTOEXEC.BAT just to get the install to run.

Arrogant programming is not found only in drivers for peripherals. Remember the justifiable hue-and-cry a few years ago when it was learned that a major online information service provider would automatically "upgrade" your software by writing to your disk when you logged on? (Now, of course, browsers, virus zappers, and many other applications routinely do this over the Internet, suddenly turning a stable desktop into an unfamiliar territory or mysteriously degrading performance without getting your permission. LLC) And then there was the operating system that would report back contents of your disk when you signed up for their network services. It matters not that you could override the option; it was arrogance, clever arrogance, to have programmed it in the first place.

Active email that executes when you open a message is quite possibly the epitome of arrogant programming. Such egotistical code not only runs itself without waiting to be installed but, of course, it throws wide the doors to entire new ways to spread viruses and worms and Trojan horses. (This was, of course, a prescient but unheeded warning that anticipated Melissa and the Love Bug by years. LLC)

More humble code is often simpler and less ambitious. It is configurable and leaves control in the hands of users. It keeps them informed without being obnoxious about it and allows for graceful undoing of the deeds it has done. It works quietly, reliably, and cooperatively with other code.

Ah, fair Beatrice, would that you were here now to show us humility.

From *Software Development,* Volume 4, #2, February 1996.

50

Interfaces Diversified

Diversity is not merely Politically Correct; it pays. It pays in teams, where it can contribute to a creative synergy, and in the marketplace, where diversity has become yet another fuzzword for flacks and field reps to use in their pitches. Now PC products are also P.C. products, and diversity has come to the user interface.

At one conference on CHI (Computer Human Interaction) in Boston, a presenter argued for customizing user interface design to appeal to diverse ethnic groups and user communities. The solution? Different user interface designs for different "demographics." The point was made by starting with a garden-variety dialog box for setting text attributes: font, size, style, and the like. Uninspired and utilitarian design, one might say: not optimal, but not terribly bad either. Then the diversified alternatives were displayed.

Circular Reasoning

Following the elegant understatement of a so-called "European" design (maybe the font was Eurostile?) came the one for women: a circular dialog box with little round buttons and text arranged in arcs. Many women said it looked like a carrying case for birth-control pills. Or a compact. How appropriate!

It is irrelevant whether, as the designer argued, women are really more attracted to curvilinear shapes than are men. A text style dialog box is a tool. The real issue here is that the circular dialog would simply be substantially harder for anyone, female or male, to use. Text wrapped around a curve or tilted is much more difficult to read than regular horizontal text, and circular scrolling is simply screwy.

This design had been criticized, as the presenter acknowledged, ever since it first appeared in an ACM publication a year earlier. As a counterpoint, he briefly flashed on the screen a fairly conventional looking dialog box putatively designed by some female staffers. But moments later, as if to argue for the basic validity of the concept of cultural customization, a dialog box tailored for African-Americans was proudly displayed, with buttons and boxes awash amidst assorted shapes in saturated colors. To justify this motif, the following slide showed the African art work on which the layout had been based. The aesthetic appeal of the African folk art is not the issue. User preferences and usability testing aside, the text boxes and buttons in this design were almost completely lost against the colorful backdrop.

This reminds me of an attempt some years ago to introduce a line of power tools for women. The company reasoned that handywoman wannabes would go for lighter tools with smaller grips. The fact that the tools were molded in "designer colors" couldn't hurt. Unfortunately, they were also under-powered and none too sturdy. Any woman really interested in doing something herself went for the real stuff: black, ugly, and useful.

Hoosiers and Africans

The kind of accommodation to diverse users exemplified by color-splashed dialog boxes and pretty pink power tools is neither respectful nor empowering. Instead of validating and valuing genuine differences, it perpetuates silly and superficial stereotypes. It lumps real diversity under artificial and largely meaningless rubrics, creating what writer Kurt Vonnegut called a "granfalloon," a false grouping.

After all, just who is this archetypal European who prefers left-justified labels and art deco layout? Is it an Italian or a German? What aesthetics and sensibilities do the residents of Sicily share with those of Stockholm? As the ad for the newspaper says, "The European—you can't be one without it." Only in the minds of advertising executives and corporate think-tankers is there a "European culture," as opposed to provincial French or Tuscan or Danish middle class.

We make granfalloons of many things, but especially Africa, an entire continent with dozens of distinct and very different nations, yet often treated in the media as if it were a single country and Africans a single people. Under this all-subsuming head, the interesting and important differences are lost. One ad in a recent Sunday supplement even touted a cruise to "exotic ports like Rio de Janeiro, Singapore, and Africa." Indeed. The port of Africa must have one humongous harbor!

Customization to varied tastes can be done well, without stereotyping users or sacrificing usability. For example, in a competitive playoff of designs for a computer-based voicemail interface, the team from Claris showed a main dialog with user-selectable "faceplates" that changed the overall shape and appearance without altering the basic functionality or ease of use. On the other end of the playoff panel, and at the other extreme in approaches to users, was one of the biggest software vendors, exhibiting a one-size-fits-all, plain-vanilla WIMP design. Ho, hum.

Good design takes into account the real needs and characteristics of users. Consider the lowly bicycle seat. Modern touring bikes are equipped with seats that, although seldom described as comfortable by anyone with an intact nervous system, are better suited for male posterior anatomy than female. A group of women, engineers and bike enthusiasts all, have come up with an entirely new seat design fitted to the shape of female cyclists. It's black, it's homely, but it's a lot more comfortable—or so I am told.

The bottom line for software user interfaces is to make it easy for the user to make whatever custom accommodations to taste and work habits make sense to them, changes that will enhance rather than interfere with accomplishing whatever they want to do with software.

Aesthetic Apprehension

Aesthetics are an important element of user interface design but should not hinder usability. I may customize the contents and position of a tool bar, but I don't want lace edges around messages. There is, I believe, a kind of beauty in simple practicality. Shaker furniture. Snap-On socket sets. Tools that work well, that truly fit the function and the hand of the user, are beautiful in themselves. We don't have to agree on all these matters as long as the aesthetics of software is under user control.

I spend a lot of my day facing a monitor. To me, the "wallpaper" on my desktop becomes a virtual window, like the cherished kitchen window over the sink that allows you to watch the garden while you wash the dishes. Sometimes my desktop window reveals a panorama of the cascades and cataracts of Waterfall City, as realized by artist James Gurney. Or it may look out on the robust but graceful arcs of Ron Walotsky's bridges and viaducts criss-crossing an imagined city. Sometimes the golden hues of an alien sun silhouette the elegant aerial arches of Jim Burns's Aristoi. Is this interface feminine? Typically male? American? European? Intellectual? Sensual? Who knows. You won't find it in any user interface guidebook. Although the styles of these artists, masters of modern fantastic realism, are all very different, there is a common aesthetic link: me. I'm the one who pulled these bitmaps together, so that I can gaze out over far vistas as I think about the next column.

If you want to sell your interface to more people, don't stereotype and don't put your design dogma between the user and the software. Give users something that lets them customize what matters to them, whether it's how the software looks or how it works. Then get out of the way.

From *Software Development*, Volume 2, #8, August 1994.

51

Wizard Widgets

An axiom of science fiction is that any sufficiently advanced technology looks like magic to the uninitiated. Even to those on the inside, who know that it's all just floating point adds and conditional logic, computers can seem a little like black magic. Some software developers would make them seem even more magical by putting wizards and agents and active intelligence on your screen.

Like a cocktail-lounge mentalist, a software wizard asks leading questions, then jumps to conclusions. A wizard in a presentation package might ask what kind of talk you are going to be making, what the main subject and secondary themes are, who will be in the audience, and what you want to accomplish. Then the wizard picks a color scheme and a slide template, then lays out your title slide for you. Maybe it's a good choice, maybe it isn't, but at least it saves you from having to think. And as long as you don't mind having visuals that look like everyone else's corporate issue, you don't need to have good taste or know anything about layout and design.

Just Acting

Steven Weiss, software methodologist and magician, once told me, "A magician is an actor playing the part of a magician." A wizard, then, must be dumb software playing the part of an intelligent actor. Even though we all know that real magic isn't real, for some reason we're prepared to believe that artificial intelligence is real when its a simulacrum on the screen.

Even experts can be credulous about on-screen pseudo-expertise in software that simulates intelligence. I once evaluated a CASE tool that included a complex expert system to automate the conversion of an analysis model, the data flow diagram, into a design model, the module structure chart. At the time, it had been through beta testing and extensive in-house use on real projects. Not one user had ever noticed that no matter how the rules were weighted or the criteria prioritized, the system always produced the same design, a trivial mechanical transformation of the input not an intelligent design, not even a very good design. The expertise of this "intelligent" software was never questioned; its recommendations had been accepted without thought or critical evaluation.

At least wizards wait to be asked to perform their magic and otherwise stay out of the way. Not so with active agents. These next-generation TSRs sit there and watch what's going on, offering help or advice or messages from time to time. In one brave new GUI, each agent is represented by a caricature: an older woman with her gray hair in a bun is meant to be the librarian, a stern male is a resource manager, and a strange character with hat down over his eyes is supposed to be a search agent. When agents have something to say, their expression changes. They frown slightly to indicate a possible error or raise a finger and seem about to speak if they have a suggestion or message. Aside from being sexist and cast in culture-bound stereotypes, is this a good idea?

Some software vendors think that even e-mail should be active, doing things unbidden on the recipient's computer, such as launching an application or deleting itself if it lies unread. Sounds like a virus to me. I don't know about the rest of the corporate world, but I don't want my e-mail to do anything on my machine except sit there quietly until I decide what to do with it.

People anthropomorphize everything from cars to cats. Many computer users give personal names to their machines and a surprising number, including no few software developers, attribute personality to software and hardware. For some programmers this may be just a cute way of talking, but for many people it is really animism, a form of magical thinking that attributes agency and personality to nonliving and nonintelligent things. It's what we do when we don't understand or can't figure something out. We're all guilty.

My first microcomputer was, appropriately, an Exidy Sorcerer. Even with its limited RAM and low-res graphics, it could do some pretty impressive things, not all of them by design. After a full day of use it would start to drop random bits from here and there in memory. I knew the real story was that some of the RAM was marginal under thermal stress, but it sure *seemed* like the thing was getting cranky and uncooperative, like an overtired child.

If it were not for my skeptical nature and my M.I.T. background, I would even have believed the Sorcerer had a grudge against a friend of mine who would occasionally borrow it to write papers. It would be working perfectly for me, but five minutes after she sat down and started typing it would start spitting garbage onto the screen or wander off into la–la land, locked up in some remote routine or another. When I tried it again, all would be fine. I know there was a rational explanation, though we never found it, but it was hard not to believe that she and the Sorcerer just didn't get along.

Dumb Terminals

Computers do not think, of course. Even the best so-called machine intelligence is nothing more than human intelligence behind a scrim of pixels and megabytes. None of the current crop of "smart" widgets has an AIQ (Artificial Intelligence Quotient) above zero. The intelligence, if it can be whimsically called that, is faked. One usability cabalist talking about "seductive interfaces" at a recent conference said it was even possible to "simulate real intimacy" with intelligent user interfaces. It's not hard to do, he assured the audience, "You know, just like you do with your wife." His wife, maybe.

It is possible that we've already come to accept mechanical and manufactured "intimacy" as real. Letters and birthday cards and advertisements are "personalized" by machine. Most of us have received one of those photocopied advertisements with a yellow sticky-note slapped on at a casual angle: "Larry, thought you'd find this interesting, J." Everyone knows someone whose name starts with J, so we're supposed to assume this is a personal recommendation from a friend or acquaintance, when it's really just another mass-produced promotion.

Windows wizardry is a form of misdirection. Misdirection is one of the fundamental operating principles of magic, the real kind, which is to say the fake kind. If magicians point to something or wave something or talk about something, it's because they don't want you to notice something else. One of the first rules for figuring out how a trick is done is never to look where you're supposed to look. By putting faces on toolbars and creating dialog boxes that simulate intimacy, we misdirect users away from questions of what the software really ought to be doing for the them. We offer them mediocrity while calling it magic. We offer them the illusion of intelligent software, seducing them into surrendering the task of thinking to the machine. Of course, the machine isn't thinking, which means that nobody is.

Maybe software should carry warning labels likes the ones required on foodstuffs and other consumer products. "This software contains routines that pretend to be smart." Or, "Use of wizards and agents and other forms of artificial intelligence is no substitute for using your head." One modest but telling bit of research found that the more users were told about the actual logic and construction methods used in an expert system, the less likely they were to trust the software blindly. Maybe there is hope.

From *Software Development*, Volume 2, #9, September 1994.

52

Future Faces

What color is your PC? Does your laptop make a fashion statement? My road horse is a dark, boring gray, and my office machine is the usual grayish-tan color sometimes called "putty" by office furniture stores. But there is hope. A new line of multimedia PCs with built-in radio, television, and VCR—true "information appliances"—will come in various bright fashion colors. Might they clash with our other household appliances, which are mostly bone white or black anodized aluminum? Don't ask.

Long ago and far away, some slide rules came with a leather carrying case that clipped to a belt, but nobody actually wore them. That was then, what next? Wearable computers and computers as fashion accessories. That, according to the keynote speaker at a conference on computer–human interfaces, is what the bright minds that gave the world the computer for the rest of us are now fantasizing.

Soft Seduction

Everything old is new again. Remember those treacly "user-friendly" interfaces that greeted you by name and told you to have a nice day even though you made a boo-boo and entered an improper date? A few of the GUI gurus who didn't get the point are now going one better, proposing "seductive interfaces," interfaces for mass markets that present the computer as friend, as pal, as partner. But do you want your computer to be a pal, or would you rather it just helped get things done?

These fantasized interfaces do not depend on any elusive artificial intelligence, at least not the authentic article pursued by computer scientists. Seductive interfaces are a marketing ploy to make software irresistible. The friendship is feigned and the seduction is simulated by customizing the interface to the personality of the customer. One audacious designer claims the programming is straightforward, since there only four different personalities anyway and everything you need to know about a person can be gleaned from about twenty questions. The last time I looked, there were at least twenty *theories* of personality and most all of them were more complex than this.

Judging from the research reports coming out of some of our major software vendors, there may be as much interest in simplified pseudo-psychology as in learning how to make software that really helps people. People want this seductive stuff, we are told. They would rather be talked to in just the right way than be able to do more. They would rather have the software take their hand and take over. But do you really want to be seduced by a computer, especially one that fakes it?

Still wilder interface dreams await: the knowledge cape, for example, a combination opera cape and truly flexible computer all rolled into one. Simply pick the cape preloaded for the occasion—advanced object-oriented software engineering for the office, current events and repartee for a party, a database of consumer reviews for that rare venture into a shopping mall. The cape would whisper in your ear to make you an expert at whatever you wanted. It could even remind you of the name of someone you ought to know, presumably keeping track of who is there in front of you through its own optics and audio input, or perhaps through some sort of neural interface yet to be devised. (It's just details; don't bother dreamers with details.) With the knowledge cape we go from computers that fake intelligence or intimacy to computers that help people fake it. What a brave new world where charm and conversational facility will devolve on whomever can afford the most RAM or the latest downloads for their knowledge capes. But do you really want to find yourself drawn to someone whose understanding comes from floppy circuitry with a velveteen lining?

Wrist Architectures

But wait, there's more, as they say in those late-night television ads. Today's cyberpunk fashion already sports tie tacks and earrings made from surplus chips and digital widgets, but tomorrow, we are told, we will be wearing the real thing. We will have complete computers in fashionable bracelets. (For those times when a cape might seem like over-dressing, I suppose.) And the wizards of interface design are even proposing that wrist computers use infrared or short-range radio to link automatically whenever they came in close proximity—using the proper protocol and digital signature verification to establish routing and the right recipient, of course. (I suppose the miniaturized versions would be called cuff links.) When friends met and shook hands, their computers could automatically exchange messages for them, giving new meaning to the phrase "handshaking protocol." What progress! Technology in service to humanity, eliminating the need for unpleasant human activity, like casual conversation or the more dread intimacy of a tête-à-tête. Wouldn't you rather swap files with a friend than talk?

The vision expands. As technology improved, the links might be varied from close range to general broadcast. You would not actually have to listen to the boor who insists on telling everyone at a party the same stupid story of how he was once stuck in an elevator with John Scully. The account would just be downloaded to your wrist processor when you entered the room. Then your own clever software, programmed to recognize the same old stuff even when it was shoveled remotely, would promptly delete it. No need to listen or even to drag-and-drop that garbage anymore.

The same wrist wonder could couple with the resident hardware when you checked into a hotel, downloading your profile to the room, adjusting the temperature and lights to your taste, and setting the wall-sized screen to the right screen-saver wallpaper. Or it might begin presenting you with personally relevant excerpts from the *Wall Street Journal* or *Software Development* or alt.wierd, as suited your tastes. In fact, one of the more common fantasies for the coming microcomputer millennium is software to search out and screen out information from the enormous digital deluge washing over the information interstates.

I already have access to such a system. My partner scans publications ranging from the *Journal* to *DBMS* and unerringly informs me about things I find interesting, enlightening, and useful. I do the same for her in other publications. Trying to put such services into computer software raises two nearly insurmountable issues. Most of the stuff that comes under the nominal headings in which I am interested is not worth reading, and many of the most valuable items fall into novel categories I could never specify in advance. Can a computer understand you well enough to fulfill this function? Would you trust it knowing that the "understanding" was faked?

Control Return

Knowledge capes or computer bracelets, word processors that rewrite your prose or software that figures out who you are—perhaps so much of this is so far in the future that we can rest easy in the knowledge that, like predicting the halting of a Turing machine, some problems are intractable in theory or in practice even if they are easy to describe. If the giant software houses can't build a presentation package without memory leaks or an operating system that doesn't flush itself into blank-screen oblivion, do we need to worry whether they'll be able to do a credible job creating software intelligence or programmed intimacy?

Alas, in the meantime the GUI designers, like fashion designers, often seem more interested in cosmetics than capabilities. Flexible interfaces adjust to the user by customization of the inconsequential. You can choose almost any color scheme you want, but don't expect accommodation to real needs and differences in working styles.

As usability guru Ben Shneiderman reminds us, people want to be in control, but they also want a sense of accomplishment. They want to be able to control real things. At the end of the day they don't want to think about all the things their software did, but about what *they* achieved. It's up to us as developers to decide what we want to accomplish. Do we want software that makes a fashion statement or that makes a difference, user interfaces that give control to the user or ones that just do a good job of faking it?

From *Software Development*, Volume 2, #10, October 1994.

IX

Culture and Quality

Introduction

Organizational culture is so pervasive in our working lives that it seems appropriate to round out this series of essays with an exploration of the cultural landscape of software development, not only in terms of the organizational culture of individual development groups and companies but also regarding some of the broader cultural issues in our industry and profession as a whole. Section III mapped out the principal variations in the cultural themes played out in work organizations. This closing section returns to the matter of culture but as it relates to the effectiveness of the whole and its individual parts and to the quality of the end products.

"Cultured" can be a term of approbation or an indication of suspect origin, depending on whether we are speaking of people or of pearls. The culture of an organization or of an industry can work for or against it. What are some of the features of successful organizational cultures? How can working culture be changed to enhance the chances of success? A development culture that values and reinforces quality work will contribute to success. An industry or profession built on such principles as responsibility and continuous learning will enhance the value and the potential of its members.

Amidst the grander view of culture and organization, however, it may be all too easy to lose sight of the person in peopleware. And so I close with a focus on the crucial roles that individuals have to play in both the transmission and the transformation of culture. Culture is not an immutable abstraction. Culture can change, and it can be changed by individual initiative. You, too, are a vital part of the cultural landscape that is software development, both as a creature of that culture and as its shaper. Whether in the large or in the small, you can be an agent of cultural change, altering for the better the profession and the business of software development.

Think difference.

53

Culture Change

When in Sydney, do as the Sidneysiders do. Years ago, when an American golden-arched fast-food chain first lodged themselves in Sydney's Pitt Street, they served up hamburgers Aussie-style, topped with beetroot pickles. More recently, American auto makers were dismayed that Japanese consumers were buying few American cars, while Japanese makes sold well in America. Of course, the cars Japan shipped to the States put the driver on the left, to fit with a highway culture where people drive on the right side of the road. To Japan, a small island country that drives to the left of the road, Detroit was trying to sell big American cars with steering wheels on the wrong side!

The simple lesson—that successful imports have to fit with the local culture—applies also to the import of new technology, tools, and techniques into software development organizations. It doesn't matter whether you are talking about software tools, conceptual tools, management tools, or marketing tools, if it is not adapted to fit the local culture, putting it into practice will be difficult.

Risk Reduction

When it comes to anything new, business decision makers are always looking for reassurance. The motto "Lead, follow, or get out of the way" has long been popular with business leaders, but hardly anyone really wants to lead. The company that leads is likely to take a wrong turn. Or get shot down. Decision makers want to know who else has used a product or a process and how they went about it. They want success stories, preferably about someone in the same industry, maybe down the block.

Before introducing object technology, or Web-based application server architecture, or visual development environments, development managers often look for a reference model: an established plan of action that will reduce the risk, or at least a story line that will make them feel better. But it can be a mistake looking for a proven standard for technology transfer. No two corporate cultures are exactly alike. Companies in the same business, selling to the same markets, can have vastly different working cultures. What fits well and will work for one may prove an unworkable disaster for the one next door.

Attempts to introduce new development practices and technology can fail for many practical reasons. You may try the wrong programming language or have trouble getting tech support or pick a vendor who is about to go under. But you can also make all the right decisions, have the right tools and the right techniques, and still get nowhere because you didn't take into account the cultural realities of how your software development group actually works.

Company culture is many things. It's the way offices are set up and who gets the ones with the windows. It's traditions of orderly desks or mountains of paper overflowing into the halls. It's casual-dress days and Friday beer-and-pizza or power ties and quasi-compulsory monthly cocktails with canapés. However, for introducing and spreading new approaches in software development groups, certain matters of culture are especially important to factor into your strategy.

Me, Us, or Them

How does an organization know what it knows? How does it control what it does? How does it decide what to do? In each case, we are interested in the principal center or primary repository of knowledge, control, or decision making. Is it the individual, the informal group, or the formal institution?

The first question of importance is: Where do you find the software development know-how of the organization? Is it carried mostly in individual heads, is it part of the collective folklore of "how things are done around here," or is it in officially established methods and procedures? In a sense, where do practices "live" and who "owns" them? How much of the know-how can we find in company manuals and guidebooks? To learn about how software development is really done, where would you have to go? Does your company rely first, last, and foremost on what bright and skilled individuals know and do so well? What would we learn by hanging out in the cafeteria or listening to discussions in the halls? Is "best practice" defined in terms of personal best. Or is what constitutes "good programming" a part of the unwritten folklore about things that work and things that don't? Is the project-to-project learning in the individual, is it dispersed through the group, or does it get built into and institutionalized in the records and revised formal practices of the organization?

We can ask similar questions about how development is controlled, in particular how quality results are assured. Do you depend on individual good judgment and the fact that you have the very best people? Are informal group sanctions operating, with people looking over each other's shoulders or frequently checking out and comparing their code? Or does the organization have written standards with systematic checks to make sure they are followed?

It's the same for decisions about what gets done and how. If a group typically designs by consensus, a top-management edict to use Groupware Gadget G will have tough sledding. A group that is accustomed to being told what the next project will be and what technology will be used to implement it may not respond well to having the question of rapid prototyping put to a vote.

Alpha to Omega

If you don't target new technology and techniques to the right spot, adoption will be slowed and chances of success lowered. For example, one approach to moving into large-scale object-oriented software engineering might be to hire a major consulting group with their rationalized, unified Object Method for Engineering Giant Applications (OMEGA), complete with seven volumes of procedures manuals and a graded series of training classes supported by an integrated CASE tool. This could be just the ticket for a group with a history of disciplined development and shelves lined with well-thumbed standards manuals, but a flock of free-thinkers who work to their own standards will duck out of classes to cut code, leave the manuals unread, and shrug it all off as "more of that corporate crud." Their approaches, like their skills and abilities, are individualized. To reach them, you don't shove them all into one large classroom to watch a video and get quizzed by a clone instructor. Accustomed to reaching their own conclusions about what is worth learning, then picking it up on their own, they have to be persuaded one at a time, then provided with local resources for individualized learning-by-doing.

What you try to introduce should be shaped to the culture, too. Take modeling tools. Tools integrated around specific methods and imposing standardized ways of working will be more fully and effectively utilized where practices are already well institutionalized. Flexible diagramming tools or custom configured suites will be a better fit with groups whose practices center on individuals or informal group culture.

Different groups will even use the same tools differently. Groupware might be grabbed with gusto in an organization already comfortable with close-knit collaboration in design and decision making, but a group of lone developers who work pretty much in isolation may find little of interest in Lotus Notes. Among a bunch of coding cowboys, an elaborate groupware system could end up being little more than fancy email used mostly for friendly flaming.

Of course, in real organizations the culture is usually a matter of degree, with some practices and decisions centered in individuals, some in the informal group culture, and some in the official institutionalized structures. Good technology transfer strategies take into account the particular mix in a particular organization.

Beetroot pickles, anyone?

From *Software Development,* Volume 2, #12, December 1994.

Change Agents

One fish, making the right move at the right moment, can change the direction of an entire school. Often the successful introduction of a new tool or a better approach to version control in a software development group hinges on one or two key individuals who act as agents for change. Effective change agents come in many shapes. Some are into door-to-door sales. They'll grab you in the hall and regale you with the benefits of Java or convince you to use a library of GUI widgets or pitch the cause of clean-room programming to every manager they can corner. Others precipitate change by just doing something a lot better than the people around them, quietly demonstrating a way out of some current dilemma or simply showing that software can sometimes be delivered on time.

But the fast-talking sales approach can be self-defeating in some organizations, and the quiet efficiency of even the most brilliant software engineer may go completely unnoticed amidst the creative chaos within which some groups thrive. As in a lot of areas where technology bumps into people, tactics and style have to fit with the organizational culture to succeed. Different kinds of agents or styles of agentry may be required to bring about change in different organizations.

It is especially important not to confuse change agents, who actually get things happening or get others to make things happen, with activists or advocates, who may campaign loudly and visibly yet have little effect. Activists for technical change tend to mimic the standard tactics of run-of-the-mill political activists. They do the obvious and visible things: sending email blitzes, circulating questionnaires, starting newsletters, or organizing special interest groups. Such tactics draw attention and may increase awareness, but often they have little to do with whether or not an organization actually changes tack and begins to achieve substantial levels of code reuse, for example. Getting smart about whom you engage to advance your technical cause or how you suit your style to fit the cause could be as important as which programming language you promote or what software platform you support.

Mandating Managers

In a company whose organizational culture is shaped like an Egyptian pyramid, executive sponsorship is probably the master key to successful change. Without a management commitment from high enough on the pyramid, efforts to introduce new practices tend to fizzle or become blocked by too many organizational barriers.

A simple mandate from on high is not enough. Management sponsorship means personal and organizational commitment, active promotion, and practical support in the form of allocating appropriate and sufficient resources. A management sponsor not only can authorize action and approve funding, but also lends the official weight of the organization to the side of change. This alone will not make developers learn and practice effective visual development, but as long as the official weight is wholly with the status quo, nothing is likely to change. At least in companies that are based on a hierarchy of authority, well-placed management sponsors are the key players in most successful technology transitions. They may be aided and abetted by a host of working agents, but executive sponsorship enables the process.

Capable Colleagues

Not all companies have an organization shaped like the Transamerica Building. In today's flattened hierarchies—where many development groups are open, informal, and highly collaborative—corporate mandates won't cut it. Used to working things out on their own in close-knit project teams, developers in such groups will want to plan and carry out improvement initiatives for themselves. The most effective agents of change in these settings are often highly respected colleagues who may function as informal internal consultants to people in the same or other project teams. They wield influence through their skills and expertise more than through their position or power, acting more as facilitators for discussions and catalysts for strategic redirection than as official sponsors or leaders.

Vital Visionaries

Visionary leaders have played highly visible and important roles in numerous companies in the software industry, but not all groups respond to the charismatic appeal of such leaders. In some companies, though, the dominant guiding force is a shared vision that keeps people lined up and pointing in the same direction. Members of these software development teams, knowing just what is needed to turn vision into reality, are able to work with smooth, parallel efficiency.

Where alignment with a shared vision is an important factor in everyday operation, the most effective change agents are likely to be visionaries themselves, missionaries who can draw the coding crowd into sharing their visions of a better method or of defect-free software. They are technical evangelists who stir up personal commitment to a new mission or a new image of the organization. Once committed and aligned with this new vision, the working developers themselves effect the transition—in the same quietly efficient way that they build software.

Fashion Leaders

In the software field, a noisy technical brouhaha is probably more common than a monastic team of developers quietly coding in their private cells. In very loosely run groups of innovation-oriented individualists, the technical charisma of a few focal developers can be an important factor in bringing new practices into the firm and in modeling them for others. Every company has some technical superstars who tend to be first into the ring with any new technology. Whether these technical fashion leaders are effective as change agents depends largely on the kind of organization in which they work. Where creative chaos reigns, informal leadership based on recognition by peers as the best and the brightest among them is often far more effective than front-office direction or even the best of training programs. If you are surrounded by ruggedly independent coding cowboys and cowgirls, yet want to see the spread of a new development practice or technology, look around to see who leads the technical fashions. To whom do others look for trends in tools and techniques? These are the natural leaders you want to recruit to your cause as agents of change.

Secret Agents

As in the world of politics and intrigue, not all effective agents operate in the open forum or the visible arena. Covert agents may work behind the scenes to advance a favored cause or undermine a corrupt regime. Agents of technical change who lack a mandate or legitimate sponsorship can still make a difference, but they may have to introduce better software practices on the sly or on the cheap. For the guerrilla developer in a corporate setting, this is one of those high-risk, high-payoff moves. You need to really believe in that new language or object technology or event-partitioned architecture or whatever it is you are pitching, because if you get found out too early in your technical revolution, or if you and the technology fail to deliver the goods, you may find yourself joining the ranks of the involuntary consultants.

From *Software Development,* Volume 3, #1, January 1995.

55

Embedded with the Best

Morning scenario: the digital clock radio kicks in at 6:30 a.m. and you drag yourself downstairs, making a beeline for the coffeemaker. You dump the dregs into a mug, then nuke it in the microwave for a minute while you hunt down the elusive remote for your TV-VCR. While swigging down the java, you catch a few minutes of CNN Headline News, then head for the car and the challenges of the morning commute. By the time you reach the office and flick the power switch on your desktop machine, you have probably already made use of a dozen or more computers loaded with millions of lines of code.

The unrecognized heroes of software development don't write for either mainframes or PCs or workstations. Their software will not be found shrink-wrapped on the shelves at Staples, CompUSA, or Dick Smith. Still, you use their code every day.

Abundant Chips

Of course, I'm talking about ubiquitous computing, the processors and pro-grams buried inside our clock radios, our microwaves, our telephones, and our tape recorders where they faithfully listen for our touch pad whims and wishes, translating them into infrared pulses or control levels for some device or anoth-er. If your car is a typical late model, it alone could have a dozen programmed processors in it, and that's discounting the cell phone you may have used on the way to work. A touch on the "TALK" button and you link through a long chain of concealed computers, starting with the one in the cellular tower itself and ending with one inside the digital branch exchange at your client's office. This is the world of embedded system applications, where computers hide away in various guises and seem to be doing everything but computing. Embedded apps sometimes make the rest of the world of software development look like the bush leagues by comparison.

The computers on which embedded applications run may themselves seem small and insignificant, hidden away inside CD players or children's toys, but the programming is not. There can be millions of lines of C embedded in a color laser copier, thousands of Smalltalk classes awaiting instantiation within a lab oscilloscope. In most of these applications, the demands for precision, accuracy, repeatability, and reliability are substantial. A bug can make its presence known in the most visible, embarrassing, and even dangerous ways when the programming controls an x-ray machine or an industrial robot or a car. Add to this the need for real-time performance that is characteristic of many areas of application, and the bar is raised yet another notch.

Despite these challenges, or even because of them, an awful lot of embedded code is impressively good. One company delivered an embedded system in a high-end office product with over one-and-a-half million lines of code and only four defects. Yes, that's right, over the two-year-plus product life only four uncorrected bugs were discovered. Why and how do they do it?

Upgrade Costs

The why is pretty easy to answer. At Hewlett-Packard, for example, a single bug in the embedded software for one of their printers could hurt big-time. If not discovered until after product release, a bug serious enough to require a field upgrade to ROMs would cost more to fix than all the profit over the entire life of the complete product line. That is a strong incentive to get it right the first time around. So they do. No really big program is perfect, but some embedded-systems programmers turn out large programs as close to flawless as we are ever likely to achieve. Anything less is just too costly.

Maybe this is part of the problem among the Microsofts and IBMs of the world: there is not enough of an incentive to get it right, especially as long as customers are willing to put up with buggy and baroque software. The software vendors can always slip their corrections into streamed releases or just send out a version 6.0a maintenance release for the cost of the CD-ROMs or put it on the Web for you to download yourself.

So how do software's hidden heroes do so well? Understand, they don't all do so well all the time. Embedded programming is peppered with its own horror stories of legacy code with layers and layers of undocumented patches and quick fixes. Modems have disconnected when passing data that happened to contain a sequence used for debugging but inadvertently left in the shipping version. There are copiers that lose track of what they are doing and have to be temporarily lobotomized with a swift kick to the power cord. Even in military avionics, missiles have timed out in midflight, and badly programmed navigational clocks have had cumulative errors. And we won't even start talking about user interfaces for embedded systems, some of which are among the most execrable and unusable on the planet. Still, compared to the shoddy stuff that represents the norm on PCs, workstations, and mainframes, embedded software looks as solid as silicon.

Some of it is built well through brute force, by dint of individual discipline that would impress even the most military-minded standards maniac. Some companies, especially in telecommunications and defense applications, have made effective use of "clean room" coding techniques that require meticulous assembly of code and prohibit programmers from touching it once it is written. Others achieve their magic by assembling systems out of great heaps of reusable components. Some of the most sophisticated and disciplined uses of object-orientation have been in embedded applications, where C++ dominates but Smalltalk has also made an impressive showing.

Down and Dirty

The challenges of embedded real-time applications seem to have attracted a lot of top programmers whose personal and professional orientations fit with an unusual programming culture. The cultural context of embedded applications mixes attention to low-level details with the need for high-level discipline. Embedded-systems programming can get real dirty, dragging the programmer down into the muck of loading registers, waiting for a shift in line levels, or rotating and masking bits. At the same time, all this bit-fiddling must be near-perfect, fit into severely limited memory, and be speedy enough not to put gaps in a display or jiggles in a missile track.

The programmers of such code tend to work carefully and methodically to reduce the number of mistakes they make in the first place. In the parlance of software quality, they have a low "injection rate" for software defects. The cheapest bugs to find and fix are, of course, the ones you don't let get into the code. A widely used tactic among embedded-systems developers is to move defect detection upstream in the life cycle, catching bugs as early as possible while they are easier to see and simpler to correct. Thorough design and code inspections are conducted repeatedly to reduce delivered defects. This practice is far cheaper and more effective than testing and debugging at the tail end. In "unembedded" software development, the popular approach to defect removal seems to be based on 400,000 beta sites doing the testing and debugging for you. In terms of total cost to the community, it is hard to imagine a more inefficient or expensive scheme. On the other hand, it is cheap for the vendors so long as customers rush to pay for the privilege of doing the vendors' work for them and so long as there is so little incentive to get it right before shipping.

Some of the success of embedded-systems programming is a matter of culture and context, but I have also become convinced that some is attributable to attitude and training. For years, I have led workshops on high-performance teamwork and taught designing for usability at the twice-annual Embedded Systems Conference. When I have remarked on how quickly teams of embedded-systems programmers come up with really good solutions to class problems, almost invariably someone suggests that it is because most of them are engineers.

There is something about the engineering mindset of pragmatism, problem-solving, and professional polish that definitely contributes to good programming. We could all gain from acting a little more like engineers. The world of embedded-systems programming has established a benchmark of best practice, demonstrating that really solid, nearly bug-free code is possible. Let us hope the rest of us can rise to the challenge.

From *Software Development,* Volume 3, #7, July 1995.

56

Columns from an Italian Restaurant

The cultural heart of Tuscany is a city of great art and great food: Florence to Americans, Firenze to Italians. Columns are ubiquitous in the architecture of Firenze. For this column, I took my inspiration from a restaurant, a model of best practices from which I believe we all could learn.

Ristorante Alle Murate is arguably the best restaurant in Tuscany. I say this fully cognizant of the history of hyperbole in restaurant writing. The truth is, as I sipped and savored my way through one particularly unforgettable evening there, I realized there was nothing I could improve. No herb could be added, no pinch of salt left out. Not even a garnish could be moved a hair's breadth to improve the artistry of the presentation.

This is a rare experience for me. Like most people in software, I cannot look at a screen without spotting something the programmers overlooked or should have done differently. As an itinerant consultant, I also spend all too many evenings in restaurants, where my own instincts as a chef are always surfacing. I am forever thinking how I would do things differently were it my restaurant. Not at this *ristorante*. It is complete and perfect in itself. It could not be made better without being made into something else, something that it is not and was not intended to be.

Three things make this place perfect, and in these are the lessons for software development. First, there is flawless attention to detail, second, near seamless teamwork, and third, the needs of the customer come first.

Last Details

In software, where the complexity and subtlety of interaction cries out for it, attention to detail seems rare. On countless products, small overlooked details ruin an otherwise sound design. An important dialog box is inconsistent with the rest of the interface, or the absence of spin-buttons for color parameters make it hard to select a needed shade, or every part of a document can be customized by the user save one. At times, even the design of commercial products seems haphazard. Such failures are not due to the wrong programming language or an inadequate methodology; they are failures of attention. They can only be overcome by meticulous—even obsessive—attention to detail.

At Ristorante Alle Murate, attention to detail is pervasive to the point of being almost unnoticeable. Each course is a miniature work of art. A fork left on a plate is almost instantly replaced. Each beverage, each wine, has a different and distinctive glass. Yet the result is neither fussy nor pretentious, only that every detail has been considered.

Working Teams

I have often written about teamwork and am always delighted by seeing good teamwork in practice, whether on a sound crew at a concert or among the sales staff in a department store. In restaurants, I am more accustomed to noticing the lack of it. Institutionalized practices, such as that of assigning waiters to particular sections or tables that are their exclusive territories, can even interfere with good teamwork. In software development, too, territorial claims can limit teamwork. Where one person is the sole legitimate expert on system architecture or where a subsystem becomes the exclusive and inviolable property of one programmer, collaborative teamwork becomes more problematic.

In this restaurant it is different. The room is small and everyone seems to be responsible for everything. Umberto Montana may be at the helm, but all the staff act as if the restaurant were theirs.

As in the best technical teams, there are specialists, but specialization does not prevent collaboration or flexibility. Sonia, for example, is a virtuoso with wine, deftly decorking and decanting with a poetry of precision. The robust Tuscan reds must "breathe" before they can be fully enjoyed, so she starts with just a splash, deftly swirling it into a ruby glaze coating the inside of the glass. Then she adds more and swirls more, always spinning the wine within a millimeter of the edge. However, if Sonia is busy—explaining the subtleties of the fish course to us, for example—someone else just steps in to do the honors at another table.

Some of Italy's greatest artists, Michelangelo among them, had a talent for fostering teamwork among artists and artisans. Umberto may be heir to that particular genius. He is the model of "management-by-walking-around," roaming the room, chatting with customers, gently overseeing the process and deftly filling in where needed. Indeed, the entire staff seems to monitor everything, drawing attention to the glass in need of filling or simply doing it themselves.

This ambulatory monitoring not only supports attention to detail but impresses me as an economical mode of collective management that is attentive and yet unobtrusive. Perhaps we could apply it to software development, depending less on sporadic and infrequent structured walk-throughs and more on continuous and mutual review of our ongoing work.

Even the customer is part of this team. Ordering resembles negotiating requirements definitions. What kind of a wine will you be having? Perhaps with that dish for your first course, you would enjoy the rolled lamb more for *il secondo?* Umberto may even, on the spot, invent the perfect dish to suit your tastes and accompany a particular wine. He goes over to the window into the small kitchen and negotiates with the chef. No, she cannot make that tonight, but what about the smoked duck? He returns to the table with a new suggestion.

In Need

Perhaps the most sophisticated and subtle of the charms that makes this restaurant perfect is the way it gives its patrons not what they want but what they need. In an era when feature-bloated software is driven by 900-number customer "wish lines," we could use more understanding of this distinction.

A truly fine Italian meal requires good wine, in fact, more than one good wine. The wine that is perfect with the pasta or the fish course will be lost in the intensity of duck stuffed with *spinacci* and orange rind. *Dolci,* the dessert course, will require a glass of Malvasia spumante or perhaps Brachetto. Not all diners might appreciate this as a necessity for the full enjoyment of their experience, however, and few are likely to order more than one wine with dinner.

So unless you decline, a glass of a pleasantly crisp white is poured immediately on your arrival, to help you into the spirit of the evening and as accompaniment for the antipasti to come. When it is time for *dolci,* another complimentary wine appears.

In software, a well-designed user interface does not present to users everything they could ever wish for, but simply all that is needed for the task at hand. A good design is a subtle compromise between what customers believe they want and what will actually work for them. This is precisely the distinction between modern usage-centered design approaches (Constantine and Lockwood 1999) and the user-centric methods they supercede.

The menu in this particular *ristorante* is simplicity itself. You choose for yourself from a modest selection of outstanding dishes, or you take one of the fixed-price options, giving yourself over completely to the experience and trusting Umberto and his staff to assemble a series of surprises and delights.

The trust, in this instance, is well-placed. With subtle sophistication, Umberto will steer patrons away from wines they might not enjoy or combinations of dishes that might jar the palate. Like the best of consultants, he quickly learns who his clients are. When we ask for a wine suggestion, Umberto remembers from a previous visit that we like powerful reds and chooses a wonderfully "fat" wine from a small holding in the north.

Perfection, of course, is not for everyone. Seated near us on one occasion was an American couple who might have been from the well-heeled section of almost any major city. A well-matched pair, she was determined not to enjoy herself and he was determined to be in control. He rejected Umberto's offer of help in choosing among the thousands of bottles in the wine cellar and, instead, heavy-handedly insisted on seeing the wine list. Neither would accept assistance in selecting from the menu. From the looks on their faces throughout the meal and as they left, they had succeeding in their respective objectives of staying in control and not enjoying themselves.

Umberto says that he sees perhaps one such couple a week, but never a second time. We, on the other hand, can't wait until next time we are in Firenze.

From *Software Development,* Volume 3, #8, August 1995.

57

Mentored Out

Mentoring. In the post-modern melange of language that seeks to verbify every noun and leave no word of action without it's nominalization, "to mentor" is a very cool activity indeed. A mentor is, of course, a teacher. But more than just a teacher, a mentor is also a guide and master—part career counselor, part coach, part colleague. In some areas of software development, coaching has become almost as popular as mentoring, even though coaching is a real word and sounds far less sophisticated. Just listen in on the conversation among a group of consultants at a conference and you are likely to hear some announce that they no longer do consulting. Instead, they provide clients with a "mentoring and coaching process." Indeed!

According to industry pundit Ed Yourdon, mentoring has become a hallmark of the Microsoft culture and the cornerstone of its approach to improving software. New hires are assigned a mentor who reviews every line of their code. And the "mentee" (but, of course!) reads every line of code the mentor writes. Here, we are told, is living evidence of a commitment to quality and improved processes at the great ranch at Redmond.

Nellie Knew

Having come neither to praise nor to bury Caesar, I'll stay out of the ever-popular deconstruction of Microsoft and instead turn to a closer look at what mentoring is and is not. First, it is not new. Despite its neologistic cloak as part of the total quality and process improvement movement, mentoring is old stuff. Mentoring is the master-apprentice model without the sting of indentured servitude. It is a dressed up version of what old-timers knew as the "Sit-by-Nellie" approach to software engineering. Ed Yourdon and I even wrote about this humble technique in the first edition of Structured Design (Yourdon and Constantine 1974). The new programmer is told, "Sit by Nellie. She knows how to program." It was, as we explained then, a symptom of a problem. Since no one knew exactly what Nellie did that made her so good, and even Nellie herself could not exactly put it into words, the best way to learn was to sit beside her and watch her code.

Apprenticeship is a better training model for the craft of programming than for the discipline of software engineering. A discipline requires that there be people who can do it, that there be people who know what it is that those who can are doing when they do it, and people who know how to teach others how to do just what it is that those who can do it are doing when they do it well. Mentoring is what you do when you either do not understand what you do or cannot cast it in a form that can be readily and reliably taught.

Naturally, the doers, the thinkers, and the teachers in software are not always the same people. Some of the best developers in our business, even some of our grand gurus, may have only vague or misguided notions of what it takes in order to do what they do. On the other hand, the best teachers may be only mediocre programmers. Teaching and programming are quite different skills.

Nellie is by now a great-grandmother, and the only programming she probably attempts is trying to get all four parts of the latest PBS special recorded on her VCR. However, the computer field still abounds with programmers and designers who do their work well but could not explain it if their jobs depended on it. And the nearer you are to the frontier, the leading edge of practice, the more this seems to be true. At one conference in Sydney, Australia, devoted to object-oriented development, mentoring was mentioned at every turn. It was promoted in presentations and in comments from the floor as the golden route to proficiency in object technology. Perhaps it is no accident that mentoring is hottest where the technology is newest and the safe ground least clear. Theory, technique, and tools lag the furthest behind the problems and practices in areas of leading edge technology. Where there be dragons, good mentors are needed.

I was mentored by some of the best. Amazingly, there were intelligent coaches brave enough and willing to take on the training of such a troublesome young man. The effects last. I am still sussing out new twists on some of the things I learned first under Jack Cremeans, Ken Mackenzie, Dave Jasper, and Bud Vitoff.

Close Tolerances

To the extent that it works at all—and it does not always—mentoring will not directly improve quality, however. It only promulgates the style and practices of the mentor. As an organizational strategy, it can be an effective way of promoting the corporate way, assuring that, for better or not, people think and code in channels consistent with the preferred culture.

This consistency in itself may represent a first small step toward a better software development process. Consistency is the grandfather of quality. It is an axiom of process improvement that before you can improve a process, you have to get it under control—it must be reproducible. As long as the process of software development is chaotic, as long as effort cannot be predicted and you never know whether or how deadlines will be met, there can be no systematic refinement or incremental enhancements. The reliability of the end product remains mostly in the hands of Fate or of legions of beta and gamma testers. The first rung on the ladder of quality that leads toward the lofty heights of level 5 in the Software Engineering Institute's Capability Maturity Model (or to software that works, whichever comes first) is reducing the variance, producing more consistent outcomes by more predictable processes. This means, of course, that both the splendid but unexplained successes and the unplanned failures will be lopped off the ends of the distribution, leaving a more stable but less spectacular medium happily in the middle.

If it fits the organizational culture, investing in a recognized and systematic program of mentoring is better than trusting to the natural instincts of spontaneous coaches. In principle, everyone needs a mentor, and everyone should have a go at being a mentor in turn. The mentoring process does not have to stop simply because you passed your first annual review without a hitch. Mentors can help you up the next rung as well as up the first. Mentoring can serve as part of an effective technology-diffusion strategy whenever new techniques and languages are introduced. Coaching can complement both code reviews and design walk-throughs in an on-going quality improvement program.

Mentoring is especially popular among consulting firms who tout it as an effective means of technology transfer. Instead of consulting to your company, they will work side-by-side with you on your project, gently guiding and helping you to acquire their advanced levels of skills. Compared to intensive, up-front staff training or intermittent consultation as problems arise, the mentoring model has obvious advantages, not the least of which being that it offers the consultant more dependable income.

So, at least for awhile, mentoring is the word. The language, though, keeps morphing before our eyes. Language must keep moving and changing lest we catch up with it, or worse, we end up being caught in the act. Smart consultants are merely being wise in renaming what they do. Money for consulting and training may have been squeezed from budgets, but the bean counters and pencil pushers have not all yet discovered coaching and mentoring. Once they do, there will be fiscal limits on coaching contracts, and mentoring will be found petrified in 13 pages of contractual obligation, indemnification, and nondisclosure.

Perhaps it was meant to be!

From *Software Development,* Volume 3, #3, March 1995.

58

In Training

The topic of the panel discussion was the immediate future, the leading edge of software and applications development practice. The question from the audience was a somewhat poignant plaint from the past. "What advice do you have for a COBOL analyst/programmer building character-based apps using a networked mainframe database?" After a full seven or eight milliseconds of careful thought, I leaned into the microphone and, using my best conspiratorial but commanding tone, said, "Retrain."

Unsatisfied, my questioner approached me during the tea break. What could he do? His company did not support further education, there was no training budget, books and courses were too expensive to buy with his modest earnings, and COBOL was all he knew.

Industry stylists have been pronouncing the passing of mainframe computing for years, but just when the coroner starts to sign the death certificate, the darn things sit up again. And mourn not for good old COBOL. Arguably, more lines of COBOL populate the planet than all other programming languages combined. (A frustrating fact driven home when the Y2K challenge reared its ugly head and brought all the old COBOL coots out of retirement. LLC) Like all living languages, COBOL continues to evolve. Now it is object-oriented and someday may even be maintainable.

Like rock 'n' roll, COBOL will never die. Of course, never has only relative meaning in a field where fifth generation languages follow the fourth only a few years after the third. Nevertheless, programming languages obey Constantine's Fourth Law: No programming language that achieves a significant user base ever disappears completely. I first learned to program in FOR-TRAN, one of the earliest "high-level" languages. FORTRAN is still in use, still fiercely supported by partisans, still viable. Even more amazingly, RPG, already grizzled when I first encountered it in the early 1960s, was still in use in the mid-1990s.

However, my stark advice to the hapless mainframer was motivated neither by pessimism nor by optimism about the imminent demise of big computers and big languages, but by realism about what is happening in the profession. The question is not whether this coding conservative can stay employed, but whether he will do so amidst expanding or narrowing options. In the 1980s, my brother-in-law made it to early retirement on just COBOL and mainframes, but that was then and this particular programmer was still standing in front of me, eager to know what to do now.

Plastics

So I told him. "Objects," I whispered, picturing Dustin Hoffman in a scene from *The Graduate*. If you are not doing objects, I continued, you will be. Or you will be among those watching the mainstream move on across the sands, leaving behind a shrinking pool of opportunities. I also talked about visual development. I even suggested there were things to be learned from embedded systems programming. I am a trouble maker.

I do not think he really wanted to hear any of this. He didn't want to spend his own money on his own future, and he really didn't want to learn anything new. He was hoping for something reassuring—perhaps some secret incantation to stem the rising tide of trends that were lapping at his boots or perhaps a dinghy in which to stay afloat just a little longer.

It is hard to know what to do. The winds shift, there are rips that can carry you out to sea. You may take up Java, learn ActiveX, and master a cross-platform GUI library, yet still be awash when the vendor of your preferred tool goes Chapter 11 or a product is dropped after the company is acquired or when Bill and Company change their minds again about how things will be done.

There are no guarantees. Still, some craft are more seaworthy than others, and you can be smart about how you steer your career. As I see it, there are really two issues here. You want to build your boat as solidly as possible and never take your hand off the rudder.

Continuous Improvement

Books, courses, conferences, and new software are what keep professionals sailing smoothly through turbulent waters. If cutbacks and business process re-engineering or a missed funding cycle have decimated the company training budget, then you may need to recreate the budget out of your own pocket. It is an investment in yourself and your future. You can't lose. It reduces the risk of falling on the wrong side of the downsizing scythe should it ever swing again. In any case, it increases your chances on the open job market or helps in launching your own new dot.com enterprise.

The problem is that so many organizations and professionals think of education as something that happens once, when we are young, and of training as a form of sporadic punctuation afterwards. In truth, the modern collective objectives of organizational learning and continuous process improvement apply to the people in organizations as well as to the corporate body. Professionals with staying power are always in training, continually upgrading skills and adding to their professional repertoires.

So, I told my erstwhile inquisitor that, yes, it is nicer if the company foots the bill for magazine subscriptions or buys the tickets to two conferences a year, but whose life is it anyway? Instead of whining about how the professional ship was sailing without him, I suggested he spend some money on learning better seamanship while he still had some money to spend.

The great thing about learning is that the more you do it, the easier it becomes. Learning becomes habit. Do it enough and you may even learn how to learn. Your first "second language," after your native tongue, is usually much harder to learn than the next and the next. The same goes for programming languages. Why would anyone *not* want to learn a new language? Pretty soon you catch on that they are all variations on a few themes. Rather than just "programming in language Z," you learn programming.

Which brings us to the other part of a more secure future. The really valuable things to learn are the most basic.

In Theory

Boston abounds with colleges and universities offering diverse approaches to education. In engineering, the leading lights when I went to college were the Massachusetts Institute of Technology and Northeastern University, two schools as different as Smalltalk and COBOL. Over in Back Bay was Northeastern, with an emphasis on practical skills and on-the-job experience through cooperative education. On the Cambridge side of the river was Tech, where basic science reigned and the stress was on theory not practice, on the fundamental principles of engineering. It was rumored that Northeastern-trained engineers were productive the day they were graduated, while Tech grads might take five years before they really earned their pay. On the other hand, in another five or ten years, the Northeastern students would be approaching early obsolescence, while the Tech tools would just keep ticking.

Theory is not the poor handmaiden of practice—it transcends practice. Theory can reach into the future. When Einstein worked out $E=m{\cdot}c^2$ there were no nuclear reactors. Before it was an observation, the planet Pluto was a prediction; in theory it had to exist based on Neptune's orbit. On a less cosmic scale, the theory of modular complexity at the heart of structured design predicted experimental results that came years later and anticipated key issues in object-oriented programming, even though OOP was not even yet an idea when coupling and cohesion were conceived.

All job security is illusory, but the best insurance policy is to be secure in the fundamentals of what you do. The word *fundamental* means at the foundation. General principles are more stable than the specific practices that are built upon them and that they support. Like flexible, reusable code, basic principles adapt to changing contexts. If you base your value on what you know of a specific language or platform or programming environment, your career foundation rests on sand, and the tides of technology will surely wash it from under you.

Whatever future waves of technology may alter applications and software development, you can be certain of one thing. If you just keep doing what you are doing now, you probably will not be doing it for too long.

From *Software Development,* Volume 3, #4, April 1995.

59

Gifted Programmers

It has been a long year. Month after month you have worked hard to deliver on project promises, and so have the programmers on your team. You are starting to think about year-end bonuses. It is the season for gifts—Winter Solstice, Hannukah, Christmas, Kwanza, or plain-vanilla New Year's—the celebrations seem to come tumbling one after another. What do you give your high-performing programmers to let them know you appreciate them? More generally, what do you do to recognize, reward, and motivate your applications and software developers? That was essentially the question posed from the audience on one speaking tour I did in Australia with industry luminaries Rob Thomsett and Ed Yourdon. It got us all to thinking about some of the more creative and effective incentives for developers.

This is a perennial problem. Many of us have a tendency to think in simple terms when it comes to incentives. Some years ago, I was working with Russian and Ukrainian managers from what were then recently privatized former Soviet-run firms. At one point, I found myself caught up with them in the ever-popular management game of "Why-Don't-You-Yes-But." I would suggest ways to work more efficiently and they would say, "Yes, but we don't have reliable lines of supply here." "Yes, but our workers do not expect to take initiative." "Yes, but we cannot fire workers and we cannot change their pay. We have no ways to motivate them." At first, these bright, motivated former-Soviet managers could see no way to motivate their workers, but when I suggested they brainstorm, they devised dozens of ways and means to motivate others without resorting to the axe or the pocketbook. Certainly we can do as well.

Toys for Techos

Most of us propeller heads love technology toys. The real test of kinship with the glorious granfalloon of dweebs and dweebettes is simple. Do your eyes light up at the thought of a cool new GUI widget or a 3-D video card driving a 21-inch flat-screen monitor or a gigahertz laptop with a 20 gig hard drive? Are you one of those who cannot wait to get your hands on the beta release of every new product that appears? Do you find yourself ripping off shrink-wrap to see if release 2.0 finally solves the problems of 1.1?

One of the payoffs for delivering your software in time might be to get on the beta test panel for someone else's new software. Or maybe the first copies of a new CASE tool or the newly purchased development suite go to members of the team that performed the best last quarter. Teams that deliver on promises might get first dibs on delivery of the next round of hardware upgrades.

This tactic will not work for everyone, of course. Some of us would rate installing beta release software on our machines somewhere between swimming in moldy oatmeal and replacing a rooftop satellite dish during a thunderstorm. I myself have managed to avoid participating in all but one beta test over the last several years. Maybe a better answer is offering a menu of new software and hardware toys. Top performers get first pick. Yet another variation would be to give the best developers more say over what tools and languages and libraries will be purchased next.

While we are on the subject of toys, have you ever noticed the feeding frenzy that results when some exhibitor at a developer conference comes up with a real cool give-away? Never underestimate the power of a T-shirt. The full range of "promotional" gimmicks—team jackets, special ties, limited edition mugs or mouse pads—can all be ways of singling out the winning teams and team members to recognize them as something special. The best team might get the chance to design its own team-insignia fashion, with the company picking up the tab for production.

Working Holidays

I have to credit Rob Thomsett for one of the most creative ways to give a bonus to your best and brightest and get an unexpected bonus in return. He suggests you reward excellence with time, giving those who deliver quality software on time the time to pursue whatever project might interest them. What programmer wouldn't jump at the chance to spend several months learning a new language or experimenting with image compression techniques or creating a new free-text search method? The project could be anything, and they get paid for it! What really turns most of us techo types on is learning things, trying things out, playing around with new tools and techniques.

Thomsett says that, in his experience, most programmers would rather have more time than more money anyway. The bonus to the company of this sort of sponsored research is not just a happy developer with new skills and ideas but maybe a new piece of software or some useful new technology as well. This approach to reward may make even more sense for whole teams. When a project team demonstrates their ability to perform above and beyond established best practices, reward them by turning them loose on the research and development project of their choice.

If time really has more value for your programmers than money, you might offer extra days off as a bonus. On a grander scale and in a larger timeframe, the Australians have an interesting custom known as long-service leave. After you have been with a company or organization for ten years, you get to take an extended holiday, typically 8-12 weeks at full pay. In a field where loyalty is lean and turnover is such a major problem, it makes a lot of sense to use incentives that help you keep the good people you worked so hard to recruit.

Electric Training

Keeping abreast of current developments in software is a challenge, but it is also one of the fun things about working in a fast-changing technical profession. It certainly is never boring. Attendance at an extra training seminar or a ticket to the next Embedded Systems Programming or Software Development Conference could be a cost-effective way to recognize hard work. Books and magazine subscriptions are another low-cost way to escalate the stakes.

Once a group has learned how to work together well, why break them up? One reward for high performance teamwork could be the option of staying together for the next project. More broadly, getting to pick your working partners might be an effective incentive for peak performance. In a related vein, a free choice from among the next projects to be started might be the payoff for doing well on the last one.

What about better working conditions, a redecorated office, or rearranged partitions that make it easier for people to work alone or to meet? The possibilities are only limited by your imagination and your willingness to step outside the conventions of traditional management thinking. At least one company motivates its professional staff through access to inside information, taking an open-book approach to management that keeps everyone informed on financial and production details, so all can see the ultimate impact of their work.

Of course, in designing rewards and incentive schemes, there is no substitute for knowing your people. One person might be quietly pleased to get a gold-lettered, best-of-show coffee mug while another would be insulted. A long weekend could be completely lost on that diehard data analyst who lives at the office anyway.

You might even ask your high-performers what they would like. Now there's a novel idea!

From *Software Development,* Volume 3, #12, December 1995.

60

Industry Icons

The conference center, one of Amsterdam's more interesting meeting venues, was a converted church, its pews replaced with theater seats and its vaulted sanctuary turned into an auditorium, complete with state-of-the-art audio-visual equipment. I was delivering the keynote for the annual meeting of a European CASE users group and could not resist commenting on the awe-inspring setting. Noting an ornately carved pulpit perched high above stage left, I started musing about what it might be like to address the group from those lofty heights. In a moment of inspired mischief, I told the audience that I had actually requested to speak from the pulpit, but had been refused by the management.

It brought down the house when I said that I had been told it was forbidden—only James Martin was allowed to speak from there.

Our industry is a world of high technology, of tough-minded business people making critical corporate decisions. We are engineers and scientists and analysts and programmers. We reasonably and rationally analyze products and processes and make our choices on the merits. Yet, underneath a thin veneer of hard reason and objective data lies a different world where cults of personality prevail. It is all about names—about gurus and followers and competing camps under banners of true belief. Rah, rah! Objects beat functions four to zip; details on the late news.

Names and Numbers

We have so many famous names, from Coad and Yourdon, Codd and Date, to Comaford, Cringely, and Curtis, from Myers, to Meyer, to Ward/Mellor,

Wasserman, and Weinberg. From newcomers and rising stars to the pantheon at the top whose names are recognized by anyone who has been in the industry for more than a week, this is a business of gurus and personalities as much as of chips and technologies. There are global gurus and those whose reputation is concentrated in specific segments. Y. Alan Griver may deservedly draw drools from among the groupies of the Visual FoxPro community, but would provoke only a "Who? Wha'?" among hardcore embedded-systems code jockeys.

The big stars get loyal followers, and they get things named after them. We have had Booch-grams and Chen notation. Some analysts followed Coad/Yourdon and others Shlaer/Mellor in creating their object models. Data-flow diagrams used the Yourdon/DeMarco bubbles or the Gane/Sarson rounded-rectangles, and time was when some business analysts would rather fight than switch. Maybe you still believe in Jackson Systems Design; maybe you still normalize your definitions to Backus-Naur form.

We have had a lot of stars and maybe even a handful of superstars, but in the constellation of computer luminaries, James Martin has been a light unto himself, reputedly commanding $25,000 a day. And what does it take to reach that level of guruship?

According to Australian journalist and industry observer Graeme Philipson, the secret is a special combination of style and substance. Just knowing your stuff or having something valuable to say will not take you far on the lecture circuit. Flash and flair by themselves actually work better, at least in the short run, but sooner or later the vapid stylist is found out and has to put up or shut up.

A signature schtick is an essential part of the game. Martin has his tuxedo, his multimedia show, and his impeccably suave British delivery. Pete Coad has his Hawaiian shirts and his plastic sirens. Among Philipson's favorites is pundit and analyst Jeff Tash, whom he described as "an abrasive and opinionated speaker whose style is to shout at his audience." As you can see, there is more than one way to impress people. I myself have been known to wear a cowboy hat at conferences, a nod to my rants on coding cowboys (see Section II).

Not Working

Admittedly, the job of software guru can look pretty soft. At the Software Methods Conference in Boston one year, Meilir Page-Jones, arguably a guru himself, finished a presentation with his own musical parody of the Dire Straits hit, "Money for Nothing." Meilir's version is the lament of the working programmer who cranks out applications day after day and then has to sit through the portable pontifications of podium presenters. "That ain't working, that's the way you do it; money for nothing and the trips for free."

Actually, software stardom can be a mixed bag. Very few people stay "on the circuit" as long as Martin or Yourdon. Part of the secret of survival may be, as Meilir whimsically reminds us, not to take any of it too seriously. It may even help to be a little clueless. I had no idea that I might be a guru until a trip to Brazil with my younger daughter in 1988. Our host, a professor of computer science at one of Rio's major universities, asked Heather what it was like growing up with a famous father. She didn't know what he was talking about. And neither did I.

I was reminded of this when a colleague at the University of Technology, Sydney, introduced me as an "industry icon." I started laughing. I have a very graphic imagination and instantly conjured this mental image of a toolbar full of buttons, my own face bitmapped onto one of them. A push on the Yourdon button gets you a warning about off-shore programmers or Y2K bugs, a click on Grady, Ivar, or Jim unifies everything on the screen. Maybe my icon could trigger a screen-saver with coding cowboys galloping across the monitor.

If seeing your face on a toolbar sounds appealing, the steps to software stardom are open. Just follow the leaders. Look at how your favorite guru goes about it, then work out your own variation.

Not all moves are optional. No matter how many systems you have built or articles you have written or workshops you have led, nobody will take you completely seriously as a guru until you have a book in print or a regular column in a major industry rag. Preferably, the column should have your face on it. The book should list your name first among the coauthors. Everybody remembers OMT as the Rumbaugh technique and recognizes use cases as part and parcel to the Jacobson method, but who can name the other authors of these gurus' influential books?

Gifts

The most enduring and endearing of the gurus have something more than style, something that probably cannot be taught and cannot be learned; it's called charisma. Over-used and misunderstood, charisma means, literally, a gift from the gods. The gift enables some people to inspire other people to take risks— to create innovative software or to strive for SEI Level 5 or to commit to an unproven programming language.

The real charismatics of the world, those impassioned true believers who inspire disciples to follow them into the hills or jail or worse, are probably a different lot. Len Oakes, a Melbourne-based psychologist who has studied the psychology of charisma, says that when you cut through the content to reach the core, the real charismatic gurus are all pretty much alike. The messages may be highly varied, but the personalities have a similar, rock-hard center. Koresh, Jouret, Rajneesh, Hubbard—such charismatic leaders share, among other things, a common defect: an impervious and self-centered view of reality that can convey to others a sense of absolute, ultimate, and inviolable certainty. In a world where ambivalence and ambiguity are what it is all about, certainty can be a heady elixir. Alas, certainty of this magnitude rests in a self-constructed reality disconnected from the real world, sustained at the cost of continuous struggle to close out new ideas or new data or new arguments that might challenge the absolute verities of personal truth.

This description may seem to fit some of the impassioned defenders of certain development tools or techniques, but most true charismatics stand little chance in an industry as fast-paced and changeable as ours. More often, the true believers are left standing in the streets or preaching to an empty auditorium. Then again, maybe the pace of change is precisely what makes us so susceptible to every savior-of-the-day selling silver bullets that promise instant applications and no bugs. Step right up folks, free software with every magic bottle.

Snake oil anyone?

From *Software Development,* Volume 3, #2, February 1995.

61

Impresario

Ours is a big business. Even in smaller companies, it can seem like one person can hardly make a difference, much less a lasting impression. I regularly get messages from people who lament that they have no influence, that they are only one small voice in a programming wilderness and have little hope of improving software development practices. Some are programmers and software engineers, eager to make a difference not just make more code. Others are managers, in awe of their technical staff, who feel they have little to contribute compared to the jack flash working for them who can modify C code in 15 different open edit windows at once.

Influence and impact take many forms. An entire industry or profession can, indeed, be transformed by the acts and contributions of one individual. Edsgar Dijkstra applied the theoretical work of Bohm and Jacopini to program style and, in his historical letter to the editor, "GOTO Considered Harmful" (Dijkstra 1968), triggered a controversy that would spark a revolution in the practice of programming. A young Bill Gates made some right moves in deploying system software for the nascent microcomputer industry, and our business was never again the same. Alan Kaye turned a doctoral dissertation into the foundations for a revolutionary language that would help turn objects into a new programming paradigm. Indeed, at the core of contemporary computer programming is really a rather small number of essential ideas coming from a relatively small cadre of innovators.

It is not always the best known inventors and creators or the most visible movers and shakers or the most active writers and consultants who make a real impact, however. Sometimes it is others, less known and less honored, who leave the deepest impressions. Consider the impresario.

Impressing

English is a ravenous language, eagerly borrowing from almost everywhere. The Italian word *impresario* means entrepreneur, another borrowing, from the French, meaning one who organizes and coordinates an enterprise. In English, though, impresario often connotes the more merely ceremonial supervision of the circus ringmaster or the theatrical host. The impresario is not the band but the tour manager, not the performer but the straw boss, not the engineer but the lab director. Nonetheless, the power and importance of the impresario may too often be grossly underestimated.

Technology-oriented visitors to Australia have often been impressed by the level of discipline and sophistication found within many software application development groups. This is not to say that everyone is first rank or that all the software is "spot on," as the Australians would express it, but just that the effective use of tools and systematic methods is remarkably widespread.

The roots of today's best practices go back to the 1970s, when some of the pioneering software methodologists began to visit the antipodes. Because the country is so small and the information technology field smaller still, a surprising fraction of Australian software professionals ended up being trained directly by these pioneers, the original developers and primary proponents of modern methods and practices. Many of those students who came under the early influence of a Constantine, a DeMarco, a Weinberg, or a Yourdon have since advanced to management positions or have become consultants and professional leaders in their own rights, shaping modern software and applications development practices.

A formative role in this culture-changing process was played by one man and a tiny training organization, both known to few people outside of Australia. DP Education Proprietary Limited was the company, and Dennis Davie was the jocular impresario who first lured Ed Yourdon and Larry Constantine down under to teach their new approaches to the Aussies. At a time when few people in the United States had even heard of structured methods and the first handcrafted "Orange Book" edition of *Structured Design* was yet to be printed, Australians were getting the structured stuff first hand. Davie was a pleasure to work with, and over the years he was able to draw a sizeable network of skilled teachers and innovative thinkers into presenting in Australia. Neither rich nor famous, Davie retired happily and quietly to Australia's

Gold Coast, occasionally teaching a class or two himself for the company after it was taken over by his son. Whether he knew it or not, Davie, who died in early 1998, made a difference for a lot of people.

Structuring

Closer to home we have other examples of the influential impresario. Ed Yourdon may himself be best known for the methods that include his name or as a prolific writer and persuasive presenter, but his most enduring contribution to the field may be as an impresario. It would hardly be an exaggeration to say that he created structured methods as an industry. The lineage of computer-aided software engineering can be also be traced back to that same root stock.

An important part of his genius was his ability to attract talent and recognize it when it was in front of him. He was able not only to read correctly the incipient currents of contemporary innovation, but to gather around him the best and brightest thinkers and teachers of the day. At its apogee under Ed and his wife Toni Nash, Yourdon, Inc., was the place to be. Almost anyone with something to say and the drive to say it wanted to work there. An amazing number of today's most influential leaders in the field got their start directly or indirectly through Ed Yourdon.

Channeling

The impresario is not of mere historic interest; the role is today as important as ever. Digital Consulting's George Schussel styles himself in this role, for example. Among other things, he was instrumental in getting a reluctant Larry Constantine back into the front lines of software development. He and Rick Friedman, yet another industry impresario, were major forces in bringing object technology to the attention of a widening audience. Orchestrating some of the most successful conference programs in the industry was KoAnn Tingley Vikoren, the former *impresaria* of the Software Development Conferences who got me involved in the very first one in 1988.

Fittingly, the country that gave us the word has it's own impresario of information technology. Giovanni Modica is not only a great Italian cook, but he has a passionate vision of helping to transform Italy into a world leader in information systems development. The means is technology transfer, which is also the name of his company. By importing the best and the brightest from around the world, he hopes to brighten the future of Italian development practices. He is likely to succeed. Through zeal and sincerity he has assembled a portfolio of world-class presenters who now make regular stops in Milan and Rome to bring the latest in effective methods and tools to Italian developers.

Gateway

Decades of research have shown that the success of a technical organization can be critically dependent on how certain key roles are played. Managers who recognize talent but are not awed by it, who can challenge the best to be better, are catalysts for technical success. These are the impresarios who can foster an organization that will always be expanding its horizons. They may not cut code or architect systems themselves, but how they push, pull, support, and resist can be the critical ingredients that either enable or disable the entire enterprise.

Of equally vital importance are the people who act as gatekeepers, conduits for technical information. Gatekeepers are the ones who go to conferences, who read technical publications, who buy books, and who bring new ideas to the attention of colleagues. Gatekeepers are often impresarios on a modest scale, the ones who organize "brown-bag seminars" and bring in outside speakers and trainers. They are not so much sources as channels, and without them there would be no communication.

Maybe this is you.

From *Software Development,* Volume 3, #9, September 1995.

Registered Peopleware

(The final "Peopleware" column appeared in the March 1995 issue of *Software Development* magazine. When the column was abruptly canceled, I had already written the draft of what was to be the April column, intending it as lighter fare in keeping with the first day of that month. It has long seemed unfair that those readers who had persevered through so many columns should be forever deprived of the chance to catch the swansong of the series. So here it is, the fabled "lost column.")

Peopleware™. Yes, believe it or not, it is a trademark. A message to this effect appeared in my email in-box just about the time I was finishing the editing for the first edition of this book (Constantine 1995). What's more, the message expressed concern that my use of the name might mislead the public. Would-be book buyers might think I had written a history of the obscure company that is the putative owner.

I was not terribly worried, nor were the lawyers at Prentice Hall. In order to keep a trademark, you cannot allow it—through wide and casual currency and lax enforcement—to fall into the public domain. Such has been the fate of many erstwhile brands, such as escalator and kerosene. To claim and hold a trademark, you must be the first to use the mark in trade, and you must vigorously defend it. If, for instance, I comment in my column that I was drinking a Coke® while writing, but fail to capitalize the word or to put the magic little "registered" mark after it, the nice people at Coca Cola™, who have their ever-watchful eyes out everywhere, will send me a pleasant but firm letter reminding me that it is a registered trademark and should always be capitalized and preferably be followed by the familiar little circle-r brand. Oh, these nice folks are not going to bring a lawsuit against every hack columnist who forgets the rules of the game. They'll save the big legal guns for the likes of someone who tries to sell Coca Cola™ screen savers without prior permission.

Peopleware, the word by itself sans any embellishing marks or footnotes, goes back many years, as the Original Introduction in this volume explains. It has been widely used, including as the title of a duly famous book by the Tom and Tim team (DeMarco and Lister 1987), all without generating lawsuits. Not that I would ever dare defy the demigods of litigation or risk the ire of trademark owners big or small, known or unknown. So, with that caution in mind as you read on, remember that all trademarks are the property of their respective owners. Or so the legal types would have us all say at the front of books and the bottom of web pages.

Mind you, I am no freeware radical when it comes to intellectual property. I have no quarrel with the Lexmark™ trademark or with registered nonsense spread in the form of such coinages of the information age as Agilent™ or Inspiron™. As a wordsmith, the point at which I really get steamed is when companies trademark Ordinary Words™, usurping for the narrow mercantile Agenda® of the moment our collective linguistic heritage, the legacy of many centuries of spoken and written evolution.

The question is whether a practice that can effectively remove common words from the public domain is really The Intelligent Choice ^{SM} for a race so dependent on language. Perhaps, but it seems to be a Paradox®. On the one hand, we need to protect commerce and the investment of merchants and manufacturers in their Good Names®. On the other, we do not want to stifle Real Communication™. I, for one, do not know what is the Smart Solution^{SM}, but I do know that we must not lose sight of the distinction between *Computer Language*™ and ordinary language, between the needs of brand identity and the needs of simple communication.

In the absence of more sense on this matter, the continued registration of everyday words and phrases could make a nightmare of everyday dreams. Imagine this scenario. One day, you crawl out of bed, your mind only half functioning after a late-night design session. You grab some coffee to Wake up the rest of your brain™. Your partner asks, "Where do you want to go today™?"

"I'd like to go back to bed," you grunt, "but I have work at the Office™. You know, the usual stuff to deal with. People, places, and things.™"

You make a mad Dash® toward the Freeway® before traffic backs up. At the office you take a call from a potential new e-commerce client looking for an Inside Track® on improving Usability by Design.™

"Like other Smart Organizations™" the client explains, "we are interested in Increasing the speed of business™. We want Real Solutions ᔆᴹ."

You respond, "You'll like the way we work.™ Here, we believe in collaborating with clients. We have a great team of designers and developers. It's amazing what we can do together.™"

"That's fine, as long as you understand that a standard Approach® is just not going to be enough," the client answers. "We've thought of everything®. We want to Transcend® me-too e-commerce to create a Buyers Advantage™. So, we need you, as consultants, to be Bold®. Think Different.™"

"-ly," you mumble. "Differently. It's an adverb."

More loudly, you say, "Let's set up a NetMeeting® conference to look over some of the issues. I'll be your Advisor™, along with my Design Companion™. Heidi®, our Office Assistant™, will be the Organizer® for the session. Of course, you can trust that we all understand the importance of confidentiality and will be Discreet™ in the complete Exchange™."

You grab a web-cam and your networked laptop and head for a free conference room to start connecting up the Plugs and Sockets.™ Once everyone is online and you get the software Working Together®, you begin to sketch out some new ideas for reworking their site. "Is this how you imagine the Web?™" you ask?

You try out more ideas. Suddenly Everything Clicks.™ "See the difference.™ I think this is The Best Solution.™ There may be nothing really new under the Sun®, but, although it may not look like much, There is a difference.™ The difference is understanding.ᔆᴹ With this, the site visitor has Total Control® and can quickly make sense of the Connections®. This is How the world shares ideasᔆᴹ."

"Have it your way.™ To me it looks like a Bad Idea®," says one of the skeptics on your own team. "How do you know this will work?"

"It just feels right™. Basically, this is a fast and simple drag-and-drop technique. Get IT, Move IT, Use IT™. We may be dealing with high-level concepts, but we need to keep Bringing information down to earth®. The objective is to supply Simply Powerful Software™."

"Of course, you need technology Built for Fast Times™ to make it function at The speed of information™. Upgrading your server-side software would be wise—A sound investment for your computer™. Nothing fancy, is needed: basically just Generic Software® so you can Set It And Forget It®. . ."

Soon, however, it becomes apparent that only an on-site consultation is going to clarify the real needs of the client. Unfortunately, the meeting has to be scheduled right away, and the client's headquarters are on the Gold Coast of Australia, a 14-hour flight from LAX.

"No problem," you say. "We'll be there.™ I already have my Visa®. I'll just have to make some Travel Notes™. And don't worry, none of us on the team ever gets jet lagged. Some people just know how to fly.SM"

You start discussing contract terms with the clients and finally they agree. "Before you take off, don't forget to bring extra contracts with you," says the project leader. "For all the commitments you make®. Is it a deal?"

"Okay!" you respond, "Partners®!"

And so it goes. Somewhere, someone is applying to trademark your pet phrase, your favorite color, or maybe even your name. You can count on it.

Guaranteed. Period®.

References

Ancona, D. G. and D. F. Caldwell. 1992. "Bridging the Boundary: External Activity and Performance in Organizational Teams," *Administrative Science Quarterly* 37(4): 634–65.

Anderson, L. E. and W. K. Balzer. 1991. "Effects of Timing of Leaders' Opinions on Problem-Solving Groups," *Group & Organizational Studies* 16(1): 86–101.

Belbin, R. M. 1981. *Management Teams: Why They Succeed or Fail.* London: Heinemann.

Beyer, H., and K. Holtzblatt 1997. *Contextual Design: Defining Customer-Centered Systems.* NY: Morgan Kaufman.

Bollinger, T. B. and C. McGowan. 1991. "A Critical Look at Software Capability Evaluations," *IEE Software* 8(4): 25–41.

Case, J. 1990. The Open-Book Managers," *Inc.* 12(9): 104–13.

Chidamber, S., and C. Kemerer 1994. "a Metrics Suite for Object-Oriented Design," *IEEE Trans. Software Eng.,* 20 (6): 476-493.

Cobb, R. H. and H. D. Mills. 1990. "Engineering Software Under Statistical Quality Control," *IEEE Software* 7(6): 44–54.

Collins, D. 1995. *Designing Object-Oriented User Interfaces.* Redwood City, CA: Benjamin/Cummings.

Constantine, L. L. 1986. *Family Paradigms.* New York: Guilford Press.

_____ . 1989. "Teamwork Paradigms and the Structured Open Team." *Proceedings: Embedded Systems Conference.* San Francisco: Miller Freeman.

_____. 1990. "Organization Paradigms and the Management of Change," *Proceedings: Software Development '90*. San Francisco: Miller Freeman.

_____. 1991a. "Building Structured Open Teams to Work," *Software Development '91 Proceedings*. San Francisco: Miller Freeman.

_____. 1991b. "Toward Usable Interfaces: Bringing Users and User Perspectives into Design," *American Programmer* 4(2): 6–14.

_____. 1991c. "Fitting Intervention to Organization Paradigm," *Organization Development Journal* 9(2): 41–50.

_____. 1992a. "Managing for Quality User Interfaces," *Software Management 1992 Proceedings*. San Francisco: Miller Freeman.

_____. 1992b. "Getting the User Interface Right: Basic Principles," *Software Development 1992 Proceedings*. San Francisco: Miller Freeman.

_____. 1992c. "Quality by Increments: Small Steps with Big Payoffs," *American Programmer* 5 (2).

_____. 1993a. "Objects in Your Face," *Object Magazine*, July.

_____. 1993b. "User Interface Design for Embedded Systems," *Embedded Systems Programming*, August.

_____. 1993c. "Work Organization Paradigms for Project Management and Organizations," *Communications of the ACM* 36(10). October.

_____. 1994a. More than Just a Pretty Face: Designing for Usability," *Software Development 1994 Proceedings*. San Francisco: Miller Freeman.

_____. 1994b. "Collaborative Usability Inspections for Embedded Systems," *Embedded Systems Conference Proceedings*. San Francisco: Miller Freeman.

_____. 1994c. "Interfaces for Intermediates," *IEEE Software* 11(4): 96–99.

_____. 1994d. "Graphical Navigation," *Windows Tech Journal*, August.

_____. 1995. *Constantine on Peopleware*. Englewood Cliffs, NJ: Prentice Hall.

_____. 1996. "Usage-Centered Software Engineering: New Models, Methods, and Metrics," In Purvis, M. (ed.) *Software Engineering: Education & Practice.* Los Alamitos, CA: IEEE Computer Society Press.

_____. 1997. "Visual Coherence and Usability: A Cohesion Metric for Assessing the Quality of Dialogue and Screen Designs." *OzCHI'96 Proceedings.* Los Alamitos, CA: IEEE Computer Society Press.

_____. 1998. "Rapid Abstract Prototyping," *Software Development, 6* (11), November.

Constantine, L. L., and Lockwood, L. A. D. 1999. *Software for Use: A Practical Guide to the Models and Methods of Usage-Centered Design.* Reading, MA: Addison-Wesley.

Cooper, A. 1995. *About Face: The Essentials of User Interface Design.* Foster City, CA: IDG Books.

DeMarco, T. 1982. *Controlling Software Projects.* New York: Yourdon Press.

DeMarco, T. and T. Lister. 1987. *Peopleware: Productive Projects and Teams.* New York: Dorset House.

Dijkstra, E. W. 1968. "Go To Statement Considered Harmful," *Communications of the ACM*, Vol. 11, No. 3, March, pp. 147-148.

Doyle, M. and M. Strauss. 1982. *How to Make Meetings Work.* New York: Jove.

Finegan, J. 1990. "The Education of Harry Featherstone," *Inc.* 12 (7): 57–66.

Fisher, R. and W. Ury. 1981. *Getting to Yes.* New York: Houghton Mifflin.

Fisher, R. and Brown. 1988. *Getting Together: Building Relationships As We Negotiate.* New York: Penguin.

Henderson-Sellers, B., L. L. Constantine, and I. M. Graham 1996. "Coupling and Cohesion: Toward a Valid Metrics Suite for Object-Oriented Analysis and Design," To appear in *Object-Oriented Systems.*

Holtzblatt, K. and H. Beyer. 1993. "Making Customer-Centered Design Work for Teams," *Communications of the ACM* 36(10), October.

Humphrey, W. S., T. S. Snyder, and R. R. Willis. 1991. "Software Process Improvement at Hughes Aircraft," *IEEE Software* 8(4): 11–23.

Hyman, R. B. 1993. "Creative Chaos in High-Performance Teams: An Experience Report," *Communications of the ACM* 36(1). October.

Jacobson, I., G. Booch, and J. Rumbaugh 2000. *The Unified Software Development Process*. Reading, MA: Addison-Wesley.

Jacobson, I., M. Christerson, P. Jonsson, and G. Övergaard. *Object-Oriented Software Engineering: A Use Case Driven Approach*. Reading, Mass.: Addison-Wesley.

Kantor, D. K. and W. Lehr. 1975. *Inside the Family: Toward a Theory of Family Process*. San Francisco: Jossey-Bass.

Kruchten, P. 2000. *The Rational Unified Process*. Reading, MA: Addison-Wesley.

Larson, C. E. and F. M. J. LaFasto. 1989. *TeamWork*. Beverly Hills: Sage.

Lickert, R. 1989. *New Patterns in Management*. New York: McGraw-Hill.

Lockwood, L. A. D., and L. L. Constantine 1993. "From Events to Objects: The Heresy of Event-Orientation in a World of Objects," *OOPSLA '92: Addendum to the Proceedings*. New York, ACM Press.

Mackenzie, D. D. 1966. "The Philosophy of Conventions," in *Concepts in Program Design*, L. L. Constantine, ed. Cambridge, Mass.: Information & Systems Press.

Newmann, P. G. 1976. "Peopleware in Systems," in *Peopleware in Systems* 15–18. Cleveland, Ohio: Association for Systems Management.

Nielsen, J. 1993. *Usability Engineering*. Boston: Academic Press.

Norman, D. O. 1988. *The Psychology of Everyday Things*. New York: Basic Books.

Page-Jones, M. 1980. *Practical Guide to Structured Systems Design*. New York: Yourdon Press.

Page-Jones, M. 1995. *What Every Programmer Should Know About Object-Oriented Design*. New York: Dorset House.

Page-Jones, M. 2000. *Fundamentals of Object-Oriented Design in UML*. Reading, MA: Addison-Wesley.

Page-Jones, M., L. L. Constantine, and S. J. Weiss. 1990. "Modeling Object-Oriented Systems: A Uniform Object Notation," *Computer Language* 7(1), October.

Plauger, P. J. 1993. *Programming on Purpose II: Essays on Software People.* Englewood Cliffs, N.J.: Prentice Hall.

Priem, R. L. and K. H. Price. 1991. "Process and Outcome Expectations for Dialectical Inquiry, Devil's Advocacy, and Consensus Techniques of Strategic Decision Making," *Group & Organizational Studies* 16(2): 206–25.

Rettig, M. 1990. "The Practical Programmer: Software Teams," *Communications of the ACM* 33(10), October.

Sutherland, I.E. 1968. "SketchPad: A Man-Machine Graphical Communication System," in *Proceedings, AFIPS Spring Joint Computer Conference.* 1963. 23. pp. 329-346.

Thomsett, R. 1990. "Effective Project Teams: A Dilemma, A Model, A Solution," *American Programmer* 3(7/8): 25–35.

van Harmelan, M. (ed.) 2001. *Object Modeling and User Interface Design.* Harlow, England: Addison-Wesley.

Ward, P. 1992. "The Evolution of Structured Analysis. Part II: Maturity and Its Problems," *American Programmer* 5(4): 18–29.

Watzlawick, P., J. H. Beavin, and D. D. Jackson. 1967. *Pragmatics of Human Communication.* New York: Norton.

Weinberg, G. M. and E. L. Schulman. 1974. "Goals and Performance in Computer Programming," *Human Factors* 16(1): 70–77.

Whitchurch, G. G. and L. L. Constantine. 1992. "Systems Theory," in *Sourcebook of Family Theories and Methods: A Contextual Approach*, P. B. Boss et al., eds. New York: Plenum.

Wirfs-Brock, R., B. Wilkerson, and L. Weiner. 1990. *Designing Object-Oriented Software.* Englewood Cliffs, N.J.: Prentice Hall.

Wood, J. and D. Silver. 1989. *Joint Application Design.* New York: John Wiley & Sons.

Yourdon, E., and L. L. Constantine 1974. *Structured Design, first printing.* New York: Yourdon, Inc.

Zahniser, R. A. 1990. "Building Software in Groups," *American Programmer* 3(7/8): 50–56.

_____ . 1993. "Design by Walking Around," *Communications of the ACM* 36(10), October.

Index

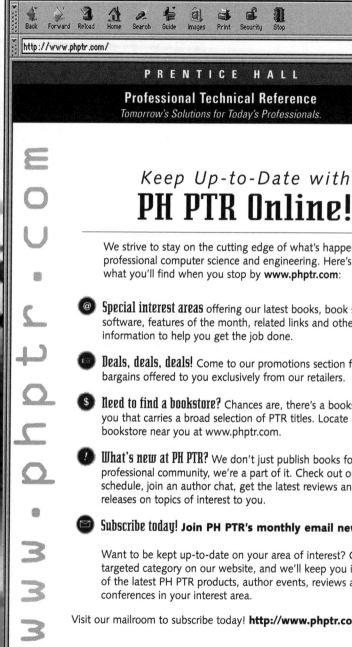

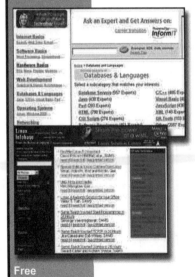